Buried Treasures

The Journey From Where You Are to Who You Are

GURU SINGH

Guru Singh – born in 1945, is a third-generation yogi and master teacher of Kundalini Yoga, meditation, mantra, and 'humanology.' His ancestry studied in India with masters in the early 20th century. He is also a musician, composer, author, and minister of Sikh Dharma, based in Los Angeles and Seattle. He met Yogi Bhajan, master of Kundalini Yoga and Humanology, in January 1969 and has been teaching throughout the world since 1970. He has studied Eastern and Western music from the age of five, and his classes overflow with musical joy and mantra.
www.gurusingh.com

Editors:
Guruperkarma Kaur
Ram Prakash Kaur
Tamara Grace

Cover Design:
Ditta Khalsa, PranaProjects.com
Marc Royce, Photography

Producers and Creative Directors:
Ram Prakash Singh & Ram Prakash Kaur

Publisher:
ReEvolution Books

ISBN: 1497594324
ISBN 13: 9781497594326

This Story is Dedicated in Four Parts

Part One - To my mother and father, Tidi and Bert, to my sister and brother-in-law, Vickie and Brian, for providing a solid spiritual foundation for the recovery and reorientation while processing the events of this trauma, the draft, and my early music

Part Two - To my brothers, sisters, and musical partners of the '60s in the Haight-Ashbury of San Francisco for challenging and inspiring me through the trials and triumphs of those early days of a massive musical revolution

Part Three - To my teachers of the Wirikuta who fiercely, precisely, and patiently guided me on the journey from where I was — to who I was to be

Thereafter - To Yogi Bhajan—my teacher; Guruperkarma Kaur—my wife; Sopurkh our son, Haripurkh our daughter, and now Scott our son-in-law, and our granddaughter Narayan Kaur, born the day this book is going to press—they walk with me through 'Now'

Table of Contents

Foreword

*G*uru Singh is a daily inspiration to thousands. We love his music, his stories, his humor and contagious enthusiasm. We laugh, cry and rejoice as we are encouraged to take—step by step—the journey home to ourselves. He gracefully and powerfully uplifts us along the way, surrounding us with love and strength.

We are blessed that 20 year-old Guru Singh (Gerry Pond) followed his heart and stayed on purpose. The book you hold in your hands is his journey and all of ours reflected in his. It is a wakeup call for the hero within.

Each one of us can courageously make the choice to follow our calling, to hear our inner voice and to walk towards the unknown, grateful for the challenges along the way that strengthen our faith and give us the determination to stay on course.

The experiences in these pages reignite the flames of our consciousness and inspire us to keep up and know that while this story is unique, its lessons are universal and beyond time.

Today, Guru Singh is a teacher, yogi, spiritual activist, husband, father, and grandfather. Through his teachings and music, he creates a space for transformation and insights so that we can access our inner light. He guides us on the journey to meet and balance the warrior and the sage within. We become more empowered and liberated through this experience.

Like the musicians in San Francisco in the late '60s, we feel that something big is about to happen and that something is all of us, making a difference, standing up!

As editor of GuruSingh.com, I invite you to join us in co-creating a global conscious community. Planet Ashram, the name we give to our online community, is a place for us to inspire, uplift, share and connect with each other. Tell us about the conscious transformation that you are part of. Share your story, your mission, your calling and how you are standing up in the world as a beacon of light for others.

We will see you there.

Love you!

Ram Prakash Kaur

Co-create with us: **contact@gurusingh.com**
http://www.gurusingh.com/planetashram/

Preface

Buried Treasures is a true story at the confluence of two epic realities; a 'near-death experience' and eleven months living with an 'uncontacted' tribe in a remote part of the Mexica. Buried Treasures — the journey from where you are to who you are — took place during the times that have given rise to the moment we are currently living in. They were the enthusiastic and dream-birthing years of the 1960s, rampant with the kind of ingenuity, music, art and lifestyle that could completely reprogram the human psycho-emotional and biological systems. These were also times, like today, filled with unnecessary wars and corporate aggression that devastated families and populations around the world.

Some back story support for what you are about to read: based on tens of thousands of research surveys conducted throughout the western world over the past fifty years, it is determined that between one and two percent of the population has experienced what is medically known as an NDE (near-death experience). These percentages have been expanded recently by the number of people who have had heart attacks and other major illnesses and then survived due to the advances in modern medicine. Every one of these survivors has a story and many of these stories have made it into books, but this is nothing new. The realms of transition that one visits between this world and the "where-ever"

have long been an active part of the human fascination as depicted in elaborate cave paintings dating back 32,000 years.

I remember my experience saying to me, *"Don't live your life
logically, live mythologically. Cast yourself as the archetypal hero in the
fable of your greatest dream. Be the sun shining every day with a simple
gratitude, and yet be ever mindful of the wandering adversaries that
haunt your dreams as a shadow in that sunlight. These adversaries are
the friends assigned to you to make you even more powerful, they will
expose your weaknesses . . . in order for you to overcome them."*

According to Survival International, an organization bringing protection and a voice for 'uncontacted' tribes and tribal
peoples, there are one hundred tribes and villages worldwide
that are 'uncontacted' . . . never having had contact with the
outside world. They live in remote, resource-rich areas, and are
today being threatened by global development. The last such
discovery was made in 2008 in the Amazon when a previously
unknown tribe was spotted at the mouth of the Envira River in
western Brazil, not far from the Peruvian border.

I've walked the path from the remote world in this story as
it turns into concrete and wanders through the known world.
I have learned to see everyone I meet on the path as my own
reflection. *"They are all a part of my total being and they're needed to
complete the equation,"* my experience would explain to me. Both
my NDE and the 'uncontacted ones' I lived with have shown me
how life is a sequence of events that lead 'one into another' and
in every one of these moments there are choices, and all choices
are interconnected all of the time.

I now stand decades downstream from my time with the people of the Taquatsi River with the hindsight of endless moments
in which their ancient wisdom was perfectly applied to modern
life. I've gone about these years finding the treasures that are

buried in every relationship, circumstance and surrounding. I've searched for ways that consciousness can replace greed, and that peace can replace war. These teachings have the power to change our consciousness. As Yogi Bhajan said, *"The guitar will be the rifle of the Aquarian Soldier."*

We are currently living in the moments that will determine the fate of the human species. We must come to our common senses right now in large enough numbers in order to prevent the devastating extinctions that are currently taking place including perhaps our own. This is a clarion moment — the wakeup time. This is the opportunity to excavate our own buried treasures of consciousness and begin to put our personal lives and this planet's life back together in a more conscientious and compassionate manner.

Introduction

$\mathcal{W}$here you are located right now in life is referred to as "fate" – the conditions, consciousness, emotions and thoughts of this very moment.

Your "destiny," on the other hand, is your destination, the reality of who you ultimately are, of who you can become.

The journey of a human life is the travel from fate to destiny – from where you are to who you are. In these pages, you will follow my journey but it is our common journey as well.

Most people are not conscious of either of these locations. They are neither where they are nor who they are. Distracted from the actualities of fate and doubting the possibilities of destiny, they live in a chaotic state. Meanwhile, life waits on a parallel track, waiting for consciousness to awaken.

The process of destiny lasts forever but the awakening can happen in a single moment. Welcome this arrival with all your heart and with every breath.

San Francisco in the late '60s was a beacon of hope for the freedom-seeking youth of the world. Freedom, like water and air, is a human requirement. It allows us to live our life as a mission and is essential to the fulfillment of life's purpose. Every human being has a statement to make and an optimal state to be in during their life.

When we face a dilemma, the Cosmos has already composed the solutions. The only questions that remain are: Which side of this event will you stand on? The dilemma or the solution? The confusion or the commitment?

Living in the current times has built up a lot of emotional and mental 'noise'. This robs us of our innate human powers. One way to respond to this is to return to our true nature by focusing our awareness on our breath. Breathing consciously brings us to a state of quiet and calm, into a sensation of dynamic silence and to a neutral mind that can think clearly and create solutions.

As you will experience through these pages, we have the power to manifest our greatest dreams or our worst nightmares – whichever ones we place the most energy in.

Thoughts receive their direction through the amount of trust you place in yourself, the world, the universe and the path of destiny you are walking on.

Become an advocate for your freedom and create a conscious society that benefits us all. Let the voice of the Soul sing the song of your life and turn you into the seeker you were born to be. The more you take charge of your life, the closer you are to living your destiny. I invite you to take hold of your immortal authority and step forward into the unknown, allowing your heart to lead the way.

One

The Imposter!

Images of life stretch into the sensations of hysteria ripping through my brain. Regret replaces opportunities that vanish into forever as I burst through the ceiling of a room, on fire with confusion. Rolling over and over, I capture flashes from above the room. I'm grateful for the distance . . . desperate to reconnect . . . all in a single preposterous moment, without momentum.

I've been here before. I remember these sounds, these smells, these people — all familiar, but I can't tell from where.

There's the lifeless body of a young man on a bed just below me but I can't see the face. Everyone around the body is working hard to revive it. I want a closer look, but I'm stuck more uncomfortably than I've ever known. Not stuck like I can't move, but like I can't exist.

When I call for help there's no voice, I make no sound. No one hears and no one responds in the nightmare below. I begin piecing together memories when a doctor places two small paddles on the body's chest and yells: "Clear!"

A bolt of electricity hunts through the room, crackling around me like a tiger sniffing for the scent of its prey. Finding my vantage, it grips me with a million hot claws and smashes me into the flesh of the lifeless body below. I shriek without sound, bones shuddering and shaking as I ride the voltage through my senses with agonizing force. Then, without pause, I'm ejected. The body lurches in seizures while grabbing my throat to block the escape. Helpless in the tiger's electric grasp, I gag as I'm pulled back in.

Thunder crashes, splitting my hearing into tiny fragments of pointless crackle; terror rips my eyes open into a blank stare. I look at the ceiling without a thought, without a feeling, without a breath, and in less than a second, I'm hurtled through it.

"We've lost him, that's it," echoes through the room.

"No, please God, no!" screams in the sadness. It fills my head with regret, but can't hold me to the Earth. I slip from the chaos into a deep, dark blackness and life vanishes, as if it never was.

Now stars stretch gemlike over the black velvet darkness. Voices pepper the sounds of infinite space . . . unnatural voices . . . more alarming than any I've ever heard. Words that have never been spoken connect to meanings that have never been understood. They enchant my senselessness, but when I listen more closely they turn frantic and terrifying.

The moon, a tiny sliver, rises gently above a vast horizon. It sheds no light from its fragile new phase on the absorbing darkness. An occasional meteor streaks its fiery tail through the dark sky and I get the sense of land beneath my feet, but that's not certain, for I'm not actually walking. I'm sliding, like on ice.

This could be anywhere, in any moment. Nothing reveals the slightest sign of identity or time. I'm glad to be free from the pain and turmoil of that room, then suddenly this too changes and a stream of faces passes before me. Faint faces, like transparent masks in the blackness of space; I recognize some of them slightly, but others I definitely know. The stream becomes a river, then a flood of these faces and voices calling out, echoing and re-echoing on into the distant darkness.

"I'm here for you," some say, while others cry out, "help me . . . help me," over and over again. When I turn to look . . . there's actually nothing but the masks and the cries rising from an endless river of agony.

They sound desperately lost as if they never existed. Their confusion burrows into me and makes me want to run, but I can't escape it. The more I slide through the darkness, the more they grab at me with their shrieks. "You promised, you promised to help me forever."

It's clear from the constant agony that they are more terrified than anyone has ever been. Agony without end, every moment . . . seemingly going on for years . . . forever. I'm vaguely not involved, but trapped all the same in its terror that pleads with me to stay.

I recall my father telling me, "When you're outside your body, move with the cold." So I do and this time — for a different reason — my moving begins to work. Getting colder and colder as I move out into the deep darkness, one tiny speck of light flickers in the distance. As I approach, I find a campfire with tribal-looking elders gathered in gentleness. Men and women dressed in simple white clothing with bright colorful trim at their wrists and ankles.

The color pleases my eyes . . . a needed relief from the chaos and darkness. It radiates bright turquoise and magenta in the firelight. Their uncut hair is tied up in loops and rolls with the same brilliantly colored yarns, hanging below their shoulders in tasseled bunches. They sit cross-legged on what appears to be the bare earth — but it's not — in a small circle; each of them wrapped in heavy blankets against the cold that now cuts completely through me.

Their sparkling eyes reflect the dancing flames with great joy and total concentration. As I search this vast darkness for a clue of familiarity, I find none. Time has become the pulsing of some ancient heart that encompasses this space forever. And those voices, the ones that were all around me, come back. But now they seem harmless, almost comical in their warnings.

"Don't go near them; do not go there. They are bad, they're evil, very evil."

The deep heartbeat continues as the elders smile and laugh and speak very gently whenever they break the silence. The firelight dances with shadows, across their dark faces, revealing deep lines of ancient wisdom. I feel as if I am looking into a jar of butterflies; my vision opens and closes with each flicker of the firelight.

I am surprised they don't notice me peering in on them this way and as I look closer I see a young woman there. She's dressed similarly, listening carefully to all the conversations; she smiles and laughs along with them, never speaking. There's an obvious leader among them and whenever he speaks, everything else stops — except the heart pulse.

It's getting unbearably cold now . . . I move toward the fire for warmth. The younger woman jumps from the circle and stands in front of me. *"Are you unhappy?"* she asks and motions with her hand that I should come forward.

"They're evil, bad, bad and evil," the empty voices cry around me.

She waits for an answer, and when nothing comes out of me, she asks again. *"Are you unhappy, my brother? Or perhaps you're trying to be okay? There's a huge difference you know . . . between truly happy and okay."*

Startled . . . I gasp for a breath, nothing comes . . . with all my effort not even the faintest whisper of air can be found. My head screams without words in a shower of terror, "I'm dreaming," blurts out, but it's a silent thought of pure agony.

"Evil, bad, the work of the devil." Those once haunting voices around me now sound like innocent children in a schoolyard.

Nothing makes sense to my frantic mind and my voice remains silent.

"That's really not an answer . . . is it?" the young woman continues with such a precise attitude. *"If you exist at all, you'll find the words here in your heart."* She rubs her hand on my chest, the first sense of warmth I've felt in what feels like a long time. *"Are you in there, or are you an imposter?"*

4

"Imposter, imposter, you're an imposter," the ghostly voices prance around me.

The question baffles me and her manners feel spooky.

"This is just a nightmare — isn't it?" I ask, again without sound.

Or is this hell? I wonder. No! This can't be — it's far too cold. I try using logic to reassure myself.

"Devil, devil, you're now with the devil," the ranting echoes.

"Dear God," I start to cry without tears. I want to hold myself, but as I put my hands together they pass through each other. I'm freezing cold . . . I want to answer her question . . . I want to say something, anything, but I don't understand. No matter how hard I try I can't utter a word. I can't breathe. I can't think and though I desperately want to run, it's impossible to move. There's absolutely nothing I can do.

"Wow, what a dream you got going here . . . right?" she asks, leaning forward. She places her ear right against my chest, listens for a moment and says, *"Ah that's what it is; your heart has completely stopped in your physical body back on Earth."*

Her words crush me to my knees. A chill plunges ice through my chest and sucks out every other sensation.

"My God," the actual words finally come pleading from my lips. "What do you mean?"

She sits down next to me smiling broadly as if she's good with this, but I don't smile back. I'm terrified now by her calmness and completely freaked out by what she's said. She's so irresistibly calm . . . must be the devil . . . such a vulgar empty way to act.

"Your spirit's crossing time," she says reverently with folded hands. *"You're about to leave the body behind."*

"But th - this isn't real . . . it's just a nightmare, r-r-right?" I stutter through words, trembling from the cold. "I can wake up if I want to . . . I can . . . yes?"

"Yes, of course," she answers. *"If you want it to be, it can be a nightmare, but that's not a good idea. You see, whatever you make of it, it will become — just like in life, only much, much faster and far stronger here."*

My fear rolls me over in relentless swells and as she is speaking these words her face distorts until she becomes beastly.

"There you go," she says. *"Now I'm a monster! It's all in your thoughts. But I can also be your angel, if you prefer. That's entirely up to your perceptions. It's really just perceptions."*

"So I can wake up and stop this . . . this will be over?" I ask again as if negotiating.

"You can always wake up," she acknowledges. *"There are no limits to the dream and no limit to being awake, but nothing is ever over. You must always remember that nothing ever ends."* She pauses to let me absorb the words. *"You'll awaken to whatever level you know . . . whatever level you believe in . . . with or without a body. It's eternal."*

"So I was right," I reassure myself with my own voice. "This is just a terrible dream."

She looks aggressively right through me with a scolding stare. *"What you're actually experiencing right now is a vanishing dream to be replaced by another — a life passing while you were sleepwalking through a waste of time — forgetful moments within an ignorance."*

"Wasted? My life was not wasted!" I shout. "I think you've got me all wrong here."

"No, I don't. I don't have you here at all. You have yourself here and you have been for some time an imposter in a larger dream. You consistently dreamt of your existence with all the joys of making it work. You dreamt all those fears that stopped your inspirations to make it not work. You dreamt that others were responsible for this and for that and now that your heart has stopped in the physical world, this is you dreaming of your tumultuous crossing."

"Are you telling me I'm dead?"

"I'm allowing you to understand that you're crossing a threshold of time," she says with the most irritating precision.

"And what if I don't want to cross, because I don't want any of this, because I want something different?"

"Your world teaches you that crossing is a tragedy. You call it death and you think of it as the end of something, but it's not an end of anything

except one simple — well not so simple — physical costume. It's like taking off a shirt and pants. You now stand naked in your spirit."

"This is crazy. I haven't had all my time yet. You can't do this to me."

"You actually had all the time you needed. All you needed was to just be you."

"That's not true. I was always willing to be myself."

"You were controlled by what you were 'supposed-to-be'. Many times you were ruled by rules, influenced by people's opinions that appeared to be in charge. These were just fears being blamed and placed onto people around you. Doubts led you away from joy. Uncertainty led you away from courage. You only occasionally owned yourself . . . the one deep inside; the dreaming you. That's the person you are born to be. That's the person you were also most afraid of being."

"That's just normal. Is that so wrong?" I ask. "Everybody's like that."

"Nothing is ever wrong," she answers. *"But it's not fully living and when you don't live your life, there's no one to blame when the time runs out. Don't worry though, the universe has forever, you'll eventually get it."* The whole idea terrifies me. The terror smashes her image into little pieces that dance around me as if taunting its power.

"Who are you?" I ask defiantly. "This is fucking crazy. I've got to wake up and get out of here."

"I'm a witness," she replies simply.

"No way!" I yell, shaking from the cold that's gotten much worse now. "I don't need a witness; I don't need any of this." As I yell, the space around me shakes and rumbles across the black.

"That kind of dreaming will bring out the beasts," she warns.

"Who the hell cares? This all sucks anyway."

Her eyes reflect my anger. *"Not yet it doesn't suck, not so much, not yet,"* she cautions me. *"But it can — it can really get bad here if you want."*

"Great — I don't need a witness — I don't need any of this shit." I look around angry like an abandoned child, searching for something to blame, to connect with, and to recognize.

I point into darkness. "I was just there, somewhere there a moment ago. I was alive. I was awake. I've got to wake up."

The confusion expands and I reach for her, but she's made of nothing and my hand passes through her. I grab for anything, everything, a piece of some tiny memory, for a moment of time. I need a thought, something to get back into life, anything at all. I am left with nothing to capture, nothing to hold . . . nothing at all.

"How did this happen? It's not real, nothing makes any sense. This is all way too fast." I sink to my knees . . . she crouches next to me.

"Time isn't real, it's just a very beautiful illusion constructed from memories. It's a tool for the mind to keep track of life: a way to build the dreams that come into life. Every moment of time contains a seed, like the seeds of all the great trees and plants. Every seed contains every single branch and leaf of every single year that the tree will live — plus all the trees of all the seeds that tree will give birth to. All of this exists inside the protection of a simple seed. Time is a seed, an infinity of moments packed into the shell of protection with all those moments exactly like all those leaves that are within the seed. Your life, and more, is in each seed of your time. Each moment of time is filled with dreams, like branches, filled with the leaves of infinite possibility. You can use them with faith and trust, or waste them with fear and doubt. Time — the illusion of moments — is the greatest gift life has to offer and when it's over, it's just over, as if it never was."

"I'm scared," I respond abruptly and the honesty surprises me. "I want to go home."

"Allow yourself to open an unknown door; don't ask how, just be determined."

"I'm cold . . . like ice."

"Without being in the heart, life is cold; the dreams in your heart are your home." She speaks more softly now and begins to actually look beautiful as she says this. I glance back to the fire for warmth, but it's not there anymore. There's just an icy white hole of light in the center of an inky black space.

"That's the same thing you did on Earth," a new voice joins us. *"Searching outside yourself to fill yourself."*

I turn back to the young woman . . . she's gone. An elder man, the leader from the fire circle, stands in her place. *"Welcome home,"* he smiles kindly, the deep lines in his face wrinkling as he speaks.

I do not like his smile. I like nothing about him. It even hurts to look into his eyes. They pierce through me. I look away like a child, hiding behind my hands.

"You must learn to be free from your slavery," he says.

"I'm not a slave," I tell him defiantly without looking at him. "The two of you have the wrong person."

"And which part of your life is free?"

"All of it."

"What about all the parts that worried without faith, that were afraid and without trust? What about the plans you would abandon in moments of doubt?"

"That's normal, everyone does that," I reply.

"Well, when you live and act in those fears, that's slavery."

"Are you kidding?" I laugh. "Fear and doubt are just a part of life!"

"Call it what you want. Being a servant to those feelings is a long way from freedom. You can realize that you are the one who feels your feelings and you get to choose how you feel if you find out how to do this."

"Feelings are feelings," I argue. "How are you supposed to choose them?"

"First of all by believing you can, then giving yourself the authority to do so."

"That's not possible."

"It's whatever you make of it. Emotions and feelings are meant to be tools for life, not the rules for life. They can be physically powerful and seem very real, but they're only memories, opinions and frames of the mind woven together. Use them to build or destroy your moments of time. Those are the seeds that contain your dreams. Feelings are not to be honored — they are to be honed. A carpenter does not worship his hammer; he uses it as a tool. It's true, the tools of feelings are helpful, oftentimes

essential, but they're not to be worshipped, or blindly followed. Since they aren't your master, don't be their slave."

His face is ancient, wise, calm, and gentle, but his words cut deep and feel cold.

"There's not that much fear in my life," I tell him.

"Yes there is, but you avoid knowing it's there — you fill your life with attractive distractions and staying busy."

"Everyone does."

"You're right, but you're not everyone . . . you are you. If it isn't love and passion that keeps you busy, you're wasting precious moments, precious seeds, and precious breath."

"I have no breath."

"Your dreams are all you can breathe right now," the young woman says, returning. *"This is the soul's domain and soul is the keeper of dreams."*

There's been a faint distant music ever since I've been with these people and it comes on stronger now as she's speaking.

"Your consciousness attaches to soul," the old man adds. *"Consciousness is the Spirit. It has a mission inside it which dreams of your purpose when it's powered by the soul."*

The young woman holds her hand on my chest. *"Purpose connects the life to the destiny; the higher purpose of your existence is held here in your heart. Destiny can be shaped and molded with your devotion and commitment, but if fear blocks this, you'll live in your fate. These are the choices you have with every breath you take."*

"Why do you make my life sound so horrible?" I argue. "It's not that bad."

"We don't make it anything," the old man answers. *"You're seeing your life right now without any filters because here there are none. It may not seem this way on Earth because everything is thick and you successfully distract yourself into the thickness. But here — without filters — it simply is what it is."*

"Is this forever?" I ask quietly.

With this question, my hope fades into a torrent of tears. They pour down through my vision of Earth like a spiral of time. At the center of this spiral, I'm once again presented with my lifeless body, a corpse of agony, with doctors working furiously around it.

"If you want forever then you have to be forever. Tragedy begs for forever, that's what that is," the young woman explains. *"You're experiencing the beggar's loss of forever as the value of all that sorrow and the reality of all that tragedy. It feels so right because it's born out of the great sadness that everyone practices, but it accomplishes nothing. Just like you feel nothing from it . . . nothing but sorrow."*

"The value of nothing? It makes no sense."

"The illusion makes sorrow appear as if it can buy more time without disappointment. See it for what it is; this is your undiluted, unfiltered view without a single place to hide. Look and listen here, you have a lot to learn."

I'm silent and weak. The sense of despair is gigantic, but that only makes it worse. I see my own agony attached to that body for what seems like forever. The idea of this being the end is so foul it has a terrible stench . . . the smell of death.

"There must be something I can do," I whisper. "I'm not prepared for this."

"Very few are ever prepared," the old man replies calmly. *"Time is a gift to be spent on the bounty of living. Sooner or later you stop dreaming, and as you run out of time the end always appears too soon. Especially if you haven't become forever, or haven't become your immortal authority."*

"Yes, it does come too soon," I whisper again, "I really have so much more to do."

"Do you want to live because you're afraid to die, or do you want to live because you're willing to live?"

"Both, but I also want to live, to actually live," I now respond honestly and humbly. "I have dreams that I've barely touched. I just never thought . . ."

"Do you have a real sense of these dreams?" he asks. *"Do you have the sense that they already exist?"*

"I want to," I answer, and then pause for a moment. "I did once — I remember."

11

"Then go retrieve them. Find a reason to live right now and then give yourself the right to live."

"Can it bring back my life?"

"If you do it with massive and unwavering enthusiasm," the young woman answers. *"To return into life, you must cut through time like a warrior's sword. It will be the greatest pain you have ever felt. You'll need to be neutral and courageous. Once inside time, you must refuse to fear, because from here onwards you cannot live if you're afraid to die."*

"I can do this," I declare. "I believe I can do this."

And with this, I'm swept away through the blackness that surrounds me. Images of my existence flash like sheets of lightning as I instinctively search among their tattered notions for the pathway back and for the strength and courage to walk it. These are the dreams and hopes I knew in my innocence . . . my younger innocence. I pass through them reaching for my very existence . . . my existence built on dream upon dream. I fly and fly and suddenly I'm back with the old man once again.

"Good!" he says, smiling very gently. *"Now, hold those that you want to live for in your heart of hearts. Hold them while you re-enter time."*

He leans into my face with these next words. *"Your body's very fragile. Hold your vision right here in your heart, even when it's engulfed with pandemonium."*

Passing both of his warm hands through my chest he says, *"Find the rhythms of your heart and restore their life into your life."*

I stare at the two of them as if I am saying goodbye, while they just look back as if to say, we will see you soon.

"Every day you'll breathe and every night you'll dream; every morning you'll awaken to a life that passes within the seed of each moment. Not one of those moments will ever return, so remember it's up to you to immerse yourself in them and do so with great courage and enthusiasm."

Hope appears as I hear these words. I can feel the faint presence of breath in this encouragement, but I'm still not breathing. "Will I always know what to do?" I ask as I turn slowly toward life.

"Trust that you will and you will," he whispers into the wind that carries me. *"Trust will be your teacher and it will always teach you what you need to know. You will be challenged when you go for your dreams and you will face this with massive enthusiasm."* His voice trails off into absolute silence while I'm left in the calm spinning wind that grows warmer and stronger with a gigantic sense of life.

"Don't die!" These desperate words surge from the distance into a maddening shriek. "Don't die, my God don't you dare die on me!" howls with such resound that it fractures time with sadness. It's all I can do to keep from being swept into its seductive fear. I've learned the lessons of sadness — I have to start life right now.

"My God, my son, my God!" the voice pleads.

I explode into time — the room that I left stands before me. Pure chaos

. . . frantic people . . . feverishly working on my lifeless body. My mother's absolute prayer has brought me back. She is bowing over my bed sobbing and wailing. The nurses tug on her as she throws her arms onto my body.

"Clear!" shrieks once more through the room.

The shock yanks me into an ocean of blood that heaves and courses once more through my body thirsting for moisture — starving for its nutrients. The blood's warmth settles around my senses as I stare back up at the ceiling. Then just as quickly as I came in, I'm ejected.

"We need one more," someone yells. "We've lost the pulse."

"Clear!"

"I can't, I can't, I can't breathe," I blurt in a paper-thin voice. The fiery air cuts my lungs as I gasp and choke for just one small breath. Pain shears my throat as it wrenches closed. "I can't breathe!"

A nurse pushes a mask over my face that blows oxygen into my nose and mouth. "We've got him," she reports. "Hold it there."

My eyes dart through a terror-filled room as nurses roll equipment around my bed. My mother, still in her bathrobe, leans hard into the arms of my father, who looks stunned. Relief draws upon the other faces around me.

My body, strapped tightly to the bed, jerks and seizes lightly. I have tubes pushed up my nose, going down through my throat, needles in my arms, and a set of wires stuck to my chest. Something is pulling hard on my guts as tubes travel into my ravaged belly.

I gag, trying to swallow as the muscles of my throat fight the thick tube that feels like a brick. Foul liquid vomits into my nose and mouth as I heave against the binding straps. Somewhere beyond this world I remember the old man's warnings while I choke and vomit over and over until my resistance fades into a soft surrender.

"Steady him now!" a voice calls, as they suction my nose and mouth. Suddenly, everything turns black as I float from my body into unconsciousness.

"Get into your heart!" the old man whispers. *"Get in your heart, right now."*

"This is way more than I thought," I answer. "Maybe it's too much and I can't make it through."

"It's not too much. You got here, now get back here — breathe and breathe and beat your heart. You will do this." His words leave no question. *"Allow yourself to open every unknown door. Don't ever ask how — always remember what courage is. Make it work. When you're motivated by even a slight possibility, you can do the impossible."*

I can't open my eyes from this deep, gentle coma, but I'm grateful to breathe and grateful that I can't feel a thing.

Two

A SECOND CHANCE

*G*od knows how much time has actually passed . . . As I open my eyes, I'm breathing through a tube with another one down my nose and throat into my stomach. The turmoil seems to be over. I stare at the room without a clue of where I am, feeling terribly drained and listening to a ping, pinging machine behind my head keeping time for something. I move my eyes back and forth, scanning, when it dawns on me that my head and eyes are the only things I can move.

"Am I paralyzed?" Fear rushes back. "What's going on . . . have I been in an accident?" Questions race — anxiety knocks me out as if I was never awake.

"You're just soul with spirit resting in your body," the old man enters my dreamy unconsciousness. *"The soul clothed in spirit and body is healing your circumstances. These circumstances, and the people in them, are your lessons. Remember to never be ruled by fears and that your thoughts within each of your moments are the lessons that will either pass or fail you."*

I awaken sometime later to a nurse snoring, softly slumped in a chair beside my bed. My head's throbbing — I desperately have to pee and can't move . . . I need to wake her.

She doesn't notice I'm awake . . . it feels helpless, but at least I woke up. That's heartening. The old man told me this was going to be the toughest time. I feel like a pair of eyes in a throbbing head and that's it — oh yes, and a bladder about to burst. There's no way to stop it so I let it go. My body's numb from my neck to my toes. I barely feel the bed, yet have a queasy sensation of floating. A little bit like my death experience.

Now my nose itches and I can't reach it . . . I need water.

"Nurse," I try to shout, but nothing comes out. My lips are so dry they've glued themselves shut over a swollen tongue inside my mouth, all caked and crusty.

"Water," I try to call again. Once more it's silent and that machine pings rhythmically behind me, seemingly louder. If that nurse would just wake up . . . she doesn't budge an inch. I fall into senselessness.

"Get on your challenges, every one of them! Do this the moment they arrive," the young woman calls to me through my dreams. *"Always ride on top of the wave of your challenges. They're wild stallions flying in time. They will be grounded and that's up to you."*

"What happened to me? What am I doing here?"

"Your appendix ruptured and you were rushed to this hospital. Your organs failed one at a time from peritonitis and you died, but you made it back. Congratulations!"

A load of sensations stir up into confusion while anxiety again races through me.

"You have two options here," the young woman says. *"Breathing and learning to deal with the world, or not breathing and leaving the world — and dealing with that."*

This startles me awake and my body has gone from numb to on fire. I don't open my eyes this time, but burst into tears of frustration. It pulls and shakes my raging gut and I realize that I can move my body but it is strapped down. The raging tears generate moisture in my mouth, just enough to slip my tongue between my caked lips and open them.

"Hey," I call out not very loudly and raspy as hell from the tube in my throat. I open my eyes and call again. "Hey — help me." These words are a tiny bit louder but have no impact on the nurse's sleep. My quivering lips grab one more faint breath as I load it into my lungs and brace myself for another try. "HELP!" screeches from my mouth.

The nurse's round face lights into a broad smile. "Hey Buddy," she says with excitement. "Welcome home." She jumps to her feet and into my face.

I can't get my bearings with her face right in mine and I've not had a conversation in awhile except with angels . . . so I eek out a question, "Am I actually alive here? 'Cause I've been dead you know."

She's plump and jovial, laughing as she answers. "No, you're very much alive, and thank God too. I mean thank God you're finally awake. You've been out there for a very, very long time. You've been gone for days. Talk to me while I call in the doctor. He's gonna be so excited that you're back."

She reaches for the phone without taking her eyes off mine.

"Say something to me, say anything at all and just keep talking and stay awake. Okay Buddy?"

She keeps calling me Buddy like it's my name. I try to speak, but little comes out. My mind's full of pictures but no words come out. I stare . . . she stares right back, like we're negotiating with our eyes.

"I died," suddenly blurts from my lips without warning.

"Don't worry, don't worry about that. The doctor's on his way and this is all under control. Just relax, but please don't close your eyes."

"This scares the shit out of me," coughs from my mouth.

"Woo," she jumps . . . you startled me there."

"I remember the death in every detail," I continue.

"Don't pay attention to that, whatever it was," she muddles around my sheets. "It's nothing, really — just nothing."

"Are you kidding?" I speak as loud as I can. "Look at me! Look at this mess!" She looks blank as a post with no response.

"A real nightmare, wasn't it?" A man's voice interrupts us as he enters the room. "Dr. Burgess," he reports quite soldier-like. "I'm the one who removed your worn-out appendix. You've been having one hell of a time here and I'm sorry we've not been able to make you more comfortable." He says all this at such a speed that the words tumble together.

"Yeah," I answer faintly. "I died."

"Nightmares . . . it's the morphine we've been pumping into you. It's a common reaction, very bad dreams."

"No, I've had plenty of bad dreams too. I'm not talking about that. I mean I really went somewhere. I had a whole experience and I saw you . . . here and . . ."

I feel excitement talking about my experience and want to say everything at once, but have trouble forming my words.

"I heard you . . . all of you . . . you . . . you people."

"What did we say?" he asks, unconvinced that I could possibly know what had been going on. "You know you were completely out of it."

"Yes, of course, but I could hear and I could see. Like when you said, 'We've lost him,' and I saw a body lying there. Then, I felt the electricity of those paddles."

By now I'm barely able to whisper, but I continue to scratch out a few last words, anxious to explain it all to him.

"I was out there. I saw this whole room — from up there on the ceiling."

He glances at the nurse with amusement in his eyes. "That's a good one," he chuckles. "You certainly need some rest."

"And when you put those electric things on me, it was horrible pain."

"Don't pay attention to any of this. You just heard what we might say when we're working on a critical patient, and you were definitely critical."

He takes some equipment from his pocket and begins to examine my eyes and ears with a tiny flashlight . . . walks to the other side of my bed and continues.

"I'll be brutally honest with you, son, as I am with all my patients. I keep everyone fully informed at all times." He pauses to look closer with the flashlight in my eyes, then inside my mouth. "It's not at all unusual, when someone's as sick as you, for the entire body to quit on us — right when we're working on it. Even the heart can stop for a few moments."

"How long did mine stop? How long was I out there?"

He looks straight at me, "Yours completely stopped for just under two minutes. That's all."

"How long? It seemed like I was dead for days."

He looks troubled by my determination. "One minute and forty-five seconds to be exact. But we don't call it death."

"What was it then?"

"Peritonitis, then the kidneys failed," he smiles that same defensive grin. "It shut you down tight as a drum, but it wasn't permanent, now was it? We were fully prepared for this and got you right back." He looks over at the nurse for some confirmation; they both nod as if trying to convince me. "There's no permanent damage as far as I can see." He turns off his light and wraps up his tools. "You'll be in great shape real soon."

"Can you tell me what any of my experience means?"

"Well, I don't know about the other side, but I know you need to rest right now on this side," he says firmly, "I'm giving you something to make you more comfortable. We'll talk about this another time. I guarantee it."

I try for one more question as he's leaving the room, but the drugs win out. The unanswered questions pulsate in my throbbing head as my eyes close and sleep fades the room to black. In the darkness of dreamtime, old man appears by my side, the music returning with their presence.

"Am I dead again?"

"*No, you're very much alive now.*"

"Why are you here?" I'm strangely happy to hear his voice.

"*I told you we'd visit,*" he reminds me. "*You made it back. Now it will be rougher, but you're fine. You did well and you'll deal with what is coming.*"

"I don't feel well, and no one's talking about it at all."

"*No, they won't, but they know — not like you know, but they know what happened, according to their measurements. They don't understand what took place because they have no words to explain what you've been through, so they simply deny it.*"

"The doctor claims that it was only a couple of minutes or so."

"*That's right — in Earth time it was only that,*" he smiles as if telling me a big secret. "*Remember what I told you about time; every moment is a seed. Here it's just minutes, but on the other side it's actually approaching infinity. And you were definitely there on the infinite side of time.*"

"Yeah . . . I remember," I reply, reflecting on the agony.

"*Don't go into pity or sympathy,*" he warns. "*Stay with brightness in the days to come. It's the only attitude that will work.*"

"Will anyone ever talk to me about this?"

"*Probably not, well perhaps your parents, but for most folks it's not comfortable. For doctors especially, talking about things they don't under-stand puts them through hell. Don't be hard on them. Their profession takes great pride in being an expert. This gets them through their lives with only a few blunders.*"

"What do you mean?"

"*Your purpose is to get well and pursue your dream, not argue with doctors. Don't expect them to understand. Science has an interesting way of denying magic when logic fails to produce the answers.*"

I smile at his explanation. "This is the kind of talk I need. It's wonderful to see you again. You make such good sense for a change, it's refreshing."

"*Yes I do,*" he replies without pride. "*You need to remember these lessons, because you'll be challenged from here on out and they will keep you on track. You can't be bothered by any of this — it happened for a reason, you'll see."* He assures me with his voice and his eyes at the same time.

"You've committed to your dream, so the universe will test that commitment. Retrieve your physical strength and do not get caught in the little upsets." He looks straight through me. *"You never had the courage for this before; now you're going to get what you've waited lifetimes for. It will come with great challenge, but it will come."*

"I'm not sure what you mean," I say as I begin to awaken then doze for a moment more.

"Ignore the small battles — they're distractions," he answers. With these words sunlight fills my room and I'm awake again.

"My God," I hear my dad's voice say as my eyes adjust to the sunlight.

Mom leans over my bed and kisses me on the forehead, holds my hand, and puts her head on my chest.

"We almost lost you there," Dad says with tears in his eyes. He reaches for my hand and carefully holds it through all the tubes and needles.

We sit and look into each other's eyes for the longest time. Family has never been so clearly defined as it is right now and with this family made up of a bunch of otherworldly yogis, I am glad to be alive. Tears of joy well up in my eyes, the warmth of family in my heart and not a thought of what could be said crosses my mind. Eventually, I close my eyes, holding both their hands tightly and feeling more comfort than I've known for a long time.

My hospital bed sits near a small curtained window. I'm aware of the passage of time only by the sunlight appearing and disappearing into the night and by its return each morning. I wake, sleep and dream for days. One moment after another wanders through my morphine-laden system. I stare blankly into the miracle of life remaining intensely aware of the gift of each breath. People visit and I don't remember them and then I dream of visitors who've never come. Every time I shut my eyes — the old man and the young woman are with me. They bring real news, stuff that makes sense while the doctors and nurses are all pretty vague.

Mom and Dad are grateful beyond belief for my recovery. This ordeal is challenging for my father. His Father was killed when he was only 12 years old and his first wife and their only son both died during childbirth. He was 21 then and he suffered so much death that he basically swore off relationships until years later when he met my mother. I see the deep relief in his face every time he visits.

"There were real people on the other side," I tell him. "They claim they are my guides."

"I figured so," he smiles back. "Probably some that I know, huh?"

"Yeah — I'll bet you do."

His eyes are so soft and accurate. He's an artist and he looks like one. Mom is a musician and that is who I am — an artist and a musician.

"Having someone you can trust is worth more than gold," he says. "These guides around you, you'll want to keep them your whole life."

"It seems like I will."

As I sleep, the music starts up again. "What is that?" I ask in darkness.

"The sounds of the universe creating life," answers the young woman. *"This is the harmony of space and life is created through harmony. As space shifts to accommodate, it creates time and time is what life is. This is the sound of that movement. We call it the music of the spheres."*

"It's incredible. How can anything be so clear?"

"Space is just that — clarity — by being just what it is and nothing else. Remember to live in the space not yet occupied."

"Not occupied?" I ask.

"Yes — it creates no contests, no competitions and no battles . . . that's harmony. From that space not yet occupied you can move into space that does not yet exist. That's where the real phenomenon is born — that's what this Earth needs. It needs phenomenon to lift the spirit more than anything."

"I want to make those sounds in my music."

"Then let music be the focus of your life and let the sounds of reality become the harmonies of life itself. When people hear it, their lives will begin to change. When you create this sound in music, you can change the world and bring harmony where there's none . . . turn conflict into concert."

"That's cool," I respond, "turning conflict into concert."

I open my eyes to the leathery old expression and dark brown eyes of a custodian staring at me while dusting my room.

"Excuse me," he says, as he politely wipes the bed railing. "I didn't mean to wake you, son." His voice is kind and gentle. "I'll just clean here."

He looks exactly like the old man in my dreams. I stare closely to determine if it's him and as I smile at his brightness, he continues to talk.

"Are you happy now?" he asks as he comes a bit closer. "I mean, I hear you've been through hell."

"That's the same thing they asked when I was dead," I whisper back, still finding it hard to talk with the tube in my throat. "They asked if I was happy. Am I dead again?"

A huge smile washes over his gentle face. He stumbles for the words to answer. "I'm really sorry you had to go through all that. Where my family comes from we know about these things, but no one speaks of it here in your country. You're okay son, you're not dead. You probably were, but you'll stay here for now. We'll be needing you."

He turns and moves toward the door as sunlight falls gently through my window, keeping the space bright.

"Thank you," I whisper as he walks into the hall. "Thank you for that."

He nods and my voice, speaking a bit louder, quivers like wind through the leaves. "I will live." And for the first time in a long time I know I will.

Three

Music is Freedom

I will live, but I also relive my death with each close of my eyes when the old man and young woman arrive. In dreams, I live in their rhythmical voices pounding lesson after lesson into my head. Maybe I'm ungrateful, or somewhat reluctant with my life just being snatched from death, but I want to slow these lessons down. The many messages are mixing up in my brain.

"Whenever there is a morning where you awaken, and you are unable to appreciate the day," the old man cautions, *"that is a morning when you are not alive. Time spent without awareness of one's mortality is a complete waste."* His eyes sparkle as he makes this point abundantly clear.

"I don't want to keep remembering my death," I complain.

"This is what makes life important each day. It keeps you at your very best, as if it could be your last. It makes each moment you spend the moment to end all moments."

"Does it have to be terrifying?"

"Terror is the result of resistance. When you stop resisting you'll experience the grace. Right now you're frightened of the unknown. Learn to find comfort in this discomfort."

I want to escape this focus on death, but he is never concerned with my desires. *"Time in life is measured by the breaths you take,"* he tells me. *"The only gifts you actually own in life are these breaths. Time cannot be saved from one day to the* next, *or passed from one person to another; it can only be spent. To gain the greatest value from each day you must remember your mortality and spend life with unreserved enthusiasm."*

He pronounces each word with precision whenever I hear the echoes of his voice. *"Enthusiasm is your clue — be in Theo — be in God,"* he pauses. *"Be enthusiastic every day."*

Days blur into weeks and I finally leave the hospital. Missing so much school, I have to drop out. When I wake up every day, I have to check to see if I'm dead or alive. It's hard to sleep with the constant dreams — nightmares really. The old man and young woman wait just beyond sleep's horizon. Even if it's only for a moment's doze, they take me back into their world, turning my world upside down.

"Death changes life," old man says. *"If you use it right, it creates a focus on the present. It insists that you release the past."*

"But memories are important."

"When memories support who you actually are and nourish who you want to be, then hold on to them. If not, release them and let them dissolve."

I remember the story of a four-year-old boy whose mother gave birth to a baby sister. He persistently begged his parents to let him talk to this newborn sibling all by himself, which concerned them tremendously.

"Why would he possibly want to be all alone with her?" they asked each other.

He persisted and insisted on being alone and finally they consented, but watched carefully through a crack in the doorway.

The boy approached the crib very gently. "Little sister," he said respectfully. "Please tell me what God looks like . . . I'm starting to forget."

I felt close to God right after I died, but time clouds the experience. I'm like that little boy as every day shifts the clarity from my mind and leaves a footprint of life's muddle. Very few people want to talk about it, avoiding their judgment keeps me silent.

This lack of understanding leaves me heavy and probably quite depressing to be around.

In the emptiness that's left, I'm on my own. Sometimes I sing till my voice disappears, but the visions of death don't fade. So I go running till I drop, and collapse in a pool of sweaty silence — cruising for a moment without gravity, but it's only a slight relief.

"Gravity is a force of nature," the young woman says. *"It's the force that eventually takes you to your grave. Your job in life is to lift it, resist its heaviness and levitate your heart. If you don't, you'll become numb with depression long before you're dead."*

"I am depressed," I explain to her.

"Okay — let's get out of it."

"How?" I ask.

"Depression is a version of life, it's a vision without a possibility or hope, right?"

"Yeah."

"Without hope you lose your will, and when you lose your will, you lose the ability to move into the future. This is depression — stuck in a moment until that moment moves into the past and takes you with it — then your present moments are empty and they collapse in on you."

"This is exactly it!"

"Here is what you must do. Take what you want to achieve and for this moment think of yourself as a bloodhound. Think of this vision — as the future of your life and study it with great attention. Connect with all the details and make mental notes. A bloodhound is very accurate with its sense of smell and now you are going to become very accurate with all of your senses as well. This will give you the true 'scent' of what you're looking for. All the bloodhound needs to find its target is a little bit of the scent. Then it follows that scent all the way to its success. The key is certainty."

With these words I awaken into thought. At the time of my illness, I was studying architecture, wishing I could be singing, but staying in school to avoid the draft. My real dream came to me at the age of five when I started playing piano. From then on it was music first.

"Connect to these values, to what is important, to that sense of wisdom," the old man's voice echoes. *"It's the connection that counts, without connection your space is filled without you — this is what depression actually is."*

"That's it!" I think out loud. "It's music."

The first time I played along with the radio as a young child I said to myself, "I can do this!"

By the age of 10, I'd stand in front of the mirror with my guitar pretending to be on stage. It's November 1965 and there is a real problem with my dreams. America is tangled in a very ugly and unrighteous war in Viet Nam. Boys my age, caught right out of school, are doing the killing. It's on the mind of everyone I know.

I talked to a soldier who was badly wounded in Viet Nam and he says he goes through nightmares every day. He also says that I should be receiving my draft notice anytime now that I am out of college.

Before the hospital, I stayed in school, unable to muster the courage to pursue my dream. I've used the war as an excuse to hide my passion and this is exactly what the old man scolded me for the night I died.

"But there's a war going on," I told him.

"It's not your war."

"I know, but the law says it's mine."

"Let those who cause this law, fight this war."

"But what about the law."

"Challenge it — law is logic and sometimes logic is out of place."

"They say that's un-American."

"America was born from the right to protest. It's an essential part of freedom and a true patriot will always exercise this freedom."

It reminded me of my college history teacher. The signing of the 'Declaration of Independence' was an act of freedom for those who did it and the British called it treason.

"There will always be a conflict when you reach into the infinite to produce your mission," the old man tells me. *"That is the nature of nature. For every action there is an equal reaction and there is nothing else*

more certain in the material world. Freedom to one is treason to another just as one finds trash where another sees treasure."

These are the conversations I don't share with anyone except my friends who just think I'm crazy.

"Every proposition, every movement forward, creates opposition; it's a law of physics," the old man explains. *"The faster you move forward, the greater the opposition against you. It's time to stand and face this law with a sense of self and a sense of humor. You will retain your power when you don't take opposition personally. Just see it as the law of what is and move around it tactfully."*

"How long will that take?" I ask.

"As long as you allow it to, just like everything. This world is your reflection, but not all the moments are aligned. You'll be able to experience this now, because you're opened by death. Most people can't feel any of this."

"I actually wish that was true for me."

"Do not wish that. Be real — the world has filtered this. They use their attractions and distractions and busy-ness to focus on because reality is just too real."

"And when it's confusing as hell?"

"It's a gift. You'll get used to it, and once you learn to walk with it, you'll understand what a blessing it is."

"What makes you call this real?"

"Everyone in this world reflects a piece of who we are. We're always most critical of those who show up with our own worst faults. This is the awareness you'll be working with from now on. Since time is only available in the three dimensions, experienced through the five senses — the timing of the reflections is not logical. Sometimes you will receive a reflection of the world from the distant past and sometimes it's from the future."

"It's lonely. What about the others?"

"Loyalty to your growth isn't lonely, this is where all other relationships begin. Fill yourself with the experience of being you and let it grow — let it overflow. People will gather because you feel so good to be around. Remember, when you don't fill up with your excellence, you fill up with your regrets instead."

"I've been there."

"Then don't go back. It is a matter of your choice."

Doctors dismiss my stories as flashbacks and panic attacks, they offer me drugs to sleep to take the edge off but they make it worse. I feel what others are feeling, I often hear what they're thinking and often can't tell the difference between my thoughts and theirs. It's really hell — it's like being without skin and bones.

"Learn to use this ability and it won't be hell," the young woman tells me.

An art student who drew a picture of me the other day said she could see right through me. In the drawing, my nerves were on the outside of my body and my eyes were turned inward.

"That's exactly it," I told her, and for a moment it was wonderful to meet a person who could actually relate. I now can sense a slight momentum coming on and have to learn to use this emptiness. I tell my few friends, "I'll deliver."

"Deliver what?" they ask me.

"My promise."

"Promise . . . . . . to who?"

"To me. Before, I thought I was out there, but I was too logical, I was too careful, planned, and safe — all that logic and safety killed me."

"So what are you gonna do now?" they ask. "You know that the Army is going to come after you soon."

"Trust and try out whatever I dream because without a dream, the rest of this 'hiding from the Army' existence is for shit."

"Now is the time to be forgiving — not angry. Anger only hides your hope," old man explains. *"You mustn't destroy hope when your prayers are being answered."*

"How can I forgive this?"

"For-give is a word in reverse. It actually means to give forth. It's a way of letting go of each bad moment. You want to keep releasing time, because time passes, and if you hold onto any moment, then time will pass you by. The more you hold on to, the less reality you're in touch with. This can get really bad when you hold grudges — then you get really stuck."

"You're saying that the world has this all wrong then."

"I'm saying that the world is living in the past. Practicing forgiveness allows you to move forward into the present moment and the present is the only moment that's alive."

"Why does anger turn everything into such a struggle?"

"It focuses your mind on the past. It focuses on the object of your anger and keeps you from living in the present. Forgiving the past will move your awareness forward to now — the present moment."

"From this perspective, the world looks like slavery."

"This world is enslaved."

"Even when I want to go back to a 'normal' life, I can't. How do people stick with it?"

"By ignoring reality, remember, 'ignorance is bliss'."

"Right . . ."

"It requires lots of distractions to keep people from being bored with a "normal" life," young woman laughs. *"So the toys of distraction pile up, along with the bills to pay for them. It's great for the economy, but it's a life without joy. Pleasure is then used to substitute for happiness leading to emptiness because it doesn't work."*

These are the messages that ring in my head and sing through the lyrics of my new songs, like the one I just wrote called "Time."

TIME© Gerry Pond

Time rushes by — waste none of it in slavery
When this time leaves it will never return
Trust and try — in the end you'll deliver
Time's all you have in this life that is yours

Song after song, rough songs or incomplete songs, singing and writing is my new therapy. The music keeps me going . . . it's my freedom.

Four

WALKIN' HIGH

I've dropped out of college and can now be that 'Conscientious Protestor' full-time, focusing on music and writing songs. The Army wastes no time in calling me up for a Draft physical.

"We're headed for war boys," a sergeant bellows across the room with a shrill voice. "Stand straight . . . I mean perfectly straight."

There are all kinds of officers hollering and banging their batons on metal desks in this large room. They've divided us into groups. The noise tightens like a vice around my throat.

"Today, I'm your boss," another yells. "And you will do what I tell you."

I cringe at this false bravado designed to drive in fear and obedience. This is the climate of 1965: those who believe in America at peace versus those who believe in America at war.

I'm standing amongst a few hundred other guys, all my age — nearly naked and totally freaked out. We're full of our own dreams and probably not one includes being gung ho for war. I've lost forty pounds from my time in the hospital, the skinniest one in the room, and haven't cut my hair in months. I look like a skeleton with a mop on my head.

"Skinny little shit — look straight," an officer mumbles, as he paces like a peacock, his eyes scowling over the room.

I'm jittery and can't help my nerves — the intimidation is working. My bladder has been full for an hour, but the Army says we can't leave the lines for any reason. We're dripping with fear and perspiration at stiff attention waiting to see the creepiest looking doctors sitting at desks nearby. They seem to be weighing and measuring each one of us for body bags.

Intense fear smells of gloom and doom, the same smell I remember in the hospital.

"I gotta piss here," blurts un-muffled from my mouth.

"You gotta shut the fuck up boy!" blasts back from an officer.

I try to do just that, but I'm way beyond holding it. Minutes pass like hours and I try relaxing as best I can. Old man taught me to breathe deep and from the diaphragm. *"It calms you,"* he said.

"When all else fails, it gets you in touch with the silence of your inner strength," his voice comes through my senses.

I need some inner strength around my bladder right now. I close my eyes and focus on breathing, inhaling the mountains, forests and streams through my nose and blowing fear, chaos and disruption out through my mouth. I breathe and blow and blow and breathe, but I really, really have to pee.

Now we are told to strip all the way down, as we get closer to the doctor's stations. Everyone's a bit self-conscious about being naked and standing at attention. The Army must do this to intimidate the already embarrassed. By now, everyone's thinking about their penis and cracking jokes out of the sides of their mouths — like 10 year olds at camp. It only makes me more aware of my need to pee.

Some pretend to be brave and carefree, but it's bullshit. The truth is we're all terrified as we're being weighed and measured for death. I'm breathing and blowing and getting light-headed when suddenly old man's voice comes showering over me. *"You're done here."*

"I'm what?" comes out of my mouth.

"I said shut up!" the officer screams back.

"*You're done here,*" the old man repeats. "*Now be who you are, not who they want you to be. This is not your place and you must leave right now.*"

Trusting what he's saying, I look for the exit. It's the same sense I had when I re-entered my body, I knew I was safe, but for no reason. The room starts to darken in my vision as I catch faint peripheral glimpses of the campfire in my death, the old man's smile and his sparkling eyes, all amongst the lines of these naked and petrified kids.

"*The power of these people is not a good power — it is not for you,*" he tells me as a tingling swoops over my face and hands.

I turn to the guy next to me and ask, "Ever think about shooting someone?"

This startles the hell out of him.

"That's what they're asking us to do, you know," I continue. "What if we all just walked out of here instead — all of us, right now?"

"I thought about fighting in war," he answers, trying not to be seen talking. "I'd just lay down and cover my head."

"You gotta defend yourself," the guy next to him claims.

"Bullshit," I hiss back. "We're invading them. That's not self-defense."

"You can't just lay there and get your ass shot off," he argues.

"There's no way I'll kill," whispers a guy with bright red hair and freckles. "I can't."

"Yeah right," another challenges. "What are you supposed to do when the bullets fly?"

"Your next, smart guy." The most obnoxious examiner of them all bangs his baton on the desk and orders me forward.

I step onto the scale and call back over my shoulder, "Lambs to the slaughter!"

"You're gonna be in real trouble if you don't shut up boy." The examiner's icy voice shoots through me as he measures my height.

"Can I take a piss?" I ask, measuring my escape options.

"Hold it," he glares as he proceeds to move the metal cubes on the scale to weigh me. Amazement paints his cold, angry face with a bit of innocence in disbelief. He slides the pieces back and forth on the scale and keeps sliding and checking to make sure it's correct. "Six foot two and a 118 pounds?" he says mocking. "What the hell you been up to boy?"

"I fucking died," I reply, looking straight into his eyes.

"No shit," he says sarcastically. "You look dead. You better fatten up because the Army only takes real men, not skinny shits."

The room bursts into laughter that momentarily evaporates the fear and his words repeat in my head. "We can't take skinny shits." My arm raises and my finger, shaking from the adrenaline, points around the room. I ask him, "Do you ever wonder about us — which ones live or which ones die? After we leave here, does it cross your mind?"

"It's not my job to think about you kid, but I tell you what, I want you to step back and shut your smart mouth." He pokes me hard with his stick, right into my belly and the surgical scarring that hasn't completely healed yet.

All the air immediately vanishes from my lungs and the pain surges as if my intestines have exploded.

I can't breathe, my throat has locked, and I bend over, nearly fainting. Rage and desperation erupt simultaneously from my gut. Agonizing voices run ferociously off the end of my tongue with no control or meaning to the words … I just rant.

Old man appears — totally calm. *"Now you're ready to fly,"* he encourages me. *"Pass through this moment like an arrow."*

I raise my head . . . certain my guts are bleeding . . . crazed. I'm now the predator as I glare into the doctor's shocked eyes. I spit through my pain-clenched teeth. "You should fucking be a doctor."

He's caught by the total intensity of what I'm saying, a man frozen like prey before the kill and for a brief moment I relish the power I have over him. My blood boiling with total commitment to victory, the scene escalates rapidly out of control. My brain's not in my body as I watch what follows from the ceiling of the room.

"Fuck!" I shriek, my eyes shooting dangerously through the room searching for escape. I race out of control; reach out my arms to clear a path. I dash past the lines of naked fear, my fingers spread like claws, and my bladder surrendering its urine. From above, this scene unfolds a vision in slow motion. No one dares challenge me for a few moments out of fear of getting pissed on or clobbered in the pandemonium. They lean away from my waving arms like corn stalks under the harvest blade. As I reach the exit, I'm tackled hard from behind, smashing to the floor. The wind and all sense fly from my lungs; my arms are wrenched behind my back as handcuffs snap into place.

I'm totally exhausted . . . and definitely excited.

The Army acts as if I'm contagious. "Get him out of here!" screams one officer.

I'm dragged across the floor by my legs, into a separate room and tossed onto a chair like a rag doll. Another set of handcuffs quickly attaches me to the chair.

I lay my head on the table and sigh, "Wow . . . what a rush." I think, feeling strangely free, like the wind.

With a ton of questions they take pages of notes about my medical and mental history. I barely mumble the answers. I'm totally spent. I've known all along that I'd never serve a day in this Army, but I wasn't sure how I'd get out of it. They all look pretty scared of me right now. Like they've been through a war, they've never seen someone like me before.

After a great deal of psychiatric commotion going back and forth, I end up at the front desk. There, awaits the news in the form of an official document. I read the first few words:

Draft Deferment Classification (1-Y)
You have been determined to be medically unfit to serve in . . .

I feel a rush of energy as I struggle to contain my thrill until I'm outside of the building. Once outside, the spell is broken and I'm yelling at the top of my lungs. The people passing on the street can't believe their ears as I scream my victory until I have no voice.

I walk the 10 miles home on silver clouds through Seattle, way too excited to take the bus. I'm dancing, running, more than I'm walking — a total state of joy. I feel higher than the clouds, my mind ringing with clarity. The words and music to a brand new song fill my head and I sing it over and over and over to make sure I remember it all.

WALKIN' HIGH © Gerry Pond 1965

CHORUS:
Here come I, walking high — seagulls fly in a pale blue sky
A little cat yellow eyed — trips along by my side
Dii dii dee dii dii

VERSE:
Riding fear's a giant wave — into your doubt your life has played
Escape the roads that make you wrong — walkin' high we'll carry on . . .

I call it Walkin' High, and it becomes an anthem, full of rhythm and enthusiasm and constantly reminding me of the courage it takes to be free. The story behind how I wrote it spreads quickly, and my friends jokingly refer to it as *'The Dead Man's Song'*.

"In order to live, to be fully alive, you must be willing to die," old man says.

"Not in a stupid war I hope."

"Choose wisely what you're willing to die for . . . because it will end up being the reason you live."

Five

BREAKS AND BRAKES

I've been writing constantly since surviving the Army draft. I write songs and test them on small audiences at coffee houses on the avenue known locally as the 'U. District' — adjacent to the college. You can just walk in with your guitar and play.

"When you powerfully maintain your dream, your dream will come true powerfully." The old man's words visit my thoughts now. This happens even when I'm awake, alongside his words, the 'harmonies of the universe'.

I'm nervous performing, even when the gathering is small; songs expose a writer in ways that are not always comfortable. You don't have control over what you write most of the time — it just comes through. This is about to take on a whole new level as I wait to go onstage at the largest 'Peace Rally and Teach-In' ever held at this University.

I was picked up at the coffee house by the organizers and now I'm here singing, proclaiming my dream with no excuses or apologies, in front of 5,000 people. I feel anxiety mixed up with freedom and complete commitment . . . quite the mix. I nervously tune and re-tune my guitar to take my mind off what's about to happen. A professor, an authority on the history of American conflicts, speaks from the stage without pause, able to ignore the ironic clarity of her words.

"In 1945," her voice rings out, "at the end of World War II, when the Japanese surrendered to America . . . our ally in driving the Japanese out of Southeast Asia was none other than General Ho Chi Minh and his armies."

The crowd stirs noisily with whistles and banners waving. She looks at her watch and back to her notes — this must mean I'm on soon.

"After the war, Ho Chi Minh wanted 'self-rule' for his homeland," she continues, "a land that France had colonized in the nineteenth century. He wanted this occupation of his homeland to end, just like Gandhi wanted the British out of India, just like our forefathers wanted the British out of America."

"By 1954," the professor continues, "the French were pushed out and General Ho Chi Minh became a national hero just like George Washington. The people of Vietnam . . ."

My mind loses track of her point when the old man's voice comes through, *"When you walk in these shadows of history, do so as a pilgrim not a slave. When you react to the shadows in anger, you are always a slave to the anger."*

". . . The people of Vietnam have the same rights as our founding fathers had, the same rights as we do — as everyone does."

I'm struggling to remember the words to my first song as well as the reason I agreed to sing here in the first place.

The old man reminds me, *"Your songs are about hope amongst these challenges — hold the space of hope."*

"I leave you with this," the speaker tells the crowd. "Colonization was traditionally about gold, money and slavery — that's been replaced with oil, money and land . . . it still creates slavery and now we have a bloodbath on our hands."

I reach for the words to my first song as I'm swept up the stairs by the energy of the crowd, but her words are all that swim in my head.

The crowd chants, "NO MORE WAR — NO MORE WAR!"

As she acknowledges their response, I step beside her to face this sea of brilliant, rebellious faces reminding me of all the guys I stood naked with at the Draft. How many of them will die in the fields of this war? I approach the microphone filled with these emotions.

"I've never been this committed in my life," I announce to the crowd, but they pay little attention. They're still talking amongst themselves about the professor. My old friends are sure to be out there somewhere, the same ones who think I'm crazy now.

"We're all aware of the war-drums," I shout. "Peace is a dirty word."

This gets their attention.

"To accept this war . . ." The crowd holds up the two fingers for peace.

". . . We're just slaves right here." I scream louder, adjusting my guitar strap with adrenaline and the cold wind shaking my hands.

"When we give away our blood like this we're slaves." Thousands shuffle uncomfortably and start yelling out their thoughts.

"I've personally experienced the sham this nation is running. A week ago, I failed my Army physical." Cheers and hissing billow like smoke amongst the flags and banners, waving in the wind that whips a light rain.

I begin strumming chords in the rhythm of my song. "We know how we're sacrificed in death fields. Right?"

"Right!" echoes back from the crowd.

"We know how we're stripped of clothing and grace, to be broken of identity and dignity." The crowd is agitated, like horses before thunder as the storm clouds gather.

"We're the children of this nation — we're the blood of the future. Right?"

"Right!" they yell.

"Let's refuse to spill our precious blood on the financial schemes of old men; old men who only want to profit from our death. This is how it's been for the thousands of years of war. When you die for nothing, it means nothing and you get nothing in return."

The crowd resembles a revival meeting — all their heads nodding together to the rhythm, starting to clap with it as if answering a 'Holy Spirit of Peace'.

"We represent the voice of reason and it's our duty to protest. They don't like what we're saying, and we need to say it louder." My guitar gets louder. The rain clouds overhead bring in a strong wind. It blows through the trees at the shores of Lake Washington as if answering the call.

"We must maintain the civil rights that allow us the freedom to be who we are." Police lines check their nightsticks; ranking officers scribble notes on little white pads and journalists take photographs of the crowd for the morning news. Everyone's ready for action.

"We're the 'Spirit of America' and we're here to stop this injustice, even if that injustice is the law."

One large telephoto lens in the distance focuses directly on my face, but it's no journalist. By the looks of him, it's the police for sure. These stark contrasts surrounding the gathering add urgency to the music and bring an unusual confidence to my voice, building and sharpening with each word.

"How is this any different than Hitler?" I call out. "Did the Jews vote for Auschwitz?"

"No!" they answer in unison.

"Did you and I vote for this war?"

"No!" they shout it again.

"We're too young to vote, but we're old enough to die."

The crowd of thousands thunder and the campus police fidget with their belts.

"Here's a song. It's about living free and oh yeah . . . how to fail a Draft physical." They laugh and whistle. "If you want to know more about that bit, ask me later."

I tune the high 'E' string and begin my song *Walkin' High*. My voice snaps from the speakers like fire. The sound carries with the wind and rain, over the crowd, across the field and clear to the lake. It's just my voice and guitar, but it sounds like an entire band — hands clapping with enthusiasm fill the cold damp Seattle air. With the final words that I sing, I feel free like never before. As I walk off the stage, I catch the eyes of a crowd filled with tears of joy. There's been a birth here, I think silently. I can make a difference."

An older man, in his forties, approaches me with an outstretched hand. "Congratulations," he says, "I want you to do that same thing in my club."

"You want me to play my songs?" I ask, still rushing with adrenaline.

"I want the whole thing. I want the talking and the singing. I want it all, just like you did here."

"Sure, I'll do that."

He smiles, "Good things happen when you speak the truth, don't they? My name's Jimmy Greene. I own the Que Queg."

"Good to meet you, Jimmy."

"Can you come over tonight, Gerry?"

"You bet, I'll be there," I shake his hand again, feeling euphoric as I walk away. "I'm doing this," I say quietly.

"7:30!" Jimmy calls after me.

The Que Queg is not a place for the lazy mind or the faint of heart. This is where the counter culture action is at for any student with an agenda. The bulletin board inside and the telephone poles outside are cluttered with posters announcing every gathering. Old man's, *Be enthusiastic* stays with me as I prepare five songs and arrive an hour early.

"Do just what you did on campus," Jimmy greets me, noticing how anxious I am. "Music is your gift, and an opportunity exists here."

When I go on stage there's about 130 people in the club. This is an entirely different experience, intimate and slightly intimidating. The first song barely comes out at all, but they applaud kindly. I say nothing between songs and forget some words to the next one. A table full of customers leaves. Sweat builds on my back, chills run through my arms. "Is this what I really want to be doing?" I think to myself. "This is hell."

After my second song, Jimmy jumps on stage and addresses the 90 or so people that are left. "I'm gonna ask this young man to say a fcw words to you and thcn sing a song I hcard him play earlier today." He pats me on the back and steps off like an expectant coach.

After a brief applause from the gathering and a little nod from Jimmy, I say some words, but can't get my tongue moving. I sing **Walkin' High** half-heartedly, walk from the stage and slump into a chair at Jimmy's table.

"Woo, that was tough," I tell him.

"Don't worry about it. This is where you start from, not where you end. It's far easier to work a faceless crowd of thousands than it is an intimate club."

"You got that," I reply, and remember the old man's words. *"Fear is just an excuse to fail."*

"Come back here tomorrow and we'll get started again."

"Okay," I reply, surprised by the invitation.

"Yeah, you're not getting away that easily."

As I walk through the tables and chairs, I feel every eye upon me. Each step seems endless until the door swings open to the evening air. "Holy shit," I shudder out loud.

Night after night I sing, struggle, and play my guitar at the Que Queg, and Jimmy keeps asking me back. It's like a performance school for me, and Jimmy's the professor. The show improves each night and crowds start showing up. In a couple of months, it's a fan club and some nights we have standing room only. I'm talking to the audience like family now. This is Seattle 1965; there's a sense of belonging that comes from a small town and every so often the cops show up just to check us out.

My songs write themselves day after day and I test them on the audience each night. Other clubs hear the buzz and ask me to play, but Jimmy's been too good, so I sit tight.

One night, I see him sitting with a small group of very grouchy looking men. "It was the FBI," he tells me later. Believe it or not, your message is getting around town."

"When you move forward you're bound to attract resistance," the old man whispers. *"This is a basic law of nature, the way reality works. Every action has an equal reaction."*

"When does it get easy?" I ask.

"When you accept each moment as the lesson of your life and learn your way through it."

The very next morning, I have the complete opposite reaction to my lesson and this reality strikes fear into my mind with a shock wave. The FBI has brought out my demon and I'm reminded of the Draft Board experience all over. I try all day to shake it, but nothing works. I call Jimmy in the late afternoon and tell him I'm sick, but I don't tell him why. I stay away from the club for three nights and don't even touch my guitar.

I take off for the country and camp in the woods by a hot spring and an icy river. I jump from one to the other all day long to clear my head. I'm a fraud without answers in a warehouse full of doubt.

"You are not the doer; you are not the dreamer; you are not the dream . . . you are the dreaming." The young woman tells me in the night.

"This isn't anything like I thought it would be."

"So how is it different?"

"It's stopped being fun, now it's work."

"Make your work your worship and dream your existence. You must give up the struggle by giving up your resistance."

"How?"

"Your life as you would dream it to be is here for you if you allow it to be. Use your imagination and meditation to design, define and refine the images. This is the power of being human."

After three days of talking to no one, but these two, I call Jimmy.

"Hey babe," he says with total innocence in his voice, "you coming back to play for us? The Feds are gone," he laughs. "You can come out of hiding now."

I'm a bit lost for words to explain, but I try. "I don't know Jimmy, this isn't me you're seeing up there each night. I'm in way over my head."

"Well, you're doing a great job of fooling everyone. Keep it up."

"Who the hell am I to be up there on stage preaching, like I'm some great performer? I'm just me and this act doesn't feel real anymore. When people find out and the illusion is over . . . then I'm a complete phony."

"No you're not — this is what we call in the business, 'coming to the end of the beginning'. This always happens with the first bite of success. It's all fun and games when you want something badly, when it's just a fantasy in your head, but the reality of getting it hits you hard and that hit has no mercy. The Feds just whacked you with a giant reality check."

"So you know this?" I ask.

"Of course I do. Performers have to be emotionally real, so they're always emotionally challenged. I'll be over in an hour to pick you up. Bring your guitar for tonight's show; there's someone I want you to meet."

He picks me up and with little conversation we drive north of Seattle to Lake Forest Park. He pulls over in front of a small house nestled in a cluster of tall old trees.

"I didn't tell you where we were going," he says as we walk to the porch. "I didn't want you to think about it."

An old lady in a long dark dress with a scarf wrapped around her long gray hair and a smile as big as the sky opens the door and invites us in. She kisses Jimmy like an old friend and turns to me with a hug.

"So," she says with a pause as she examines me from top to bottom. "Looks to be a real one. I'm Anita."

The house has a soft musty smell. The room is quaint with tidy knick-knacks all perfectly placed and telling their stories.

"Sit here," she motions to a large overstuffed chair as Jimmy goes for the couch. I sink, up to my shoulders in velvety cushions — she sits opposite from me and looks me up and down, left and right. "I see you brought your two friends with you," she says as her gaze continues.

"Wow," I think to myself.

"Yes, those two there with you; the older one and the other — looks like a grand-daughter."

"You see them," blurts out with relief and trust. "That's so cool that they aren't just my imagination."

She just laughs at my surprise. "I'm going to talk with them for a while," she says, closing her eyes and leaning her head back on the dark velvet. She's silent for probably 10, 15 minutes at least and then she comes back as if waking up.

"Death saved you," she says very matter-of-fact. "You must never go back to that life that ignores your desires."

"What do you mean, death?" Jimmy asks.

"Be quiet, Jimmy," she cautions him with a smile and an open hand, and then turns back to me. "He'll tell you what he wants you to know."

She looks deep into my eyes and smiles. "It's not up to you to move those mountains, you know. It's up to you to be dreaming, don't demand the results, but keep the scent and learn to trust the process."

She sounds just like the old man; my mind races with questions as she speaks in her low sweet tone.

"We all pass through life, leaving traces of wisdom in the immortal memories of each other's hearts. Do you ever wake up with a bad day on your mind?" Her eyes dig into mine for the answer.

"Yeah," I respond softly mesmerized.

"What do you do when that happens?" she laughs.

"What do I do?" I repeat her question.

"Yes — do you choose to live a different day in a different way, or do you stick with the bad one?"

I shrug as she laughs and then continues. "Your life is only made up of moments and breaths. You have an originating amount, so you don't ever want to waste one. When the demons of fear, embarrassment or doubt go dancing around you — you don't ever want to get in the dance."

I'm spinning with this conversation.

"Be the solution in life, like water in the rivers; be so flexible and persistent that you never discourage." She stops and changes her expression, pressing me into the deep cushions with her eyes. "That's what your friends have to say to you and you have got to listen."

"My friends?" I ask, but know exactly whom she means.

She stares back for the longest time without saying a word, then slowly closes her eyes and it looks like she's fallen asleep. Every once in a while she mumbles something and begins to speak again. "This is an ancient dream of yours, a dream that you're helplessly involved with now. This is not something that you have a choice in. Do you know this?"

"That's what it all feels like," I respond.

"You've been after this dream for a long time. When you were much younger it was so real that you'd live in it."

I'm amazed by what she's saying, so clear and true yet I've told her nothing.

"You have those two guides helping you right now and there will be many, many more because you'll need them," she warns me with a wink. "Guides and angels are real, you know."

"I know," I answer.

The room's very dark — not so dark that you can't see, but the kind of darkness that comes from heavy velvet pulled over windows in the middle of day. A weak bulb in the table lamp adds almost nothing. In this pale light, I swear she's gone to sleep. Jimmy later tells me she's a shaman, whatever that is.

"War," she says and then goes silent. After a minute or more she continues, "Men fixate on competition. War is competition with blood as the ball. The side that causes the most blood to spill wins. Women don't do this, because a woman's blood spills to give life, not take it."

She goes back to sleep and this time she actually snores then opens her eyes. "You'll travel with your music — not stay in Seattle, but this place will always be dear to you. You'll create a powerful opposition to what you have to say — some of this opposition will be very dangerous, filled with people who can't understand you. This will be unavoidable."

"What does that mean?" I ask.

"You'll be scared a lot of the time because this is going to move very quickly. Ancient dreams tend to do that, like they're predestined. Use the dreamtime and use your prayer work to identify your passion. You're on your path of fulfillment."

She's saying so much I want to take notes, but there's no chance.

"These are the perfect environments to take drugs and alcohol in, but you must never touch them."

"I don't."

"Good — they would murder you. Your pathway to the spirit-world will never close down now that you've died. If you were to take drugs now," she waves her arms, "you'd be right out of your body for good."

"I'm not interested," I reply softly.

"You don't have to be," she replies, "just remember what I've told you. Temptation wears many masks. You must remain committed to being you . . . to holding your vision."

"That's what the old man said when I was dead," I reply.

"I guess we're from the same place," she laughs and then goes completely silent.

We wait for a while, probably 20 minutes, but she doesn't say another word. Jimmy motions to me to get up and we make our way quietly to the door. As we open it she speaks softly, "Leave it open — I want the fresh air."

On the ride back to the club I have a million questions, but Jimmy only answers a few. "I had no idea all that happened to you," he says. "I thought you might be getting into drugs when you started skipping the club."

"No drugs," I laugh. "Just a little death."

Six

FOLLOW YOUR LOVE

*A*nita is the boost I need and my shows become the best ever. One night there's a management company from San Francisco in the front row. Jimmy's handled every detail, another angel in my life.

Anita said I'd leave Seattle and that's exactly what's happening. I push my seat back as the plane bounces rhythmically toward San Francisco. I'm excited and anxious all at once. Two GIs sit across the aisle, drinking nervously and boasting about the war they're headed for. They glance over and snicker at my condition — a sharp contrast to their crisp GI look. It's been months since my bout with the Army, and from their conversations, they could've been at the Draft Board that same day. God knows what's on their minds and I have an urge to talk, but I don't say a word. I just nod and let them know I understand. They smile back nervously to let me know that I'm the least of their worries.

The bouncing rhythm of the plane closes my tired eyes and the face of the young woman immediately takes me away into her world with its fierce stare.

"We're filled with new possibilities," she says. *"This is the time, no matter what happens, you must remain true to your promise."*

"Promise?"

"*Your promise.*"

"But that's what I'm heading to do. Why do you say, 'no matter what happens'?"

"*Because the outside opposition will become brutal now. When you initiate real progress, you face the real challenges; nature's law comes from within you. People expect it to get easier when the momentum increases, but it's the opposite, now your commitment will be tested.*"

"How can I expect it to look?"

"*However you least expect it.*"

"Why?"

"*Because you're being tested for reality. It will be testing your weaknesses as well as your strengths.*"

"Is that right?"

"*This plane you're riding in has been tested in the worst of situations so it will hold up in all situations. If not, it wouldn't be safe.*"

"I'm not a plane."

"*In order for you to advance in time, you must be able to stand the test of time. You must strengthen the worst of your abilities, as well as be skilled in your best.*"

"This is fair?"

"*Reality isn't fair — it's real. It's important to know your weaknesses. Without this knowledge you're playing at life and expanding the control of weakness by playing it safe. When you're not testing your potential, you don't know your limits or your abilities.*"

"So this is it?"

"*For a while . . . you made your promise; you guaranteed your dream and the purpose of your life.*"

"Yeah?"

"*Well, now fear might dare you to turn away — to run back into ignorance. Now is the time you will shine or shrink.*"

"How will I know?"

"*You'll learn from your pain by remaining aware of the lessons embedded in your dream.*"

"What will pain tell me?"

"*It will tell you what parts of your life are in favor, and what parts are against you. Be careful of blame here.*"

"This doesn't give much to go on."

"*This is your walk into the unknown, just like you promised. It's always filled with opposition and mystery, that's why it is the unknown. Faith is essential — trust your promise and the innocence that made you promise.*"

"But why so much mystery?"

"*When you're stagnant, everything is familiar . . . you don't move. When you grow, everything is new.*"

"And scary?"

"*That's why most people do not grow, it scares everyone. When you move into the space not yet filled, your demons dressed up as fears, worries, doubts and excuses, want to return you to safety, to hide you in the familiar. But your death showed you that safe isn't really safe at all. Right?*"

"Right. So what do I do now?"

"*Use the tools you're learning about. Meditation is your power; prayer is your guide and silence is your messenger.*" She smiles with a huge stretching swoop of the arms. "*These tools will sweep you forward if you let them. They're your angels, and more important to maintain than all your talent, your manager's money or any amount of knowledge combined.*"

"I'm working hard."

"*Don't kid yourself. This is the big world you're heading for now. You'll be joining people who may have worked harder, planned smarter, and studied longer. Some will want to compete with you, and others will be jealous. Then there are those who will want to crush you. Your job is to recognize them all. They're all players in the story of your life . . . all placed there for a purpose. Intuit who are angels and who are the slave-makers. They will all look alike for the most part — so you must be alert. Slave-makers mask themselves to look just like angels in the real world. The only tool you have for this job is your awareness.*"

"Can I keep this straight?"

"Make sure to spend time in silence each day to erase all the noise and confusion. No matter how exciting it all seems, or how fearful you might become, you must set aside time for silence. Sharpen your intuition in this silence and you can see the meaning inside every action, and the real purpose between all the words and the worlds."

"But I don't know these people yet. How can I see all this about them?"

"You do — they are just you. When you're sure of yourself, you know everyone else. Self-assuredness never meets a stranger."

"That's what my dad says."

"And the people who are angels, what about them?"

"There will be many to help you focus and be on purpose. They'll help you breathe your dream as if it is life and they won't distract you. The cycles of nature guarantee everything if the intent is held long enough. Everything dies to be reborn."

"Great words . . . what does it mean?"

"What is before you — always — is the lesson of your moment. Learn your way through it no matter what."

"So why would I ever give up?"

"Because it seems easier to make money — and that's extremely attractive. You can lose yourself for years in this chase. You can live in this slavery while your thoughts tell you you're free."

"Why can't time support me?"

"The only time that you are truly free is time you spend in your heart. That's the exact meaning of the word courage . . . cour—age."

"Why does nature test it?"

"To produce a perfectly clear connection. If you're not tested, you don't know your strength."

"This is walking into never explored places."

"Just like you promised when you died, and you were told about this."

"Don't people become bitter from tests and failures?"

"Only if they take the laws personally. Only if they think that they're being singled out."

"That's easy to do."

"Sure, if you see it all with your brain and your logic. But love is the answer here. If you follow your love, even though you're being tested, life is pure child's play."

Those last words turn into a song as I wake up. I must write them down. The songs in my head compose melodies with the words.

Everything's dying to be reborn
Infant day is the early morn
It's dark as night when the day shall end
Into the light you'll be born again
Fa la la la la la la la low your love

"Hello, sir," I hear a woman's voice and a strong tugging on my arm. "It's time to deplane sir . . . we're in San Francisco." A stewardess jiggles me again.

"Wow," I sit up to an empty plane. "I'm the last one."

"Yes you are sir. Are you okay?"

"Yeah, I'm fine," I smile up at her.

I stand up dizzy . . . pause for a moment and pull my guitar from the overhead and walk out into my new city. At baggage claim, I pull out my guitar and the song from my dream emerges.

FOLLOW YOUR LOVE © Gerry Pond 1966

Miles south of Heaven's reach — here upon this Earthly beach where
All the lovely ones have flown — into the wombs waiting to be born.
Comes the morning sunrise caller —
finds a prize the round sound dollar
It'll buy you gleam for in your eyes — to see reflected from the skies
Bellies of the birds so blink — and catch one there within your wink
Oh, open up set it free — looking after you can see
Love dancing endlessly
Love's the song been sung the long while — We've been sittin' here

Looking for love the stone Heaven's thrown —
You can hold it to your ear
Sing along with love the song — and see oh so clear —
Pure child's play is life when love's your game
Love's a gentle wave washing you my way oh, oh
Everything's dying to be reborn — Infant day is the early morn
It's dark as night when the day shall end —
Into the light you'll be born again
Fa la la la la la la la low your love
All you gotta do is fa la la la la la la la low your love
All you gotta do is fa la la la la la la la low your love
Fa la la la la la la la low your love

Seven

HAIGHT IS LOVE

I shuffle through the terminal at San Francisco International, exhausted from the sleep that never really comes on full strength anymore. I look around a room full of strangers, all with something else to do. It's daunting to chase uncertain treasures without clues except barely believable dreamtime fantasies. The old one tells me, *"Courage has no guarantees. That's what makes it courageous.*

"'Coeur,'" he explains, *"means the heart, so to have courage means to have heart."* Courage is exactly what I need right now. Going for this dream of mine has huge emotional risks that feel like being constantly in harm's way of unworthiness. It's a sensation that clings from the inside.

"It's natural to feel guilt and shame around death. It happens when someone else dies, it happens when you die, and it occurs when you're attempting something great because this is also a death . . . a death of your old normal. That's when something old has to die. *"'Original sin,'"* he'll always laugh when he refers to this. *"That's what some cultures call this sensation."*

The young woman always laughs. *"Can you imagine the absurdity?* *"The innocence of a newborn life being originally guilty of anything?"*

A lady named Julia is to meet me here; I spoke to her on the phone from Seattle. I catch a glimpse of a woman in her twenties banging down the aisles of luggage as she navigates her way through the waiting passengers with great determination. People around her move back and forth to let her pass, distanced by the fervor of her intent. Once or twice she engages in a battle of frustration and the long hair that hides her face flips back and forth as she strides along to keep track of the luggage she's narrowly avoiding. It's a dance that's coming closer to where I sit and now I see quite clearly: this frustration clashes with everything else about her; she appears flawless, like a painting of transparent skin, behind thin gold rimmed glasses, covering eyes that contain a total focus. She tromps down the final aisle and straight toward me holding up a sign with my name.

"Is this you?" she asks.

"Yeah, yeah — that's me," I answer, a bit embarrassed by her spectacular entrance. I stand up and lift my guitar case as proof of identity.

"You must be Julia," I smile innocently, glad to have someone to talk to.

"Right," she answers curtly. "You're really late — the last one off that plane."

It's as if my lateness has insulted her.

"I've been checking everywhere for you," she continues. "Everyone else has been off your flight for at least twenty minutes. How did you manage that?"

"It wasn't hard. I was sound asleep."

As she scolds me, her voice changes from angry, to elegant, to flustered.

"I was worried that you missed the plane," she continues as she dumps the sign with my name in the trash. "And we have a schedule to keep . . . Bob insists on tight schedules." She pauses, motioning for me to hurry along. "How was the flight?"

"Good . . . I guess," I reply, distracted by my name sitting in the trash. I reach in and pull it out as I walk by.

"What do you want that thing for?" she asks sarcastically.

"I don't look good in the garbage," I laugh — but she doesn't smile.

"What do you mean you guess the flight was good . . . don't you know?"

I'm thrown off by her attitude and my inability to answer.

"Are you just a silent artist with an attitude?" she asks sarcastically. "God, I hope not."

"Well, Julia," I respond immediately this time, trying to cool her, "what I remember of the flight was fine, but I fell asleep — the crew had to wake me up after every one was gone."

My welcome to San Francisco feels like a boxer caught in a massacre — she's bashing the hell out of me.

"That's gutsy," her words tumble out without missing a beat. "Sleeping on planes is not my thing."

"Hold on! I didn't come down here to get my ass chewed out."

Without a blink, she shoots back, "We all have our strengths and weaknesses. Mine have just become obvious to you."

"Okay, okay, this is way too hostile — we've gotta slow it down." I set my guitar case on the floor, methodically fold the sign and put it in my pocket without looking at her. I clear my throat and say, "It wasn't gutsy for me to sleep on that plane, Julia," irritation ringing from every word. "I haven't really slept well for months; so when it stopped moving — I slept — it wasn't a choice."

"I don't like being stuck in something I can't get out of," she explains, "so planes give me the willies." She's walked ahead of me by this time, almost talking to herself.

We make our way through the terminal without another word. It makes me feel foolish — like a child running behind its mom. I guess that's exactly how she likes it — total control.

"We've lined up the musicians for recording tomorrow," she says.

"That's fast." I answer, nervous about the idea of recording so soon.

"Not really," she replies. "You're ready to work, right?"

"Yeah," I answer.

"That's good, because when Bob believes in something, he's on it big time. We're successful because Bob's a predator that way."

He's taught you to be one as well, I think to myself. Her description of my new manager is disgusting. Just what I need — an Army sergeant!

"By the way, he wants you to give up on that 'one man — lonely guitar' routine," she explains. "He thinks it's too folksy — so we're putting together your backup band for the concerts too."

"Backup?" I ask.

She doesn't answer and fiddles with her keys at the trunk of a large white Rolls Royce. It shines and sparkles while being blatantly parked the wrong way in a red zone. She pops the trunk and states proudly, "This is Bob's, but he has two." She waves two thin, taunting fingers as she moves to the passenger door. "I drive this one and it's extremely cool." She opens the door and taps me on the chest with one of those taunting fingers. "Hop in."

This is unreal, I think, bitching one minute and flaunting the next.

"You never get speeding tickets," she continues around to the other side, "you never get hassled — and as you can see, you never search for parking. That's very convenient in San Francisco."

The conversation pauses briefly while we climb in. She looks over as if I already know her next revelation. "Nobody tows these things, ever! They're too afraid of who the owner might be."

I settle back into what has to be the most comfortable car ever. "My God," I respond. "Seduced by a car. That's a hoot."

I remain quiet absorbing the sensations of the new location as we drive out into the wet, gray San Francisco day. The fragrance of leather fills my nostrils with the scent of pure wealth, soft music plays on the radio, and the heater is on high against the rain and cold. The drive into the city is cozy, silent and plush. With everyone on the road gawking at our chariot, it's clear that Julia loves the attention — what a character. My mind travels back and forth between here and Seattle. I've become a big deal in that little club back home, but down here I'm totally unknown and starting over.

"It feels a lot bigger down here," I declare softly with obvious concern.

"Don't worry," Julia replies quickly, seeming glad to offer comfort now. I can tell she's a big talker by the way she drives — always looking over waiting for a chance to start something as her hands nervously fidget on the wheel. "We've got everything covered, and Bob has complete confidence in you."

"Yeah?"

"Yeah! Remember, you come highly recommended. Why else would we fly you out here?" Julia's only about five years older than me at most. "Jimmy Green swears by you," she adds, "and Jimmy knows music."

I lean back and stretch my legs way forward. "Jimmy Green — just hearing his name makes me wish I were back in Seattle."

"Jimmy's great," she continues, sounding a lot softer, "but he loves Seattle too much . . . he never leaves."

"Yeah, I love it too," I answer. "He's probably biased, I mean about me."

"Why do you say that?"

"I don't know . . . he got super excited telling everyone about me even when I didn't sound that good."

"Then he must've heard something you didn't."

"Yeah . . . the night your company came to see my show he was like a little child. He didn't stop all evening, going on and on about who you guys were."

"He's sweet," Julia chuckles, with the first real smile I've seen from her.

"Yeah, I walked on water that night, the best performance of my life. Those folks from your company flipped."

Julia looks over at me and winks — her second sign of warmth. "I know," she assures me. "I heard about that show ten minutes after you finished. They couldn't even wait till morning to call us with the news."

I'm starting to feel more at ease with her as she lets her guard down. Without thinking, I let mine down too and say, "That was a profound night. I hadn't experienced that much since I died."

There's abrupt and total silence, like when something goes very wrong and nothing can be done to make it right again. Barely a breath passes between us. Julia finally looks over in complete shock. "You what?"

"Oh . . ." I pause, "Jimmy didn't tell you . . .?"

"Not a word," she responds. "He might've told Bob, but I very much doubt that."

"Jimmy has a crazy side so you never know," I laugh nervously.

"What are you talking about?" she finally asks. "I knew you acted different, a bit worried I thought when I first saw you in the airport, but I thought it was just your eyes — they're intense — you stare a lot."

"I've learned to live with that," I reply and take a huge breath. "People generally think I'm nuts these days, with my stories that don't make sense. They often think I'm too much to deal with." I adjust my position and continue slowly. "I actually died in a hospital . . . a few months back. My appendix burst . . . and they didn't get to me in time." I take a few more deep breaths. "My heart stopped and I didn't breathe for a couple of minutes. I went out of my body and crossed over in a really violent way."

"No shit! Pardon my language," Julia whispers staring straight ahead, her sophistication crumbling. "I didn't expect this. This is very weird."

"I saw things during all this I can't explain . . . stuff that's changed me forever, I guess. At least my life hasn't been the same since." I pause, feeling exposed and naked. "I'm not used to telling this story. No one believes it except Jimmy and my parents. I actually thought Jimmy would have warned you guys." I try to justify my predicament. "Or I'd never have said a word."

"I'm sure no one knows about this in my office," she responds. "I'm absolutely certain of that."

"I rarely tell a soul," I admit. "A while back I wanted to quit music entirely. For a solid week I couldn't get on stage. Jimmy got freaked out, so I had to tell him what was happening."

"Why quit your music?"

"I stopped believing I could do it. I was filled with doubt and it still happens on occasion. Your head gets crazy when you've seen what I've seen. It's hard to feel real when nothing else seems real. I started doubting everything; I doubted I was a singer; I doubted my songs made any sense. I got up on stage, went blank and walked off."

"Are we going to have this problem here?"

Tears come to my eyes when she asks this. "I can't answer that Julia. What I went through in the hospital still gives me huge nightmares. When Jimmy heard this he took me to a psychic, a shaman, he called her. Her eyes were intense like mine — it was like looking into a mirror. Jimmy just thought I was on drugs."

"Were you?" Julia asks in an even softer whisper, knowing she's prying into very personal ground now.

"Nothing, nothing at all, not even a little," I repeat the point to make it extremely clear. "I've seen reality and non-reality. I don't need drugs."

"Well, that makes you a 'Lone Ranger' — just like me," she proudly reports. "And I thought I was the only straight one in town. You don't want to mention a word of this to Bob," Julia warns me. "He's very cool, but extremely pragmatic; if you can't see it, touch it, or spend it, to him it isn't real and he'd just freak out if he thought you were weird. He can't handle that at all."

My stomach churns as she describes this man. Dread returns with the old one's warnings, *"Get to know the people who touch your dream."*

"What happens now?" she asks.

"I don't sleep much — I'm always tired — my dreams don't rest. That's why I was last off that plane."

"Oh . . . sorry about jumping on you. I just thought you were another musician kid with a huge ego — you know, making me wait and all."

"Right," I reply.

"Bob thinks you're important so he made me do the airport duty and that upset me too."

"He sounds like a piece of work," I tell her. "I wish Jimmy could live here instead. He's great for my head."

"That's my job now," Julia replies. "I'll do that for you."

"Really?" I question. "How can twenty somethings replace what Jimmy's taken years to master?"

"I'm good!" she laughs.

"OK, first of all . . . these musicians . . . can they really work with my songs — they change every night. I've never found any-one who can keep up."

"No problem for these guys," Julia answers. "Bob's found the best you can get in San Francisco. This is music heaven here."

"You're sure about that?" I ask again.

"Absolutely," she answers. "San Francisco's the place. We've got everything, all the charm of Paris without being big — all the talent of Manhattan without being crazy." She looks over and takes hold of my hand. "You'll do just fine here, I'll see to that."

I close my eyes with a smile. "Okay," I whisper quiet as a prayer, "but I'm still doubtful."

"There's the Matrix Club," she raises her voice and points. "You'll be playing there in a week. I'm excited now. I don't often get like this, but I know you're gonna be big. You're just crazy enough to get big."

This sends chills through my spine. "That's my dream, Julia," I laugh. "Bob did a cool sales job on me too. His exact words were, 'San Francisco's gathering the new musicians and from what I've heard of you, I know you're one of them.' That moved me down here."

"You're a trusting soul," she laughs. "I mean with those voices and moving here — you really don't know who we are."

"I'm chasing a dream Julia. I have no choice. If San Francisco's the new music center, it doesn't matter who you guys are. My dream brought me here, that's what I know. I'm scared a lot of the time, that's something else I know, but the rest of this is clearly out of my hands."

"I appreciate that attitude," she answers. "I can work with that. The people who've seen you perform say your music's got attitude too." She picks up my hand again and says. "We're the ones who can do it for you — we're that good."

A dense fog rolls in over the hills north of the Golden Gate, breaking like an ocean wave over the highway. We crash into it like a wall of blindness, turn on the headlights in broad daylight and exit at the highway to Sausalito. Down a windy hill toward the water, it looks like we're driving through the moors of Sherlock's Baskerville.

Julia clears her throat and asks, "Why do they sometimes call you Tiel?"

"My eyes." I answer with a grin, my mind still crawling through the fog. "It's my eyes. They've been really big and blue my whole life. My friends created a ton of nicknames over the years, Frog Eyes, Bug Eyes and Tiel just stuck."

"But I saw how you write it and that's not how you spell it. The color is spelled T-e-a-l."

"Yeah, it's an unusual color." I laugh. "And at 10 years old who knows how to spell?"

Eight

THE STAR MAKER

*W*ithin a flicker of our headlights in this thick milky fog, we've motored through the main road of tiny Sausalito and off the streets altogether. Driving out onto a pier, we're heading straight for the water when Julia announces, "here's your new office."

Stopping the car and turning off the engine, she points to a building hanging precariously from the end of the dock. A gold-leaf sign over the front doors understates a reality that gloats of success with the simple words, *BOB PHILLIPS, INC.* We walk down a sweeping stairway of a surreal art deco structure — navigate two large glass doors, slip through an elaborately mirrored lobby, smile at the receptionist sitting behind a desk overflowing with photos of stars, and enter the future . . . floating on the water.

"Wow," tumbles softly and involuntarily off my lips as I stare at the immaculate headquarters of my new brain trust. The large room before me contains at least fifteen people working at stark glass desks, not a paper clip, a cuff, or a collar out of place — spotless neat freaks to the last one of them. Three sides of this room are constructed of floor-to-ceiling glass facing the panorama of San Francisco Bay. It's hard to gather perspective with this backdrop extending on so dramatically; boats move behind people working at their desks, as if floating through the room. It's a puzzle for the brain to capture as the scene dissolves into the water.

A tall elegant figure rises within this labyrinth and motions for us to meet him. Thin and about my height with the bright sun shining from behind makes him look even thinner. He peers over gold-rimmed glasses like Julia's, or more likely hers are the copy of his. With a confident stride, he moves to meet us halfway. The star maker, I'm thinking, as he arrives with his self-assured smile.

"So this is you," he says offering a gentle handshake.

"Meet Bob Phillips," Julia says with a proud tone.

He's unpretentious, but extremely convincing with a sincere childlike charm mixed in. This shows me why Julia speaks as if he belongs to her — rather than working for him. I suppose their deep connection allows her unconventional charm to run un-checked, but beyond this he's definitely in charge. Julia winks, as if appreciating my attempt to absorb it all — I might look like a deer caught in headlights.

Everyone rises from their work, eyes galvanized on our meet-ing point . . . time kind of stops about mid-stroke, phone calls terminate, papers are set aside and conversations end on cue. Remarkably businesslike desks are camped in a semi-circle around a long glass conference table that appears to be Bob's station. Gold records hang from thin invisible wires in front of the glass walls and appear to float in midair. Photos of music stars decorate every flat surface in the room. The staff gathers in closer for a meet and greet. They look quite surprised with my appearance, like mute creatures observing something they don't understand.

"Perhaps I'm not what you expected," I express — a tad self-conscious.

I'm definitely not the image in those photographs on their desks — all highly polished musicians in colorful performance suits. Here I stand in my blue jeans half tucked into saggy unpolished boots, big bloodshot eyes unable to hide the travel fatigue and scarce sleep, curls jumping out of my uncombed head. I'm a protest rocker, not a Vegas act. Everyone inches forward for a closer look with smiles that look like relief.

"Bob's not what I expected either," I answer my own comment since no one else has.

He's in a tailored suit that appears to refuse wrinkles, clean cut to an extreme. A corporate lawyer-like statue with all the required soft edges for persuasion purposes. A dangerous mismatch I'm thinking, when he calls out gently. "Listen up everyone, I want to introduce our next star." They all clap on cue. "This is the young man I told you all about and you'll make him into a player in the game, the new music-man in this town."

He pauses and looks at each one of them individually. "Take a real good look," he continues, "because you'll rearrange it all." He turns back to me and points through the glass walls. "Here's your threshold son. If you cross this with any speed, your game begins and if you continue the crossing, your game will never end. I've got artists that have been touring with me for 20 years."

"That's persuasive," I tell him, as the staff claps again and even louder this time.

"We've all heard the very bad recording of your very good music," he smiles and turns a 360 to include everyone, "and we solidly believe you can take the next step."

They clap for a third time as I clear my throat and say, "Thanks, I appreciate you overlooking the quality of my tapes."

"Your tape was no problem son," Bob replies, "I can spot talent within a whisper even if it sings over a phone line. You have a terrific sense of melodic pulse and rhythm."

"That's my main focus when I write a song," I explain. "I always start with the pulse."

"Well, we start recording tomorrow morning," he says, not fully acknowledging what I've said. "So I want you to get a good night's sleep. I've promised Warner Bros, in Los Angeles, a demo in a week."

"Wow . . . sure," I respond without thinking, then add, "the vocals might be raspy, — I'm tired right now."

"Being tired is part of the job, son — your voice will be just fine. Don't be insecure."

"Okay," I respond, letting the point drop. I can see Bob doesn't actually listen, he's probably seen shaky nerves a million times.

"How old are you son," he asks, "about 20?"

"Almost 21," I answer, getting amused by his 'son' references.

"Getting up there," he laughs, as if he'd made a joke. Everyone smiles with him. "This is good, we need you to play clubs and that means 21."

"Not really my audience," I answer back, but he's moved on quickly to something else.

"How long have you played music?" he asks.

"All my life," I reply.

"Then I'm sure you can make some little changes I need," he states almost in a whisper.

"Changes?" I ask, puzzled by his remark. Again I remember the young woman telling me, *Watch the people who touch your dream.* And the old one saying, *Fear is simply an excuse to fail.* So with this I jump in with him, "I don't expect to change much of my songs."

"Remember one important fact, son," Bob speaks quietly as if telling me a secret, as he places his forearm on my shoulder. "We love your songs," the room nods in agreement. "We can't push politics right now though."

Ice blows a harsh wind through my chest with these words.

"So I want Los Angeles to hear your talent, which is huge," he continues. "But not all the words in your songs are understandable. We'll have to take the time to explain them and right now we don't have that time."

I'm now outside of me watching his lips move, but can't hear a thing he's saying — my mind is leaving the room in disbelief.

I catch Julia, out of the corner of my eye, backing away slowly and from the firm gentleness in Bob's voice; I see little room for question.

"We want to distance ourselves from that war stuff," he continues. "Politics and music aren't a good mix for us right now. We need good love songs to begin with."

Julia now backs completely out of the picture, pretending to have something else to attend to. She sees my eyes flare — I can't hide this reaction. I'm raging, but silent.

Bob tries to soothe the obvious by saying, "You know what caught my attention when I first heard your music? Like I said, the rhythms and the melodies — those are pure hits, I know that."

The breath sucked from my lungs, I have no response. This has been a surprise attack from hell, but I might've guessed as much. It's the exact picture Julia painted of Bob, very pragmatic and only business. I hold on for dear life as the furious adrenaline reaches for my reaction trigger. My breath returns just as fight and flight both stalk me . . . begging me to run. I haven't felt this trapped since the Draft Board, but I don't make a move. Why is this back in my face? I have no idea — but this time Bob, my new manager, appears as the enemy.

"What song would you like?" I ask blankly, really wanting to say — go fuck yourself.

"Well, what matters is that we pick a great song. Right? What do you think, Julia?"

"I like 'Walkin' High'," she jumps in to rescue me.

"We have a problem with those words too," Bob replies. "It sounds like a drug song."

"I'll sing it anyway," I declare, "If there's questions about the words, I'll just explain them. They're not about drugs you know, they're about pure joy and inspiration."

"Okay, we'll see," Bob agrees with objection ringing in his voice. He turns back to Julia. "Now," he pauses, "we need some great head shots, but with a different look. Arrange for the hairdresser to meet us . . . umm . . . day after tomorrow, okay?"

She nods while Bob's eyes sweep off into the distance, as if searching for a sailboat, or a perfect word. "We need a straighter look." He says with a bit of difficulty, still looking out the windows. "I want those curls out of your hair for these photographs." He says turning to me.

I stare back, having just gone from the next star to a mannequin. "Another photo for your desks?" I ask as the room goes dead calm.

Bob fills the silence as if his point is clear and undisputed. "Julia will get you settled into your home tonight, and she'll be your helper from here on; she's assigned to you," he winks at her. "And when you have a need, just tell her and it'll happen. I'll meet both of you at the studio in the morning, 9:30." He shakes my hand, motions to one of his staff, and returns to his conference table as if running for safety.

I greet each one in the office on the way out the door, a state of apprehension drifts over us as Julia does introductions. "These are the people who'll light your star," she says as they smile from behind their discomfort.

"We are the details in your career," one of them says with a timid grin. "The details you won't have to worry about."

We leave the building through the parking lot. "What in the world was that all about?" I ask as we get to the car.

"That was all about your success in the music business," she states.

"But Bob's way out of touch with what's happening today," I respond.

"Out of touch? Are you kidding? He's a star maker. He'll make your career fly if you put up with him. I've seen it happen countless times before."

"But those times are different now, it's all changing," I tell her, but more quietly now. My eyes are heavy from the long day that started hours ago in Seattle.

"Tell me straight," she asks, "What are you interested in?"

"Music," I reply without hesitating.

"Exactly," she interrupts, "and Bob will make your music happen."

"Yeah, but there's a message that's gotta be in there too. The war is killing kids every fucking day."

"Whoa," she almost shouts. "Hold the language. This is me."

"Sorry," I concede. "This just wasn't expected. I thought my fight was over and that's what brought me to Bob."

"Well, the only way to move your music forward in a big way is with a person who deals in reality," she explains. "Bob's a reality check — there's lots of things that you'll hate, a lot of things you won't understand, but he's a big success."

"Yeah, okay," I lean my head back, deeply troubled by all this and remain silent all the way back into the city.

"Don't worry right now," Julia speaks into my contemplation. "Your aim is bigger than these details. Let Bob get you started and then you can do your thing." I barely hear her.

"The outside world is your mirror," the old man speaks to me. *"It's constantly reflecting who you were in the past, who you are in the present, or who you hope to be in the future. It's a maze you are to navigate and only your commitment can do that."*

"Commitment?" I ask.

"Yes . . . the commitment at your core. It's the sensation of knowing it will all work without any reason, the ability to feel connected without any proof."

"These people aren't what I expected," I respond. "I'm really disappointed."

"Your vision never moves off target when you commit no matter what. It never fails you when the storms of chaos, or opposition confront you, and they will confront you hard. Remember I warned you — this is all part of going for your dreams. Disappointment is making a choice to take away your appointment. Is that what you want?"

"But these people don't get what I'm here for."

"Don't blame the outside — you'll be disrupted and thrown off course. Turn to your commitment — move your purpose ahead."

"You talk in your sleep," Julia informs me, as we pull into the driveway of a large Victorian house.

"Yeah, that's a habit lately," I reply. "Talking to my less reluctant helpers — it's not real sleep . . . more like taking notes in a dream class." I add with a smile.

"Well, I'm glad your smile is back. You were carrying on such a conversation — I thought you were talking to me," she laughs. "But then I couldn't understand a word."

We pull my bags from the trunk and climb three flights of stairs to the top floor of an old mansion, all the original, intricate details perfectly restored. Carved banisters, pressed metal paneling, stained glass and beveled windows everywhere — we arrive at a large dark mahogany door where Julia hands me a key and says, "Welcome home," with a huge grin.

"In my other life," I tell her, turning the lock and swinging the door open, "I studied these old buildings."

"What life?" she asks.

"Architecture in college," I reply, "when I was hiding from the Draft."

"You'll have the entire top floor to study now," she says as we enter the front room. "Bob fixed this house up for his clients. This part's yours, the penthouse suite." She chuckles and points around a large room of thick Persian carpets spread out over polished hardwood floors, overstuffed furniture scattered about in the magnificent light of dusk that streams in through large bay windows overlooking the city.

"I can live with this," I joke.

We make our way down a short hall and into a bedroom. A large wooden four-poster bed stands nobly in the center, flanked by a matching dresser and hutch.

"Bob doesn't miss a single thing, does he?" I say.

"You just wait and see what Bob can do," she says and disappears into the closet. "You can have as many clothes as you want here, these closets go on forever. This one's as big as my bedroom."

We continue the tour down the hallway and into the kitchen. "There's fresh food here, but you can give me a list of what you want. Jimmy tells me you're vegetarian."

"Yeah, since I was thirteen or fourteen."

"How'd that happen?"

"I was raised by yogis. My mother was first," I explain. "She read a book, 'Autobiography of a Yogi', back in the late 1940's and that did it for her. It took me a while longer, but I can't imagine eating animals anymore."

"I'd like to try that, but I don't have the discipline, not yet." She pulls open the curtains and exposes another gigantic view; this time a park stretches out below the window. "You can shower if you want and I'll grab some takeout for tonight . . . Chinese okay?"

"Yeah, that's good," I say, caught up in San Francisco's lights cascading over the buildings and hills into a magnificent sunset. "It's all coming true," I say to myself with a bit of a shudder of excitement. "My dream is coming true."

The excitement is only slightly tempered by the brief realization that I'm starting all over here. No one knows me yet.

"Have courage," the old man's voice deep inside reminds me. With a chuckle, I express my relief. "You are an angel."

Julia hears this on her way out the door. "That's sweet of you to say," she smiles, thinking I mean her. I leave it at that. No need to spoil it.

Tired from the long day's activities and the plane ride, I stretch out on the couch and wait for dinner. Like always, they're right there, just over the edge of sleep. *"This is the chance you've been waiting for,"* the young woman whispers in my mind. *"It's right here for you, waiting to come true."*

"I'm excited," I reply. "But Bob's a piece of work."

"You must not blame him," she insists. *"Everyone is a part of your puzzle. Take time each day to breathe and see how the parts fit together."*

"It's not easy," I claim.

She laughs at my excuse, *"Easy is for boring lives, and challenge is for destiny."*

I don't wake up until sunrise, the first great night's sleep I can remember. I'm greeted by the smell of stale Chinese and a note explaining how to work the oven and a note . . . *"Didn't want to disturb you . . . see you at 9:00 am sharp. Love, Julia"*

I pick up my guitar — aided by the inspiration of morning sunlight pouring through my windows – and write another song that Bob won't understand.

PEACE ON THE EARTH © Gerry Pond 1966
We're gathered here today
Celebrating peace to pray
For a world completely free - children safe at play
We won't have it any other way

Joy to the World
Peace on the Earth
God Bless the Children
How we Love them

Children can't grow in war
They simply can't take it anymore
We have to find a new way to settle score
Just can't fight it any more

Joy to the World
Peace on this Earth
God Bless the Children
How we Love them

Mothers can't feed babies in a fight
Their houses bombed - burning in the night
Screaming sounds of terror - people running for their lives
Crying - God please bring back the Light

We're gathered here today
Celebrating peace to pray
For a world completely free - children safe at play
We won't have it any other way

Joy to the World
Peace on this Earth
God Bless the Children
How we Love them

Love from Heaven imagine that
Everybody living for each other hand in hand
With joy in our world coming back
Peace on this Earth is now a fact

Joy to the World
Peace on this Earth
God Bless the Children
How we Love them

Joy to the World
Peace on this Earth
God Bless the Children
How we Love them
God how we love them

Nine

TEXAS AND THE FROG

Shortly after I arrive, San Francisco awakens with Bob's pre-diction of a musical renaissance. The elderly certainly take note. Youthful musicians move into the old neighborhoods and revive their sleepy lives with loud guitars and a carefree spirit. Though none of our adventure has been exposed outside of town yet, there's a sense that it's imminent. The feeling in my gut is the feeling on the streets. It's in everyone's eyes — seeds of something big about to happen, of dreams beyond our imagin-ings, all preparing to sweep us away. It's great to live in this in-ventive atmosphere. From my fairy tale perch atop this old house along the edge of Golden Gate Park — a park that fills up each day with musicians from all over — I write the songs that will soon make up my records and concerts.

A sense of family is found in the clubs and dance halls that wait each day to ignite with our spirit at night. It's our musical freedom pestering the need to express itself. It's in our pleas for 'world-harmony' and 'civil rights' and a love that bonds us together. We're a hodgepodge gathering of the nation's mis-fits — placards for peace emblazoned on our smiling eyes. I feel connected and right where I need to be.

San Francisco lights up when the sun goes down and our music starts. Show time is magnificent — displays of raw genius playing for a few bucks a night and a chance to reap the larger rewards to come. Not one band is famous yet, but Bob Phillips, Inc. has sprinkled enchantment on my career. I have a car driving me where others hitchhike, a house of my own when many just crash on floors, and a personal assistant instead of barely scraping by.

From the beginning, there's conflict — Bob knows music, but clearly doesn't get me. I'm sure I scare him, but we struggle through each episode and seem to move on with confidence. He has many acts that have made it big — Las Vegas is the style he knows best. He always puts the pressure on me to conform. "Isn't there something you can do about that hair?" he asks over and over.

Mine's curly, wild and impossible to tame as it continues to grow uncut. He's crazy about the clean look but the world's moved on . . . the clean look is history. He had my hair straightened when we did the publicity photos and I don't recognize myself in any of them. The old man just reminds me, *"Follow the current of silence through the ocean of noise."*

Then there are the studio sessions — here Bob's the master — with an incredible gift for pulling talent together. He makes my music so much larger with great backup musicians. I've never heard these sounds in my songs before and it fills me with more ideas. I call home telling Mom and Dad how I love studio work, but the stage is another story. No matter what size the audience is, it still frightens me. Within days of my arrival, I've recorded 'Walkin' High,' which immediately impresses one of America's largest record labels. They sign me on the spot, and my dream takes another giant step forward with national distribution and radio connections added to Bob's management machine.

I'm the first of the new singer songwriters in San Francisco to get a record deal. I listen to my songs over and over, tweaking the lyrics and setting everything just so . . . all to get my point across more clearly. I write, I record, I rehearse and a fast train begins to pull out from my little life station. The only rub is the constant conversation surrounding my lyrics — the constant pressure to change them. Julia usually jumps in to defend me; she's become very cool that way. Weekly phone calls go out to Jimmy Greene back in Seattle for the needed encouragement. I try hard to connect with the San Francisco pace, but with my fast track getting faster, I find myself wishing for a simpler life.

Vietnam rages on and the passion to stop this senseless war grows stronger all over San Francisco with each passing day. In the local peace rallies, I regain my inspiration to speak out. This keeps me sane in the frenzy surrounding my music. Peace is becoming a second career for me.

The first citywide peace concert, featuring six new bands, is in the planning stages and I make the cut. San Francisco doesn't know much about me, but they've heard the gossip about my record deal. I've been playing clubs and small audiences — this rally is set for a huge ballroom called The Avalon.

"The label is nervous about your politics," Bob warns me, but I know he's speaking more for himself.

The old man's constant message, *"Get to know the people who touch your dreams,"* is exactly what I'm doing; getting to know those who might only see the big bucks in my music. Money is fine, it takes money to live, but I question whether they're seeing the other more essential parts of the art.

"You won't believe this singer who just hit town," Julia exclaims as we drive to the concert. "She's a Texas monster, that's what I've heard. We've got you playing right after her."

I don't talk much before a show, I'm too scared and I can barely even eat. It never gets easier and always goes away once I start singing. I listen quietly to Julia go on about this crazy monster playing before me. It replaces the panic in my stomach with some humor.

We enter the ballroom where posters are hanging from every available wall. The wild art announces the evening's event with paisley patterns weaving words and pictures together — nearly impossible to read. My name's right there in red, white, blue, pink and green — turbulent colors jolting the eyeballs. It's kind of an ugly collage depicting Uncle Sam bombing foreign lands with all our bands hovering over them as protectors. I'm staring at my name with a hundred thoughts, when, "That's her!" Julia hollers over the music. "Can you believe that voice?"

I can't imagine what I'm hearing. Some young, wild blonde running the stage, taunting the audience with her voice — like a roadster without a muffler. I completely forget I'm here to play and just stare at the relentless creativity everywhere in the auditorium, authenticity spewing everywhere.

"Welcome to your new world," whispers in my ear. I'm excited and intimidated.

"What did I tell you?" Julia yells in the noise. "She hitch-hiked here from Texas — her band, they're from San Francisco."

I barely hear their words; the volume from the stage is so loud. I'm staring at this singer and my guitar case dangles from my fingers getting heavier by the second, but I don't notice. I can't take my eyes off what's happening in this room. The sight of this many people celebrating to the music with pain and joy and talent all mixed into a nonstop sound.

"Are you still with us?" Julia asks as she pulls on my arm.

"Yeah," I respond quietly. "Yeah, I'm right here."

I catch the remainder of her act from my dressing room. As I tune my guitar and have a moment to think, fear comes back in full force. The other band members are right at home. This is their territory. Amused by my concern, they try to relax me with humor.

"How you gonna play your guitar if you can't move your arms?" Andre, the drummer, jokes.

As the set comes to a close, the promoter addresses the crowd. My heart hits my throat as he says, "Here you have it folks, the greatest display of San Francisco's new talent here to put an end to this bloody war — because we don't kill mothers, and we don't kill their children. Is that clear enough?" The audience roars as he pauses for them to respond. "This music is our secret weapon, the guitar is our rifle," he yells into the mic. "But it won't be a secret for long. Our next performer releases his first record in a few weeks, so give him a warm San Francisco welcome."

"That certainly gives us something to live up to," William, the bass player, declares. Chills run through my body as I stand up to go.

"Here's the deal," Andre smiles at me. "We set the mark so high here tonight, that all the others will shoot for it."

"Let's boogie boys," Bob calls out as he walks into the dressing room.

I'm soaking wet in a river of sweat running down my back. My mind races, madly agonizing over the words to my songs and blanking on most of them right now. I died for God's sake, I think to myself, why am I so scared of singing?

"Because this is your dream, and that scares people more than death," the old man answers in my head. *"This is not a test of your talent, it's a test of your commitment . . . commitment to being you."*

I'm jolted by a hard bang on the door. "You're on!" someone yells and then bangs again. "Get your ass to the stage!"

"Yeah, I'll be right out." Fear tightens my throat.

The rest of my band runs out the door and down the hall . . . I haven't left the room. The door swings back shut. My hands shake as I fumble my guitar. Julia grabs it and hands it right back. "You'll be great . . . just sing like you do," she says.

My head runs through dumb thoughts like — "I can't follow that singer, my songs sound stupid, it's over after tonight." Dumb thoughts. I trudge through the door under this negative weight, forcing one foot in front of the other. Suddenly the hallway rips open and the blonde from the stage comes bounding down. "Wow! Check you out," she hoots, climbing up in my face. "You must be that new guy — I'm new here too."

She's loaded, at least with alcohol, and I try to squeeze by without answering, but she latches onto my sleeve. "You okay man?" she asks loudly. "Can I offer you . . . ?"

Julia pushes me forward. "He's cool, he's fine."

"You don't look fine," she argues. "You look scared shitless; that's what I see. You don't want to go on stage looking like that, they will eat you alive." She enunciates each word carefully to make sure her drunkenness does not destroy the point.

"Really, I'll be okay."

"I've never seen eyes like yours before," she says. "They look like a Texas bullfrog, I swear to God."

Now she's pissing me off and it takes my mind off the fear. "I've heard that all my life, but right now I've gotta go sing."

"I'll bet you see right through people with those eyes, don't you?" she continues.

"We've gotta go," Julia pushes her aside.

"Well, don't waste any time standing here then — and don't let anyone get in your way down that hall," she laughs at her irony and lets me pass. "Take that crowd, Mr. Frog!" she yells after me. "But I get 'em back when you're done. You tell them Janis sent you." She performs a huge bow to an empty hallway.

"What a crazy woman," I say to Julia, as we hurry to the stage; I begin my first song without even acknowledging the audience, a real no-no in a new town — my voice comes out tight. I'm thinking the entire audience must hate me as I struggle to keep from running. I see their eyes — a thousand little dots on a rolling sea of bright clothing, but I don't see smiles. They're staring closely, examining the new kid in town. They don't seem to dance either as my words come out rough, without rhythm. I'm not used to the new electric guitar, my fingers can't find the right strings. My chords distort something fierce. The moments pass like agony. I keep playing, but I want to quit. I turn my back to the crowd and breathe deep between songs. The look on my band's face is one of those 'Oh shit' looks. I'm a disaster. Then, a voice rips through my brain. *Do you think any of this is about you?"* Again, it's the old man's voice. *"This is not about you,"* he explains, *"it's about inspiring these people. So get out of your way, release your heart and sing."*

Fear vanishes . . . in fact, everything vanishes and the whole room fades to silent black. The voice in my mind yells louder. *"After what you've been through, what's to fear? You're alive — so be alive."*

Then it all comes back the way it left — the room, the music, my band, and the dance floor full of people. They are clapping wildly at the song I've just finished. I've sung the second song and completely blanked out. The crowd roars and San Francisco has just been born for me.

The energy surges up my spine and what's left of a 40 minute set passes like one stroke of time. The room shakes and vibrates. I can barely keep track of where I am on my song list, but it goes on playing by itself. We end the show with my new single, *'Walkin' High'.*

A holler rings from backstage as we hit the final note. "No shit man, that's it – that's it man!" the scream comes from that damn Texas blonde. The crowd stomps and whistles, and chants, "More, more, more, more!"

"This is when you give them an encore," she jumps from behind the curtain and grabs a microphone. "Don't you know shit — Frogman? You need some taking care of!" The crowd loves it — seeing the two of us together stirs them even more.

I ignore her and start my song *'Great Day In The Morning Glory,'* but she doesn't leave the stage. Loaded to the gills, she does her best to counterpoint with my words and halfway through she learns the chorus.

Great day in the morning glory halleh luuu
Day's breakin', that's its story — how about you uuuuuu

I see the crowd below, their teeth smiling broadly and singing along. We crank up the guitars to deafening levels and love it.

As the song ends, 'Texas' hugs me. "You made it Frogman," she declares. "You're in up to those eyeballs now."

"Thanks Tex," I respond sarcastically. "Couldn't have done it without you."

"Name's Janis!" she yells over the din of the crowd as we walk from stage.

"What?" I holler back.

"Tex," she replies, leaning into my ear. "I like that name . . . and I'll call you Frog."

I hear the promoter in the distance. "And now my fellow lovers of life, here's the 'Grateful Dead'."

"That's a cool name for a band." I say to the new friend glued to my arm.

Ten

THE HUMAN RACE

*M*onths go by as I settle into San Francisco's new life. It's now the fall of 1966 and the hype surrounding my career is a constant exaggeration of fact and pressure. I'm trying hard to remember the real reason why I came here in the first place. I campaign hard on the anti-war front, but that world is getting crazy too. Bob's totally against this and creates hell when we record songs with a political message. He talks about my career and how it can be the biggest this world has ever seen, but it's very clear that Bob doesn't understand the purpose of my music. He's just fond of the traditional boy meets girl songs and that's fine, but it isn't me — there is a larger picture now.

My songs rant to every audience. My Mom and our record company say the FBI has its eyes on me at every concert. And San Francisco is loaded with people thinking and acting just the same. Concerts and rallies raise awareness, the Diggers and the San Francisco Mime Troupe increase the pace of action. The promise I made at the Seattle Draft Board is in real time now. When we all get together, we come close to breaking the law and then we say "fuck it" and break it anyway. The birth of this nation was about breaking the law too — big time. Two hundred years ago breaking the law gave birth to our current freedom to break the laws that shouldn't be.

Every move I make causes insecurity in my management and when Bob gets insecure, he has this uncanny ability to alienate people. Even my band takes the hit. Tex, on the other hand, just cruises through the bullshit like it's so much mud. She says she's seen worse crap on a good day. ". . . Bob's nothing. I'm grateful for his attitude." Bob is threatened; Julia keeps us united; I write, record and perform — it seems to work.

Bob has assembled a great band, we perform all over town now. When he first found me in Seattle, I was just a voice and a guitar. Here we're a complete sound, a big sound. I appreciate this masterful side of him and chuckle now when he says. "Love your sound — your lyrics need the work." What he really means is that words offend the establishment. I tell him song writing is my job and management is his. He reacts by telling me that building talent has little to do with song lyrics. I react to his reaction by declaring that we have no problem then, and laugh . . . ultimately he does too. Like I said, it all seems to work.

Moving toward winter, most places are hibernating. But not San Francisco; here, there is a birthing of a radical new culture. It feels powerful living here, like we're a gigantic force of nature cutting through time. Music is the centerpiece and the attention forces me away from my fear. The acceptance from audiences affects my writing too, the lyric poetry cuts deeper into issues. I play concerts for the joy and against the war and at many I headline.

Never a dull moment . . . as this shifts too. "Are you crazy or stupid or both?" the record label asks one day. "Do you want this to all come crashing down, just because you weren't able to take it slower? Remember, you're the first with a record on the charts, and the first one is always the pioneer. No one in America likes this war, but they're not all willing to agree with what you're saying quite yet." This conversation with my record company supports Bob's position, but I'm getting tougher too, and fueled by my success, I'm committed to my purpose and style.

"I really have no choice," I respond to everyone. "And this means I only have one choice and that is to keep up with who I am."

"This is dangerous ground you're breaking," the record executive answers back. "We may not be able to go the distance with you on this. We're getting huge pressure from the Feds."

Strangely enough, this very same day, I receive a desperate phone call from an old friend. Dave and I have been buddies since we were in Cub Scouts. He's been drafted and went through basic training. He's now sitting at Fort Ord, a few miles south of San Francisco, scheduled to leave for Vietnam in two weeks.

"You've got to be insane, Dave," I yell back over the phone. "You're Japanese. You've got a zero chance of staying alive over there. You will be shot at from both sides."

"I know," he says. "But what can I do?"

"Well for sure you're not going to Vietnam," I reply confidently. "Get some time off, grab a bus, and come to my place. We'll work it out somehow when you get up here."

He arrives a few days later and comes to my concert. It's an eye-opener for him. He hasn't seen this much freedom in months, if ever at all. Afterward, we talk all night. Friends drop over until the sun comes up and the collection of opinions runs from radical to absurd. The radicals talk of disappearing by changing names and the absurd ones speak of anarchy. The next morning, all of this fresh in his head, Dave's off through the streets of San Francisco to become a different person. The Army never sees or hears from him again and this marks a major escalation in our campaign. With this, the solution has come home.

Our shows raise awareness for radical organizations in San Francisco and the West Coast. Dave connects with this in a big way. His closest Army buddies hear his story through word of mouth and the word spreads rapidly. They connect to other operations smuggling soldiers and draft evaders into Canada and through Dave's connections, a complete system for new identities develops.

The possibility of any success in stopping the war does not go unnoticed by the authorities. The FBI begins paying regular visits to my mother's office in Seattle. They hope to find my friend Dave and figure out how I'm involved. They know my songs are the 'enemy' so they go after my mom with scare tactics. They tell her they'll destroy my career and put me in jail.

One day on the phone she tells me, "Several men came into my office without any introduction other than — we're the FBI. They closed the door and started asking questions." She's a tough woman and totally believes in what I'm doing. "It really got testy very quickly," she says. "When they asked me, what kind of mother are you . . . not knowing what your son is actually doing? I said, what kind of government are you to send our sons off to be killed?"

"Good work, Mom," I tell her. "You're doing a great job . . . I'm proud of you. Give my love to Dad."

After this encounter, the FBI is certain she knows more than she's admitting and begins harassing her every week. At the same time, I receive a warning from Julia. The FBI is also pressuring our record company. Some insist they abandon all artists considered subversive. That's exactly what I'm now considered.

"Julia, I'm proud of this label," I tell her.

"I know, and that's what scares me now. I have a feeling the FBI will take this beyond threats."

"We have to be willing to face everything if we want to have an impact on anything," I tell her.

With this challenge my dedication is born at new levels. San Francisco's loaded with musicians soon to become famous, and we're planting the seeds of peace not war, civil rights not prejudice, and love not hate. I'm on a fast track; my band's strong; our music's solid and the audiences adore us wherever we play. The words to my songs cut deep into the war machine whenever we play. I hear my song, *'Walkin High'*, on the radio several times a day and each time I relive the walk home from the Draft Board. I state this vision every time we step on stage, making it clear — we get high on life and down on war.

After one such show, I'm walking down the hall of the auditorium, making my way through the usual crowd, talking to fans as I go. I reach my dressing room expecting to hang out and relax, but Bob looks like a ghost and Julia's in tears. "Did someone die?" I ask.

"Yeah," Bob responds sarcastically. "We did. There's a problem with your hit record. Radio stations are refusing to play it because of your lyrics."

"The FBI got to the FCC and now the stations are afraid for their licenses and are saying you're promoting the use of drugs with *'Walkin High'.*"

"Those idiots," I react. "They got to them, they actually got to them."

"It was the lyrics," Bob repeats.

"They don't believe that at all," I argue. "They've read my interviews. They know what I'm talking about. They know I'm talking about my walk home from the Draft Board and that is exactly what is upsetting to the FBI and Hoover."

"You're right," Julia agrees. "The label says the authorities got to them and it's because of your anti-war stance. You're absolutely right."

"They want to wipe the peace movement out of the picture," Andre says. "Just like they want the Black Panthers out. Black people like us are considered a threat because we want too much freedom, too much peace and that's not what makes this place work for them."

"Right! A threat to the nation," I respond flatly. "They're the fucking threat to this nation and to all of its children."

"Maybe so," Bob agrees for once. "But they're determined to stamp all this out. They're finding a way to stop you and everyone else like you. We have to figure out how to counter this right away."

"This won't happen! They will not stop me!" I don't say another word and just put away my guitar and towel the sweat from
my face. I'm filled with anger and hope all in the same moment.

"We'll find a way around them," Julia says with confidence.
"That's what freedom is all about. You have the right to have an
opinion and voice it however you like."

"It hasn't actually stopped us," Andre replies calmly. "It's
definitely going to change the game, but we're not dead by any
means. The audiences love us and we can still perform."

"You're right, Andre," Bob agrees. "But we have to consider changing something if we want to continue making records.
Records are about radio play and without that we are not in that
game."

Bill Graham, a concert promoter in his 30s, sticks his head
in through the dressing room door. "Your music was sensational
tonight! We have to talk."

I glance over at him, concealing the rage in my eyes. "Great
to hear that." These words break the mood.

"I'm just trying to talk your team into some reality . . . that's
all." He winks across at Bob. "The world is going to meet you in
that *'walkin high'* place and you'll be playing your music when
they arrive."

"That's not our direction," Bob responds.

"Yes, it actually is," Bill answers, looking directly at me. "Forget
the road to Vegas." He gives Bob another sarcastic wink. "That's
not the road this music scene is headed toward." He stands at attention, gives me a boyish style military salute and leaves.

I take a really deep breath and am so glad he made the point.
I look back at the empty doorway and have an urge to run after
Bill to get more of that reality. Now that the stage adrenaline has
worn off I sit with my pity, like an old friend, but it's not a great
relationship. At least 10 minutes goes by without a word when
two figures fade up into my view like a dream. They stand just
beyond the doorway dressed in very traditional native clothing,
which is not so unusual in this moment of history. One's a tall

intense looking man with piercing brown eyes and a single braid down his back, tied with bright colorful ribbons. The other's an amazingly exquisite woman with two long black braids. As I stare at them without speaking, the room fills with a strange peace, but I'm not sure they are real.

The man speaks kindly, "Excuse us," as they walk through the doorway. "I hope it's okay to come in this way." There's tremendous respect and smoothness in his words. "We wanted to express our deep appreciation for what you're saying in your songs, that's all."

"Thanks," I respond. "That's good to hear." I try to conceal my mood, but it's not completely possible.

"We heard your music on our radio in New Mexico and came here to see you in person," he continues.

I stand to embrace them as Andre says, "I guess you won't be hearing it on the radio anymore." They come through the doorway with such grace and delight, I catch them both with a group hug.

"Nothing will ever stop you," the man says softly as if he knows exactly what's been taking place. "Not when you live in courage. Fear stops everything, but courage never spends a day without freedom."

These words startle me, but I only say, "That's a long way to travel just to see my show."

"We're glad we did," the woman answers. "Your music is even more powerful in person." Her face reflects every bit of the sincerity in her words.

"Your songs are about our life," the man adds. "We wanted to see if you were for real." He says these last words with a smile. "You are."

I catch Bob out of the corner of my eye looking very uncomfortable. This doesn't make any sense to his way of thinking. They've travelled over a thousand miles to see me perform. *"Get to know the people who touch your life and touch your dreams,"* echoes through my mind.

"That's exactly what you have to do now," the man says as if he has heard my thoughts and smiles very slightly.

"I'll see you early in the morning," Bob says abruptly as he gets up to leave without acknowledging anybody. "We've lots of work to do here, so don't be up late."

"See you in the morning," I reply.

I turn back to the couple, far less angry about the radio scene, but I don't know why. It just left me, replaced by the fresh attitude of these two strangers.

"Am I real?" I ask them jokingly. "Did I pass your test?"

Only smiling at my joke the man answers. "Yes — very, very real and we'd love for you to visit our home in New Mexico. Our land does wonders for the spirit and we'd be honored to share it."

"That sounds great," I quickly respond. "When I'm ready for a break, can I call you?"

"We don't have a phone," the woman replies. "We'll draw you a map and you can come anytime you're ready. We'll be there."

All this amazes me as if we're speaking totally different languages from completely different worlds. Their world is real and calm while I'm in the middle of a crisis based on lies. They're asking a stranger to visit, based on love after travelling a thousand miles to hear one concert. "Really? That's great, but it's kind of hard to go all that way without some assurance that you'll be there."

"Oh, we'll be there when you come," she assures me. "That's for certain, but if you need to, you can leave a message at the store in town, they have the only phone."

"This visit to our land is very important for you," the man speaks with total clarity, as if knowing what is happening in my world. His piercing gaze commands the room. "You must live up to those words of yours and have the courage to believe it will all turn out."

This resonates clearly with me as if it's one of the lessons from my dreams. I look really closely at them without saying anything. They smile and bid everyone in the room good night, with a respectful bow. As they leave, she hands me a small piece of paper that she has just written on . . . it reads, *Paul and Adrian White Elk, Servilleta Plaza, New Mexico*, with a little map of some highways.

I stare at it and go back to putting away my equipment. A moment later, Tex bursts through the doorway. When she's 'on her game' she's a beautiful woman — even her insecurity comes out delightfully, but Tex is loud in a quiet room.

"Wow, what a great show, Frog!" she says slumping into a chair. "Absolutely the best you've ever done. You just keep getting better, that's all."

"Lot of good it will do," I reply sarcastically.

"What's with the shitty mood?" she asks.

"He's been banned," Andre says.

Without really hearing what Andre said she asks, "Who were those people that just left?"

"Fans from New Mexico," I answer. "Said they loved the music and drove all this way just to invite us to their ranch."

"Sounds great to me! They actually look more like fans from the old Texas," she says laughing. "So when do we go there?"

Noticing that I'm not joining her good humor, she grabs my arm. "What's happening? What does Andre mean, banned?"

"Shit's happening," I say with a look of frustration. Shrugging my shoulders, I grab her hand and start for the door. We stop along the way to acknowledge the people still hanging around the hall. Two of my band members hug me as we exchange looks of determination. I turn to Tex with a nod. "We could go there tonight! Let's blow this town." We walk down the hallway and into the San Francisco night. John Lennon's song, 'Norwegian Wood' is playing on the radio of a passing car. My songs were playing there too, just hours ago.

Eleven

INNOCENT TIMES

Consumed by thought, Tex and I walk the streets of San Francisco for an hour without a word. This is usually the freedom time — the sort of euphoric innocence that's experienced after every concert. It's our time to unwind, but we know this freedom won't last long, for it will vanish with the stardom that chases after us now. Though we're committed to waking up the world, the job is becoming more chaotic with our increasing popularity.

Tex is a warrior, but the really tough outside only protects her painfully extreme sensitivity. We love each other and count on that love — a clear understanding that's been there since we met. Tonight we don't stop walking until we reach the Golden Gate Bridge, a favorite spot where we cast our dreams on the waters and watch them float out into the world beyond.

I'm the first to break the silence tonight. "You know that couple in the dressing room?"

"Yeah," she replies.

"There's something very unusual about them."

"We're unusual, Frog," she laughs. "They're just out of their element."

"That's not what I mean. There was something that happened in that room, the moment they came in."

"Yeah right, you know you don't smoke," she laughs. "What are you telling me?"

I grab her hand as we run across the bridge to the ocean side, carelessly splitting the traffic like two wild animals. We catch our breath as the adrenaline rushes.

"We're insane!" she yells, bending over to pull oxygen into her lungs. "We're out of our minds."

"It was like they just appeared," I continue. "And the moment they arrived, Bob couldn't get out of the room fast enough."

"No shit man!" she yells above the noise of the cars. "Bob's just paranoid. He's even afraid of me."

"I'm telling you these two just appeared. After that the whole room turned calm." I pause for a moment. "Before they came in we were exploding with rage and after they entered . . . there was none of it . . . nothing."

"So what's your point?"

"I'd like to go to their ranch. That's my point."

"We have work to do right here," she says sounding defensive. "Don't forget, you're the one with the record. That's more than any of us have right now."

"That's all changed, kid. It's been banned on radio."

"What's been banned?"

"My record, it's dead. They say the words promote drugs, but that's not the reason. This is about war."

"I'll bet the record label's pissed," she says.

"Do you think that couple is for real?" I ask.

"Of course they are," Tex answers, brushing off my question as she walks away and then turns to face me. "Bob will work this out. You're too damn good to be blown away. You got nothing to worry about, besides you can't control their shitty little world, so screw 'em."

Tex walks further onto the bridge then shouts. "I need to be pushed like you're getting pushed. You got shit happening."

"What's that supposed to mean?"

"I need this too. That's what it means."

By now we're at the center of the bridge with the entire bay, a huge light show all around us. Tex spins in full circle on the back of her heels, pointing at the lights and the city beyond. "Hey you!" she screams as she twirls. "Watch us now. We're coming after you San Francisco — then it's the world, the whole world!" She plants her feet and stops with a laugh as her voice pierces the night like she's on stage. We all have this in our mix of bravado . . . it lurks just beyond obvious notice.

"You've gotta pull real hard and pull me along," she stops with a perfectly straight stare. "Will you promise me that?"

"Absolutely!" I respond more calmly now. I've almost forgotten my own dilemma with her little performance. I walk up and put my arms around her and lean against her. "We're together here kid, we have no choice." Her emotions have worked for me — the radio dilemma seems silly in this moment.

This is 1966, nothing but dreams to live on and our momentum to lose. These are the days, too early for success, but you can feel it coming. It's breathing down our necks, just beyond the shouts of our madness. We're certain we own the world one moment and get lost in a torrent of total doubt the next. I wipe the tears from her eyes and we walk back through the night, more silently now as the adrenaline wears off. We move through the San Francisco hills, combing the quiet streets with our dreams.

It's three in the morning when I leave. I can't imagine sleeping, so I end up at Dave's. He's rooming with an ex-Army ranger named Stephan who's seen his share of battle in Vietnam. He now works against the war; knows the inside as a matter of fact and is great for information. He cuts deep into any subject. They're still up when I arrive, somehow I knew they'd be.

"Hey, what's going on?" Dave lets me in with a hug. "You look worried, what's up?"

I just found out that the Feds put a ban on my record and radio won't touch it now."

"No shit, why?"

"They say that it's drug lyrics, but I know that's not it."

"You got yourself on the wrong side of Uncle Sam's fence," Stephan says, entering the room.

"That's what people tell me."

"For sure," he continues. "This is real for them and it makes those guys do nasty things. I've lived with them. Those fuckers kill what they believe to be a threat. They're like an animal when it thinks you're threatening their young."

"What a drag," Dave says.

"Yeah, this is not the pretty face of our country," Stephan continues. "This is the ugly side, and not even as bad as it could get with these guys."

"I battle my management, the record company and now this. It's affecting every moment. I'm getting cynical."

"You got to be," Stephan replies. "You got to know what your enemy is thinking before he's thinking it, or you've lost the battle."

"But my music depends on me being me — being real," I respond, "and this shit isn't real, it's bullshit."

"Well buddy, with all respect, I don't want to spoil your dream, but this bullshit is very real and you'd better get used to it if you want to play the game you're playing." He stops for a moment as if to ask himself if he should say more. "As a matter of fact, if they think for a moment that this isn't going to stop you, then they'll pull out the bigger guns, and I mean guns."

"What's that supposed to mean?" I ask.

"Check out JFK, he walked beyond their limits and paid the ultimate price."

Stephan's a man most would call crazy. He never wears shoes, no matter where he's walking. He spent years living in the jungles of Southeast Asia behind enemy lines, surviving on whatever he could find in the wild. One thing is certain here, this man knows a story from the inside.

"They are afraid of the worst case scenarios here," he explains. "They're in this war for the long haul and worried as hell about your protest spreading across college campuses, soldiers have radios — so they don't want you to become very popular."

"How far are they willing to take this contest?" I ask.

"Well, first of all, they don't consider this a contest. To them this is war and you are the enemy." He looks around the room as if to compare it to something. "How far do you go with the enemy in a war?"

"You kill them," Dave answers.

"Exactly," Stephan replies. "And that's how far they're willing and able to go. They're counting on the fact that you won't take it that far, but if you do, they have an answer prepared. You see they run all the scenarios across the table and prepare for them all. That's what they are paid to do and that's what they do."

"So where do I go from here?"

"Well first of all, do the math. They have millions of dollars and huge manpower; they've sent agents to your mom's office, your record label's offices, and to the FCC. They'll spend whatever it takes and never worry. The national debt is just their way of getting a job done."

"You, on the other hand, have limited funds," Dave adds. "What you do will have to be paid for in real dollars, not this Monopoly stuff."

"But this is what I've committed my life to, like getting out of the Army."

"Then you have to do it out in the open," Stephen says. "Do it with a high profile — do it in the open. This won't stop them, but it makes their dirty work hard to hide."

"That's not comforting," I reply.

We talk for the rest of the night and I never get to sleep. I discover that my options are slim, but I have to do this. The sun has long been up when I head out the door for my house.

Twelve

On the Road

$\mathcal{B}$ob calls as I walk through my door. "We have to meet," he says. "Where have you been?"

"I've been up all night with this thing," I reply.

"You haven't slept?"

"Not a wink."

"Well, put up with it . . . we start work this morning. Let's talk at breakfast, I'll pick you up."

"What's the plan?" I ask, not wanting to wait.

"Lots of repair work. I spoke with Frank in L.A. this morning and they're going to go to bat for us. We do interviews over the next two weeks and they're putting together several promotion concerts . . . lots of cheap tickets to get in the crowds on short notice."

"What are the interviews all about?"

"You'll talk live on-air to DJs about the lyrics and the meaning of your songs and we'll just pray that the people in charge are listening."

"And the concerts?"

"We play nine cities, with radio stations promoting each concert. We'll do Portland, Seattle, Salt Lake, Denver, Oklahoma, Albuquerque, Phoenix, San Diego and Los Angeles. We've had to call in some favors, but that's the plan."

"This is fast," I say. "Did you help do all this?"

"I've been on the phone with the label nearly all night and morning. They're pissed off as much as they're scared, but they're not giving up on you. When they get angry, things tend to happen quickly." He pauses for a long moment. "They told me they want all the shit about Vietnam to go on hold for now."

"Or what?" I question.

"Or they can't go any further, they won't invest another dime. The FBI's been up their nostrils. It's not just our label, they've hit all the big companies, telling them that they're not going to tolerate this communist propaganda."

"Communist?" I reply. "Do you really think they believe this for a minute?"

"Listen, the label defends you, but this is serious."

"You bet this is serious Bob," I reply. "This is America where we are supposed to be free."

"The FBI holds all the cards," he answers. "They mentioned a friend of yours who's gone AWOL." He pauses as if waiting for me to confess to something, but I remain silent. "Their very words are that they're watching you closely."

"Well they'll have to buy a ticket, just like everyone else," I say with a smirk. "We're not cutting these guys any special deals."

I hang up the phone with a sense of accomplishment. I'm glad to hear that this is all in line with what we talked about last night. Stephan said — "keep it out in the open," and that's exactly what's happening. I sit down and jot some new notes to a song I've been working on for a month.

The chorus:
Great day in the morning glory hallelu-jah
Days breaking that's its story
How about you, yeah
Great day in the morning glory hallelu-jah
Sun's rising that's its story
And I love you, yeah

Just days later, with the tour in place, our bus rolls down the highway to the next town on our schedule and I'm working on new songs. "I'll mix these love songs in and they'll think I'm changing." I laugh with the other band members.

"Yeah, sure they will," Andre responds. "They're just gonna claim that you're promoting the use of Morning Glory seeds."

We laugh and go about our bus routine, which is a lot of fun for 75 percent of the time and total boring hell for the rest. We goof around, play music and try to sleep, but you get very little rest on tour. It's actually good this time to get on the road, when I get to see the audiences outside San Francisco, where the scene is totally different. It's like going back in time and I realize what a bubble San Francisco is right now. I enjoy being back up north where I started and Jimmy Green's ecstatic to see how our music has grown.

Julia has become the nervous one now without Bob around. She's freaking out about which side she should take when there's controversy. While we prepare backstage for a show, Julia ends up talking to a couple of local radio programmers. "We've got problems with some lyrics, do you think we could address this with him?" they ask her.

"Problems?" I yell, overhearing their request and everyone backstage turns to look. "Definitely not any problems from the fans out there." I point to the curtain I'm about to walk through. "They've filled this place to hear these songs."

One of the men reaches forward to shake my hand. "I'm a big fan — I love your work. I hate even asking this, but we're forced into an image game right now. If you work with us, this will all blow over."

"I'm not into image, other than being myself." I say backing away from the conversation. "We might talk about my image later, but right now we have a show to do." Without another word I walk to the curtain.

Julia runs after me trying to sound calm. "Do you realize what this means to blow a show?"

"Yes," I fire back, "and I know my music too. So give me some room to move and we'll go over all this later."

"Don't take this personally," she insists. "This is just business. They've gone out on a limb to work with you here."

"Is this about business or music, Julia?" I ask bluntly.

"Without radio there is no music. This is the way the real world operates. The real world is about numbers."

I stop in the middle of the stage curtain and turn to Julia. "No Julia, don't go there sweetheart, the real world is not about numbers. You got it wrong now and you know that the real world — the world that I live in, that you live in, is about being honest. Numbers are slavery and neither you nor I are going to go that direction . . . are we?" I don't look back, but walk onstage, I'm furious as I approach the microphone and take hold of the stand to calm my hands. I begin to speak. "Good evening, thank you for coming tonight. I want to share something with you before we start. There are people here in my world who want me to sing to you without a message. They're not bad people, they're just following orders from those who want you to die in war." The crowd boos loudly. "To die for absolutely no reason." A few slurs emerge from the audience. "I agree, and those people back in Washington want my message watered down because they're afraid. They're afraid that you'll wake up and discover what is really taking place. They want me to use 'nice' and 'approved' language so that no offense is taken and no one wakes up from this trance."

A loud hissing of disapproval comes from the audience, as they become restless. I continue and acknowledge their disap- proval. "Well, I'm not listening to them and I hope you under- stand, so if I offend anyone here, you can complain to someone else because I'm just who I am. That's honest and that's that."

Cheers erupt, my band hits the opening chord of 'UNCLE SAM' and the beat begins furiously in total protest.

So you think we believe that Sam don't care
Or what he'd say if Tom Jefferson was here
Sending us to die because if we can't afford school
Is that coincidentally keeping me a fool?
Is that coincidentally making me a tool?
In your war — well I'm for peace
I'm no slave — I'm my release
I'm your son — I'm not to kill
I'm the words of your church upon your hills
I'm your son — I'm not to kill
We're the words of your church upon your hills

The crowd sings with these repeating words and the band keeps the chorus going longer so that they can join in. There is such good communication between me and the other players that we know exactly when to do these kinds of things. The enthusiasm builds and to the right of the stage I catch Julia's eye in the middle of this song, she's dumbfounded. The others around her are looking on in total disbelief. The concert rocks forward to a thrilled audience with song after song met with a joyous response. The radio programmers are caught between the fact that this is what people will pay to see and listen to, and being told this is anti-American — not to be aired.

After the show, Julia is the only one on the bus in a bad mood. The band's ecstatic about the show.

"That was the best," Andre claims. "Did you see the hope on their faces?"

"Yeah, well that cancelled the radio show for tonight," Julia warns.

"That was vintage," William adds with a huge smile. "Don't worry Julia, the radios will be begging for our time real soon . . . just watch."

Our bus rolls down the highway and on to our next stop. Julia tries to sleep, but the rest of us don't bother. We're high from the adrenaline of the concert and we continue to play music and carry on with the sweet taste on our lips. Andre beats out the rhythms of our songs on a cardboard box and the songs last as long as the box does.

We perform to sellout crowds all the way through Denver and then we're scheduled into Oklahoma City before turning back for the West Coast. Some cities have been more receptive than others as far as the radio DJs go, but the concert crowds are champions of the music. And when we do get on the air, I'm able to answer most of the questions with ease. Overall, it's becoming more obvious that there's a tremendous gap between the government's agenda and what the people believe in.

Thirteen

BUSTED

"Why Oklahoma?" I ask Julia, as we prepare our bus for the road.

"Well sweetheart, you're going to Oklahoma, but I'm not," she answers with a smug look. "Bob wants me in Los Angeles to organize your recording sessions in advance."

"Right, but why Oklahoma? It seems so far from our base."

"Oklahoma and Texas are the states that started the radio problems." She says with a shrug. "They're the ones who think of you as a commie rat. You're entering the mouth of the monster to set it straight, if that's possible."

"Wow, Tex will love hearing that her home state started my problems."

We finish packing the equipment on our bus, and we're ready for the road to Oklahoma. Julia prepares to fly west to L.A.

"Give 'em hell," she says with a salute. "But make it sweet, so they don't throw you out."

"You know me Julia," I say, laughing. "I'm always sweet."

"Right, and that's our only trouble." She hugs me, waves, and we're off.

I'm relaxed with our shows nearly complete and look forward to turning this tour back west where consciousness rises more easily. Our bus rolls hypnotically across U.S. Route 70, out of Colorado, and onto the vast flatlands of Kansas putting us all to sleep. I haven't encountered my guides since the tour began. It's actually a relief, for I've slept perfectly and the tour is going the best we could imagine.

"Are you grateful for the silence?" the voice of the young woman softly vibrates in my ears.

"I have no choice," I reply.

"You do have a choice each time you take a step," she echoes back. *"Uncovering the seeds of reality in the midst of the dreams has always been a human challenge."*

"Is there a lesson in here?" I ask.

"There's a warning," she replies. *"You're entering your deep doubt here and your senses are at odds with your dreams."*

"I've got a concert in Oklahoma tomorrow night. What doubt do you mean?"

"It can't exist when the doubt is too strong," she says.

I struggle to wake now, but can't. "Our concert is a scheduled fact, right?"

"Life is a deep labyrinth fashioned from time and time is fashioned from memory of the past that is creating anticipation of the future." Her words are exact and do not waver even slightly. *"Weakness will always be forced to grow stronger and that's the evolution of our consciousness."*

"What you're saying is such a riddle," I respond, trying to make sense of it.

"There are powerful moments," she continues, *"within the fabric of our production of time that appear as fear. They are always lingering around us, but when we believe in their power they become powerful and we fall victim to this fear. Then our lives are disrupted until we can once again realize it as an illusion and shift our belief."*

Her voice fades from my ears — my confusion fades into silence and I fall into a dark unconscious sleep, unable to continue this meditation of lessons and I'm gone. I sleep until the bus slows down some hours later. Signs of a city appear on the horizon and the crew is assembling in various parts of the bus. I'm uneasy with the dream, but the rest of the band looks great. I've never had a warning such as this, not since the night I actually died.

"Are you ready for rednecks?" Andre asks. "This is the flattest land I've ever seen. I'd go nuts living here."

"We already look nuts." Pat Dave, our horn player, pokes at me with a microphone box. "Wake up man! We gotta look sharp here. Julia said this is the monster's headquarters."

Everyone busts up silly, in a way that happens when you're groggy. As if on cue, police sirens blast through our laughter with short bursts. Our bus driver brakes hard and pulls over, our loose belongings being tossed around the compartment.

"What the hell did I tell you?" Patrick shouts. "There's the monster now."

It's sunrise and the flashing police lights make red strobes on our ceiling. "Will you look at that?" Andre says, his face pressed up against the window. "Did one of you rob a bank while I slept?"

"What's going on?" I yell up to the driver.

"I was doing the speed limit . . . I have no idea," he answers and swings open the front door to get out.

A rough and fear-filled voice burst into the bus, along with the cold morning air. "Everyone step outside slowly."

We look at each other, smile and proceed. "I guess they want a preview show," Andre says, beating his drumsticks on anything in reach as he moves forward through the bus.

We step out into a morning of glaring fear-filled eyes and are immediately turned up against the bus and frisked. They move us quite forcefully into separate locations. No one says a word. The ones doing all the action are in business suits. There are uniformed police here too, but they're standing away and watching everything with lock-jawed attention. As this continues to unfold, more police cars arrive, park, and light up the dawn sky with a bright red flashing light show. The police radios bustle with excited conversation, giving the sense of a movie set filled with real criminals. This isn't real, I think as I remember words from my dream. *"Its power parades before you as fears. In the world of this fear, greed gathers weapons as an answer."*

"What's this about?" I ask, trying to make sense of the ridiculous.

"We don't need to answer that just yet boy," a burly, suited agent replies. By this time the men in suits are inside our bus, rummaging through everything . . . our belongings are being tossed around with abandon. We're being watched very closely, as if they're hoping we'll make a sudden move.

"You've got to stop this and let us know what it's about," Andre finally says. "This is not legal."

The blunt end of a nightstick plunges into Andre's gut, bending him in half. The uniformed cop turns to the rest of us and waves his big authoritarian finger. "Anyone else have questions?" He then looks directly at me through his reflector glasses in the dimly lit dawn. "How about you, smart ass, you got any smart questions?"

"In the world of fear, greed gathers weapons as an answer," rings in my ears.

"It's okay," I call out loud enough for everyone to hear. "This is what we have to go through and I'm okay. How about you guys?"

"Me too," Andre calls back.

"Yep," William and Patrick both add.

"Shut the fuck up!" an officer holding a shotgun shouts.

Seeing this could go very badly, really fast — with scared police on high alert — we all go dead silent. The clear indication is they're looking to get violent with any excuse they can find and they may do it even without one. By this time, four or five more patrol cars have arrived. We're each cuffed and put in separate cars while they continue to search the bus. Two more very plain cars arrive with men in suits and they gather together for a meeting that takes at least 20 minutes. At the end of this time, an officer gets in my car and we drive off toward the city.

"Ever heard my songs on the radio?" I ask my driver. He remains silent.

"I have a concert tonight, right here in town, if you're interested," I continue.

This gets his attention. "I don't think you'll be making that one, son," he says, looking at me through the rear view mirror.

"Really?" I comment, looking out at a sign that reads, 'YOU'RE OK HERE' Welcome to Oklahoma City. So this is the beginning of the new phase I've been warned about. I close my eyes for the rest of the ride.

Without further conversation we end up at the City Jail. I'm placed in a holding tank after I make my one phone call to Bob. I sit through the day without contact with my band. In this environment with nothing to do, the dreaming comes much easier. Old man seems to like the jail, his messages are deep and detailed. At the end of the day, I'm taken to a four-person cell where I spend the night.

It's completely obvious that the FBI wanted to keep me from giving my concert and although they succeeded on that level, it's no big deal.

72 hours later, without any charges, I'm released. The rest of the band was released shortly after being brought to the jail and spent these three days in a hotel. Bob had done everything in his power to bail me out, but the system would not budge.

As I'm leaving, the officer signing me out at the front desk says, "I'm not expecting you back here — we don't like the trash you sing." He hands me a bag with my wallet. "You're an asshole, son, and that means you're full of shit as far as we're concerned."

I walk out through the front door greeted by Julia, the band, and our bus. Everyone's great except the bus has been trashed. The Texas concerts have all been cancelled while Albuquerque and Phoenix were postponed to accommodate the jail time. Dave and Stephan, hearing of my arrest, meet us in Albuquerque to lend their support. The remaining concerts sell out on the news of the band's jail time. Paul and Adrian, who live nearby, are backstage the whole night.

There are banners of support everywhere like a huge party of the like-minded. One reads, 'We Don't Die For Lies' and it floats through the hall attached to the back of a fast moving dancer on one end — a helium balloon on the other. Everything I say between songs is wildly applauded; Julia, impressed by the massive support, comprehends our movement more deeply.

"We're making progress," Stephan comments, during a break. "That was definitely the Feds who orchestrated your jail time."

"Yeah," I reply. "It's falling apart on one end and coming together on the other."

"Don't be concerned about the falling apart," Adrian assures me. "You can accomplish anything now — just hold the vision."

"I'm pleased with the success," I say, as I go back on stage after break. "People come together more when the opposition is aggressive."

Later in the evening, we're interviewed on local radio and the show closes with a final caller who sounds like he wants to pick a fight. "You better watch your back there, son," he says over the air. "There will be no place that people like you are going to be safe."

"Then we'll just have to keep walkin' high," I respond. "That's our anthem and it gets us through each day."

Fourteen

BLACKLISTED

*W*ith the remainder of the tour, we established victory for the freedom to speak our mind and my confidence grows stronger with each success. People I've never met initiate a fight with the radio censorship by signing petitions at the concerts. With these petitions in hand, we arrive in Los Angeles to record the final songs of my album. I feel certain we can change the momentum. The band, in great shape from the tour, works like a single player on many instruments. We build the songs into their final arrangements . . . the recording session arrives.

I'm doing what I now know is right and it's working with every audience. I sing about peace; I sing about being real; I sing about living high on life and of loving without ignorance or prejudice.

Conflict starts the day but as the day unfolds, it gets out of hand. The record executives are masked with disapproval. My band and I are heading strongly in our direction while the record company runs for the cover of playing it safe.

Adam, the head of A&R, and Frank, the president, search through my song sheets for words that might create a problem.

"My songs are what they are and the recent tour proves they're on target," I argue. "It proves they will sell."

"You can't sell them if radio won't play them." Adam says. "If radio doesn't play your music, no one knows your music exists.

"The FBI's so far down our throats on this we've all got headaches." Frank adds. "They won't let us breathe left or right. They want to shut down anyone who's actively against the war."

"Let's take the lead then," I respond. "Let's turn this around with public opinion."

"It's too late for that," Frank points out. "The radio stations have already caved in. They were our last hope. We thought they'd hold out for the freedom of speech, but they didn't."

"So that's just radio." I respond.

"No, that's the market." Adam says. "Without radio we have no way to reach the market."

"Maybe we need to challenge the censors then," I say. "Let's throw them a party," I continue pushing. "I'll play them new material for radio."

"Unfortunately you've given them too much ammunition and we're just not in that business," Adam responds, shaking his head in disgust. "We're a huge company — you have no idea how much is at risk here."

"Then you're making it really clear, aren't you Adam?" I respond angrily. "I'm with the wrong fucking record company." Deadly silence swoops through the room. I've crossed the proper etiquette line, but I'm way beyond caring at this point.

Frank's hand shoots up as if to deliver peace. "Hold everything right there. We don't need to take it to that place, not now," he says, more determined than I've ever heard him before. "Maybe we can do something with a few of the stations. That's not a totally bad idea."

"Now that was easy," my drummer chuckles sarcastically, perhaps to relieve the thick tension that now stifles the room. "Let's cut to the music and finish this."

Frank walks back into the control room where Adam already sits fuming over his notes.

"He's right," Frank says. "These lyrics sell the record."

"He doesn't call this shot," Adam says angrily. "You heard him. He could let it all go to hell for the sake of principle."

"That's exactly what we're trying to avoid. We'll talk when we've finished the album and take it one step at a time." This ends the conversation for the moment.

Both Bob and Julia are going to pick me up at the San Francisco airport, so I prepare myself for a tense discussion. Much to my delight everyone's on their best behavior.

"What do you think we got from the sessions?" Julia asks.

"I think we have the answer to our problems," I quickly reply to establish the attitude.

"I'm on your side," Bob adds. "I've heard two of the songs over the phone. They sound great." He pauses and makes eye contact with me before continuing. "When you get Adam backed into a corner, there's no place to go. Frank on the other hand tries to be open. He tells me that they're going for your suggestion on a radio promotion."

"Perfect!" I exclaim.

"It's next weekend," Julia adds. "I'll find a location by tomorrow."

When we get to my apartment the phone is ringing — it's Jimmy Greene from Seattle.

"What's up, Jimmy?"

He never has time for small talk and begins with what's on his mind. "This trouble you're having with the record isn't necessary," he says. "The word's out around the business — you know there're no secrets."

"That's for sure," I laugh.

"Your people are handling the FBI all wrong," Jimmy continues. "The way they want to present you doesn't fit San Francisco or your music."

"I know Jimmy. The audiences on the tour were great, but the record company's buckling under the pressure. They say it's the FBI."

"Yes it is the FBI, but they're letting this happen. Someone should stand up down there and reap the benefits of a career that's ready to take off . . . there's no place for this mess up."

"What can be done?" I ask.

"You might require a smaller label and new management," he replies.

"It's so good to hear this," I reply. "I thought I was going crazy."

"Times have changed and Bob hasn't. He's good, but he doesn't have the vision of your music. He has a formula for financial success, not a social movement."

"Why don't you take over then?" I ask.

"I'm not a manager, but I'll find you someone if you want me to."

"If there's any way at all, I'm all for it."

"Good luck my friend. Call me in a few days."

Fifteen

A SECOND EFFORT

Our car rolls slowly up the last few miles of a narrow road. The driver worries around each corner about the approaching traffic he can't see. He uses the horn incessantly. Julia and Tex look over at me every few moments to see how I'm holding up.

Deep gray clouds break up the pale blue winter sky. The final bit of this road finally arrives with the appearance of a human touch amongst the thick natural forest. The evenly planted trees wave their branches over the entire roadway. It's been at least twenty minutes since we left the main highway and headed into this isolated location in Marin County.

Radio executives and DJs arrive at the home of an eccentric friend of Bob who's agreed to host this gathering. Working hard to counter the radio ban, Bob spared nothing to set this up.

"You'll have to be convincing," he says with his camera smile. "This is the moment."

There are no like-minded fans here in love with the music I play, just executives judging whether my music can be played.

"They need to see you're up for the fight," Bob instructs me.

"For some reason I feel like a criminal under investigation," I answer.

"Then enjoy every minute and give them everything to remember."

We enter the main room where the band's equipment is set up. Frank and Adam introduce me around. Tex, feeling the pressure, slips into the background.

Small talk mixes with gossip around the room — chatty honesty blended with honest discomfort — each conversation wanders without a whole lot of meaning. This turns into a blessing as I quickly lose the caution I came in with. I stand silently, for a moment, in the middle of this grand room and realize there are no rules in this game. People make it all up without protocol and no one really has a clue. But if you believe it, it becomes fact. My disgust for war mixes with this realization and I determine to wake up the room.

Several of those present are ones who've pulled my songs from their play lists. I lean over and whisper sarcastically in Bob's ear. "Don't miss a moment of this — it's the Vegas show you've always wanted . . . the harmless Las Vegas show."

Julia grabs my arm. "You need to work this room like a pro and stay away from attitudes that don't help."

"Remember, this was your idea," Bob reminds me calmly. "And it's a great idea too — San Francisco could become the new Vegas."

Julia looks worried as she continues in a forceful whisper. "If you give them reasons to play your songs they will. The Feds gave them a big scare, but they are music lovers."

Our conversation ends with Adam tapping the microphone. "We're starting any moment now, please have a seat," he announces.

I step on stage sensing their curiosity and a bit of the embarrassment from the executives. I remember Tex describing them as "ass kissers in expensive suits."

"Watch this kid," I look to her and chuckle through the mic.

"Go for it," she calls back. "We got your back."

"Good day and peace be with you," I begin. "This is your opportunity to see the bad guy . . . my opportunity to play one." There's a slight laugh . . . not much.

"Here we go," Julia says leaning over to Bob.

I continue with a smile. "You've misunderstood my music . . . or not. But 'Getting High' is a way of life to me — not about drugs. I sing about getting high on life; about taking charge of yourself; of thinking for yourself." I stop for a moment to adjust the stand.

"Frankly, it's not about what you think of me, but about what's happening in this world. My music is dedicated to change the way we live. It's about making people important and having the government answer to the people. This cannot turn into another McCarthy era of making accusations of disloyalty, subversion, or treason without proper regard for evidence."

By now I have their complete attention. "There's no way you're going to stop the change that is already here. It'll happen no matter what. We're in a time of great upheaval. Someone has to be a voice of peace, non-violence and reason. Right now that voice happens to be mine and the audiences have shown that they love it. But I'm not the only one with this voice. You better get used to it because it's coming from everywhere and very soon there will be no way to drown it out with record banning." I look straight into the eyes of the closest audience I've worked in months and I've got them. "You may stop a few songs, but you're not actually stopping anything. At some point there's a lesson you'll learn from this. I'm only one pioneer and there are many more, believe me. Anti-war is not anti-democratic, it's all about democracy and you'll feel the same way the moment they come after your sons. The crime scene of this war has our prints all over it."

Adjusting my guitar strap, my bass player and drummer start a strong beat. The band's ritual blessing begins just like every one of our concerts. Song after song fills this house up on the hill. I'm singing on the edge of my anger without sounding angry. The songs, even the lyrics, meet their approval as they tap their feet. Those sitting stand up and once standing they move and dance. At the end of my final song they deliver an ovation over the top and the job's done.

One after another, they express their love for the music and the lyrics, although they suspect these are still probably too strong for the censors. They say things like: "We look forward to playing this on our station — the audiences will love them as long as they last." They stand smiling like the criminal we are all feeling faint sensations of.

Julia rushes up. "That was so incredible — that was the best I've ever heard you play. Maybe you should get angry like that at every show."

"Yeah . . . maybe, but the Feds are still going to ban the songs."

"They can do what they want," she replies. "The stations are on our team now."

"We'll see . . ."

Julia puts her arm around my shoulders. "We'll talk tomorrow, let's get out of these woods."

The old man comes to me in this moment, *"Laugh with your life's joy when it arrives, for God's sake. Laugh in the face of all the false power and you'll weaken it."*

I've got to succeed, I scream in my mind, and throughout the drive home I mull over the human struggle we've just witnessed . . . amplified and accelerated inside the microcosm of my music, radio play, war, and government. We all want to do the right thing, and though we might view it differently, we mostly mean for the best. I see the reality of happiness is simply a little courage mixed with some well-placed enthusiasm. The dilemma of failure is but fear mixed up with doubt. There are the nets of this rational illusion, draped over humanity like a blanket, weighing them down and smothering life. The political world is using these unfortunates, trapping them in massive networks of belief slavery. It destroys the memory of why we came and replaces this memory with an empty pursuit of pleasure. There's nothing else outside this enigma. Summoned by these sensations, I sleep for the last part of our drive.

The young woman takes hold of my hand and walks me back into the world inside my dream. Like a holiday showing of Dickens' *"A Christmas Carol"* we tour the things to come and the options we have. There are constant police raids in the world I'm facing and even an orchestrated murder. There is absolutely no way that the government is going to give in to our efforts to stop their efforts . . . no way.

As the dream builds I'm left with a sense of darkness; my achievements are not so large; my world is far away from the music that I heard outside this world; and as for making a dent in the war — that remains a question. 'I thought San Francisco was my move' I mumble as the car comes to a stop at my house.

"Talking in your sleep again," Julia says as she looks over to find me in a very bad mood.

"Right now I don't want to hear a word about business," I state flatly. "I just want rest." I leave her without a "good night," or a "see you" . . . not a word.

In the morning I wake up empty. At our morning meeting, though I haven't spoken to anyone, there's an obvious understanding of my change of heart. The mood's deathly quiet when I express my hesitancy to return to the same hustle.

"You know this is my life," I exclaim. "But it has to show signs of getting better . . . I have to have a glimmer . . . sometimes."

"Aren't you thrilled about last night?" Julia asks.

"I need some time to clear," I continue. "To refocus around my purpose."

"You know you have two concerts coming right up in Los Angeles."

I look sarcastically straight ahead with a smile. "Right."

Her tone turns even more businesslike. "I've already checked and there's no way to get out of this. I know it's been hard . . . I'm really sorry, but . . ."

"You'll have to hold off . . ." I interrupt her with my arm stretched out, smiling to show less anger. I close my eyes to indicate that I'm not interested in conversation at the moment.

"I'm sorry that I have to talk business, but the world continues to turn," she says.

"I'm not clear enough to be concerned about worlds turning. I'm going to rest a couple days and we'll talk later." I rise to empty faces looking for some sort of relief in my statement, but there's none. Having been shown so far into the future of this effort, there has to be a recalibration. Crazy government surveillance, constant harassment, arrests at my concerts, and even murder — there's no way I can mention this shit and where it comes from. I can't confide to anyone here that I'm betting a career on the accuracy of two "out-of-body" guides. Holy shit what a story this would make. I live by the direction of dreams that take place when I'm awake and when I'm asleep. So I just give everyone a hug and walk out of the door.

Sixteen

SECOND THOUGHTS

It's a very long walk. It reminds me of Draft Day in an odd way. This time, however, I'm where I wanted to be back then and now I'm questioning the journey. Mulling over my options, I know I need time outside the fire. The New Mexico offer sticks in my head over and over.

When I finally get to the house, Tex greets me at the door looking deeply shaken. Julia called her. With a desperate hug, she says nothing. After minutes of silence, she stares into my face. The words and tears pour out of me all at once, "I'm going to New Mexico. I think you should come."

"What the fuck are you talking about?" she asks.

"We'll spend time on the ranch. You know, the friends from backstage."

"That's it?" she asks. "That's a fucking — gonna fix it all — plan? That won't work at all, we've got too much at stake right now," she argues.

"And that is just the point, we have so much at stake right now I have to get clear to work. I need to strengthen how I'm dealing with all this in the first place — because now I am not dealing with it, I am just reacting." I pause to see if any of this makes sense. "I'll do the two shows next week in L.A. and then take a short break."

She's now matching my tears, but embarrassed to let them show, she starts acting silly. "This is a huge deal," she wipes away the tears, looking uncomfortable with her emotions. "You have to think this through." She sits me down on the couch and continues, "Look at you, you really look like shit." She pushes my hair back out of my face. "You really do look like shit. I'm telling you the truth and you are in no condition to be making these decisions."

"Thanks love," I smile. "I appreciate the tender honesty."

"I'm sure you don't feel any better than you look," she says standing up from the couch. "Let's get some food into you."

I pull her back down on the couch and look straight at her. "You know the strangest thing Tex . . . the music out there . . ." I point off into empty space.

"That's great, Frog, but do we all have to die to hear you play it?" she laughs.

"No, but we've got to be able to make that music. You know we're good Tex, but we don't come close, not even slightly close. It's for the best," I say smiling. "I thought this was my dream, and it is, but the message in all this challenge says I'm losing sight of some important detail. We've gotta get out of this chase."

"Well, we aren't doing badly as it is — the fans everywhere love us," she says. "If your songs step on too many more toes they'll do anything to shut you and your big mouth up."

"Yeah . . . and that is why we have to regroup. I've been warned again and again and now I believe it. I believe we can imagine a way through this mess, but not with all these people on us every single day."

"Don't forget you promised we'd stick together," she says with a worried look. "Remember?"

"I do," I whisper back. "And I promise it's still true, but right now I have to take a long deep breath. I can't ignore the message,

I'm slowing down." I see tears welling up in her eyes again, like she is feeling abandoned.

"Frog." She rarely calls me by that name. "Damn it, everyone loves you." Tears are rolling from her eyes.

"Sweetheart." I smile at her tears. "I'm not quitting. I just need to regroup." I sit back up and take her hand, holding it tight. "I'm under attack from the inside too. My demons make the FBI look wimpy. This is just the time I need to get my life back."

She turns her head away, trying not to hear what I am saying. "If you take a break now I don't think you'll be back."

"Then come with me and I'll have to come back," I reply. "Then we'll join together and deliver the message."

"You want me to go with you?" she asks.

"Yes, to the land of New Mexico."

"For how long?" From the tone of her voice, I can tell she wants an exact answer.

"A couple of weeks or so, whatever it takes to get clear. I don't know if they are real, but I keep getting warnings and this solution makes the most sense."

"To hell with your warnings, Frog," she says angrily. "I'm just getting started with my dream and I can't leave in the middle."

I hold her hand, close my eyes, and fall asleep in total exhaustion.

After this, Tex comes over at all hours during the next few days. She hopes I'll stay but she is aware that this is the end of something. One day, I'm trying to explain my world to her. "You know the judgment of my life is what this whole experience is. It's not that I've done wrong," I say. "The worst offense was not believing in myself. It was the things I didn't do because I didn't trust that I could. That's what hell is."

"You are joking?" she questions. "Isn't this a bit too imaginary?"

"Maybe so, but I am being given information to live my life with and I have to trust my gut here. I need to face being challenged."

"Well," she pauses. "Since you're being challenged right now, why not get tough — that's what I do — show what you can do with it."

"Right," I respond. "I've got to get to the place where I can walk right through this, but I'm not there yet. Life's too precious to leave it puking your guts out on some floor and that's where the opposition wants me."

"Maybe that's the risk you have to take to be great," Tex responds.

"Maybe . . . and there's always a risk. I know this," I answer. "But life has to make a difference. I look closely at her. "You better come with me. This place is dangerous right now for both of us — the FBI might kill me and the booze will kill you."

Tex rubs my shoulders — her voice sounding like the innocent honesty of a little girl. "Hey Frog, you promised me, you promised to help me get there. You can't forget me. You promised."

On the way to Los Angeles, I inform Bob, Julia, and my band that I'm taking some time off to rest. This causes outrage with everyone, but it doesn't stop my two concerts from selling out . . . controversy is always great for the music business.

Seventeen

RUN FOR YOUR LIFE

"I'll be right back," I say to Bob and Julia, but it somehow sounds totally insincere the moment it leaves my mouth. The L.A. concerts proved that our position on the war is both valid and widespread. There was not a single vacancy in the auditorium for either show. I feel freer than I have in months and can't explain this as they drop me off at the Los Angeles airport so I settle for, "See you in a couple weeks."

The flight to Albuquerque is rough as storm clouds sail across the sky with the plane. They look magnificently mythological as they unfold on a blue stage. It gives me a sense of the true value in this mission.

"Welcome home, brother," Paul says as I come off the plane.

I respond with a hug, it feels like greeting family.

Seeing my look, Adrian says, "Don't explain a thing. Whatever's happening are the sacred things. It only makes you crazy when you try to make sense of the non-sense." She flashes a huge smile and her entire face lights up.

We walk through the airport with Adrian's arm draped on my shoulder as if to secure the depth of family. "By the way," she whispers. "You should know our real names since we're family.

We are Palqtlo and Adltleena. We're not Native American, we're Indigenous Mexica. You can pronounce our names very easily if you deeply relax your mouth and tongue and let it roll out like water — it's 'Paul-ka-tlow' and 'Aadal-tlee-na' that's all there is to it."

"Why the Paul and Adrian then?" I ask.

"You can imagine," Palqtlo says. "They are so hard to pronounce and impossible to spell in the English language that instead of having every conversation about the name we just made it simple. It's just easier, no other reason. Otherwise, we spend our entire lives pronouncing and spelling," he laughs.

"When we meet someone here in America," Adltleena adds, "it's more important to get the person, rather than going round and round about names."

"Cool," I say as Palqtlo nods in my direction.

"English is a business language," he continues. "It has concepts for the senses and business of these senses, but it has very little for describing the Spirit. Spirit deals in pure experiences; our language is only about these experiences of Spirit."

At this point, Adltleena is laughing delightfully and holding my shoulder even more strongly. "It's so good to have you home with us. We've felt you being here, ever since we first heard your songs on the radio in our truck. We knew you were something special right away."

We walk into the parking lot where an old rusting pickup truck sits patiently. It looks like a loyal dog and has about as much earth on it as the mountains in the distance. The tires are new, but that is about it.

"What a change," I exclaim. "When I got to San Francisco, I was picked up in a Rolls and felt like shit. Here I'm picked up by one of the dirtiest and oldest trucks I've ever seen, but feel very fancy."

"There you go," Palqtlo laughs. "That's the humor of a human."

A large green sign greets me as we leave the airport 'WELCOME TO NEW MEXICO, THE LAND OF ENCHANTMENT.' "That's how I feel," I tell them. "Enchanted."

"New Mexico has earth that sticks with you," Palqtlo says, referring to the dirt all over the sides of the truck. "It's been raining."

"It sticks to everything," Adltleena adds. "I hope you brought a tall pair of boots that you don't mind getting wet and muddy."

"Just the ones I'm wearing," I respond, showing excitement in my voice. "The dirt will be good for me."

"Well, those will look just like this truck within the first five feet of our land," Adltleena says as we drive north on US Highway #25 — the signs read 'Santa Fe, 60 miles'.

The wet ground and dry air of springtime in New Mexico makes for the face and hands to feel alive and lined. It reminds me of old photos of Native Americans with their deeply wrinkled faces. Even this early in the day, the heat is making the distant land shimmer and wave as we roll up the highway through the green fields of sage into the hills of Pinion. The mountains are deep blood red. I'm born into new life.

We pass quickly through Santa Fe. "This is the town where artists come to settle and fashion their skills," Palqtlo says. "A more realistic vantage of life than the big cities."

"But still just a vantage," Adltleena says.

This land is so real that I breathe it in, savoring it like a meal. Within an hour of Santa Fe, we come to the tiny community of 'OJO CALIENTE'. My high school Spanish makes me ask, "Why is this called 'Hot Eye'?"

"The hot spring waters are said to come from the Eye of the Earth," Palqtlo tells me.

"This land is covered with hot springs," Adltleena tells me. "This is where Geronimo surrendered a hundred years ago."

"Now there was a magic man," Palqtlo adds. "He believed his visions so strongly that they would come true. He only surrendered to save the children, but this never really worked because the government couldn't keep their word."

"I know all about that," I say. "That's the battle now."

"Greed has a way of turning treaties into traps," he adds gazing into the sage and trees.

A few miles further we pass through the tiny village of La Madera and the pavement ends at a sign, 'Servilleta Plaza 10 miles'. The arrow points into a set of muddy tire tracks wandering off into the forest.

Pointing to the ruts in the dirt, Palqtlo says, "This is the exciting part."

It's as if we are a train on tracks. Once we're in the ruts, we're obliged to go wherever they take us. They're deep from the tires and rain and hard as cement from the heat of sun. We heave and bounce as if trying to jump from their restrictions. From one side to the other, we bounce our way up the narrow roadway surrounded by a large mesa. The earth here is nearly blood red and the sky a robin's egg blue, an outstanding combination for the eyes of a city boy.

"I see these ruts as my teacher," Palqtlo points out. "Always keeping me in the exact path that is set for me. No matter how much I struggle with the discipline of the path, I'm firmly and without hesitation pulled back into flow."

Cresting one of the many hills, the valley below spreads out revealing a large white teepee in a sea of sage, surrounded by a few small wooden structures and an adobe house. The red adobe land with dusty green juniper and pinion trees is a cozy invitation that glows straight out of space. Several dogs run yelping and jumping down the road toward our truck. Taking in the sights I remember the way these two greeted me backstage in San Francisco. They walked in so natural and calm, just like this country. They had approached me that night saying how impressed they were with my message, now I'm the one impressed by theirs.

"That's home for the moment," Adltleena says waving at the exquisite picture before me.

"Welcome to Planet Earth with a capital E," Palqtlo says, his eyes glowing with the same excitement I'm feeling. "This was a good idea to come and visit the land. We've been praying you'd take our offer and here we are, from dream to reality."

'From dream to reality,' I'd hear him say this often.

As we drive closer to the house, three goats run among the dogs and Adltleena says. "I can't keep them in at all. They're absolutely convinced that they're dogs."

"Even though they get milked every morning," Palqtlo adds.

"Do they have names?" I ask.

"Taka, (life giver) Taki, (life) and Taku (living). This is all in thanks for the blood they turn into milk each day," she adds with reverence.

Unable to hold back my joy any longer, I say, "This is just as I remember the two of you. We only talked for a few minutes that night, but I remember your attitude being so clear and calm." I pause to take in more of the moment. "I'm glad to be here — a little spaced out — but I knew I had to do this the moment you made the offer." A tear surprises me as it rolls from my eye. "This was not a small decision," I add. "There are a lot of people upset by this."

"That's the nature of business," Palqtlo states flatly. "You always owe someone for something. If it's not your money it's your time, but the purpose of the game is debt. Debt in your consciousness creates debt in your world." He stops the truck and turns off the engine. "You're a debtor in this world until you come to the realization that this Earth belongs to no one. No one can buy or sell it . . . we're just renting a mask." He points to his face. "And some space." He points to the land all around us.

Such a great way to look at my issues, I think to myself. Trying to say something meaningful in response. I simply blurt out, "This is remarkable. I've just flown back in time."

Just as I say this, an elderly woman steps from the teepee with a small child strapped on a board.

"That confirms it," I say pointing at the baby.

"Yes," Adltleena acknowledges. "Meet our daughter."

"What's the purpose of the board?"

"The papoose . . . that is the greatest invention for a child," she says. "There are hooks all over our property and that papoose can hang from them anywhere. It puts her at eye level and therefore never overwhelmed in a world of giants. Our children learn from the time they are born that they are equal to everything."

"Sounds harsh to me, I say. "The wrapping's so confining."

"That's always the opinion of those who've never grown up with this," Adltleena tells me. "The wrapping keeps her from being distracted." She looks lovingly at her daughter. "Even at this age children enjoy a time of focus, not to always be confused by the wild movement of the untamed arms and legs. She gets plenty of time for movement also. Your Bible refers to this as swaddling clothes."

"Listen brother," Palqtlo quickly adds. "Where you've been in this world is harsh. There was nothing to prepare you for that pressure." He reaches out with his hand on my shoulder. "With this kind of disciplined training when we're young, we learn that there's nothing to enslave us when we grow up. We handle the pressure of this world and it doesn't even seem like pressure to us."

I settle into the New Mexico pace over the next few days. The experience of incredible harmony between life and Earth begins to heal my anxiety about San Francisco, the FBI, my music and mission. One evening, around the fireplace that sits in the center of the main room, I begin the conversation. "Ever since my experience of death in Seattle, my mind cannot focus or relax because it's obsessed with finding the peace that never comes."

"Everyone else should be that fortunate," Adltleena responds. "Most people are simply obsessed with finding money." She reaches out and soothes her daughter's forehead with her soft touch. "Peace is way down most people's list. They become a slave to this money chase and a prisoner to the doubts that keep them running."

Palqtlo smiles, his eyes reflecting firelight he says, "Just as the prisoner is limited by the prison walls, each human is limited by the walls of their own doubts and fears." The room is filled with peace — firelight dancing over brightly colored blankets that lay across every piece of furniture in the house. It's magical to my senses in its splendid richness. I'm dizzy in a good way.

Noticing my dreamy state, he continues. "You can travel beyond these emotions. You can find peace in your greatness, but when they hold you with their doubt, fear and betrayal, they feed upon each other. Then, in the game of your life you're not a player, you're just the ball. That's when the real trouble begins."

Adltleena hands me a glass of water as she says, "You really need to drink more fresh water. This is very good for grounding and calming your nerves."

Palqtlo continues, "At this point you begin to feel powerless. This is the world of business and the greed makes it even more toxic. As the ball, you are kicked from one end of the field to the other."

"When it's based on greed it robs you of your life energy," Adltleena adds. "And your connection to your purpose becomes a blur."

"I was able to handle it until I wasn't," I say — thinking it sounded a bit weird.

Palqtlo laughs. "That's what everyone thinks. They claim that they can handle it, but it's really always handling you."

"You slowly become its captive," Adltleena says.

"So you're saying that there's no way to get through this process successfully?" I ask. "That a person can't live and work on this planet without becoming a slave?"

Palqtlo stretches as if to indicate that this might take a while to explain. "Listen," he says leaning forward in his chair. "It's within these emotional walls that the slaves of humanity dwell, every one of them thinking the same thing . . . that they can outsmart it." He looks at Adltleena and smiles. "Everyone's feeling they've found the way to not be caught in the gears of time's wheel. This all takes place in the imagination of the mind. To actually play the game and not get caught requires mastery, massive courage and total commitment."

"Wow!" I blurt out. "That's exactly what the old man says in my dreams. It repeats over and over in my head ever since."

"Well that's what you need," Adltleena says. "But it's huge — it means relating from the heart in every moment, even the ones that are very painful."

"How do you know you're in your heart?" I ask, not expecting the question can be answered.

Palqtlo takes up the challenge. "To live in the heart is to practice and fail and fail and practice and fail and fail and fail until you're able to sit in a neutral state. You have to be beyond the fray, otherwise the mind will override the heart with its opinions and conclusions every time. It'll claim that the heart will fail because it's too soft, too uncertain and too changeable."

Adltleena picks up the conversation like they're a band of musicians sharing a solo part. "The heart is in fact the most absolutely certain and the most organized organ in the entire human body. It can't ever rest or take breaks and so it's historically been connected to the idea of bravery and endurance."

Palqtlo adds, "The mind in its negative state is not aware of such wisdom. Only in the neutral state can the mind grasp the power of the heart."

We spend hours talking about my career and the strange twist it had recently taken. I wish Tex could experience this and I decide to invite her out here once again.

I'm exhausted and fall asleep on the couch. The next morning I'm awakened at 5:00 by the birds that are louder than I've ever heard in my life. As early as it is, I'm surprised to see I'm the last one up.

"We thought we'd let you sleep in," Palqtlo says smiling.

I can tell that he's not joking so I ask, "What time do you get up around here?"

"We get up before the sun gets everything else up. This way we accomplish several things," Adltleena says. "Most importantly, we're able to set our attitude with Spirit and prayer before we take on the worldly duties."

"Where do you come up with all this knowledge?" I ask, a bit stiff from a night on the couch.

"We were raised with it," she replies. "Our people have been living in this way ever since people and time began."

"Where's this?" I ask . . . my curiosity totally peaking.

"Well, according to the mythology of our elders," she answers, "The original name of our area is Wirikuta, which means the home of angels."

"Where's this?"

"It's actually located in the wilderness of Central Mexica — what is known to geography as the Copper Canyons."

"Mexico?"

"No it's actually Mexica," she explains. "The mythology says that angels would come to the Earth for visits in order to obtain the sweetness of the human vision. Then one time, a few thousand years ago, some of the angels became enchanted with the Spirit of the humans and decided to stay on earth and live among them."

"Do you believe this?" I ask.

She continues without answering, a habit I'll get used to. "According to legend, our villagers are the descendants of those angels."

Palqtlo adds, "These ancient legends speak in terms of time as one time, no past, present, or future. The clarity of legend is the power to unite the air so that all creatures can breathe, to heal the land so all creatures can eat, and to clear the waters so all creatures can drink."

The elder lady from the teepee enters the room carrying a bucket of fresh goat's milk.

"This is our birthplace that Adltleena speaks of," Palqtlo says. "We visit it as often as possible."

"Why would you want to leave it and live up here?" I ask.

"We were sent here, by the Maraakame. From their dream-time they received the vision of this mission."

"Who?"

"The elders of our community," he says. "These are the medicine people."

"Why come here?"

"To connect this knowledge to some in the out-world," he answers. "That's our word for civilization. We call it the out-world."

This interests me intensely. I completely forget I want to call Tex. "Are you a Maraakame?" I ask feeling suddenly like a child in the presence of a grandfather.

"We both are," he says motioning to Adltleena.

"This is one of the reasons we're so interested in your music," Adltleena adds. "You have a heart message without burying your head in the sand and that's very important for this time."

"You're interested in me and now I'm really interested in you," I laugh.

"You reach people with your words, but you're getting caught up in the business mess," she says. "It's the government control and the greed of the company that you can't work with. Some people can put up with this and survive, but it's got to be obvious to you by now that it'll end up killing you."

"Why? Can you tell me why I can't take it?" I'm irritated at the thought.

Palqtlo speaks calmly, paying no attention to my edginess. "The elders in our village say when you're very close to the sun your shadow is eliminated. Without a shadow, you find it hard to identify the darkness. You end up getting burned in the process."

"What's that supposed to mean . . . am I too close to the sun?"

"Not too close, but just too close for the game. You get caught in their wake without knowing it. If you want to play you'll need to get tougher, but that has problems too."

"So there's no way . . . is that what you're saying?"

"Anyone can get tough and play the game, but this carries a debt. The only way to master the game is in the neutral mind and the open heart and that takes all that practice and failure that we spoke of last night."

"How do I get there? I want that!"

"Years of work." With that comment the conversation shatters my hope.

"Time out!" Adltleena shouts from the porch. "Take him in the river and cool him off before breakfast . . . take Aramara too. She'll love the water."

Taquatsi Aramara is their daughter. They call her Aramara for ease and I'm told that it's the place from where all life comes from. She's named after Palqtlo's grandmother.

We walk through corn and squash fields to the edge of the mesa rocks and there's the river. It's mainly a stream about ten feet across and two feet deep, but there's a rock pile dam making it twice as wide and about fifteen feet deep.

"This is the way you get in," Palqtlo says handing me his daughter. He somersaults into the water feet first. As he climbs out and scrambles up the rocks, the smile on his daughter's face is as big as the sky. "Now it's your turn," he says reaching for Aramara.

I hand her to him and jump in feet first, no flip. As I hit the icy water the shock of the temperature is more than I expect. "GOD!" I yell as a rush-like electricity goes up my spine. "This is fucking freezing!"

"Stay with it for a minute till it stops being cold!" Palqtlo yells over my yelling. "This is the best thing for your nervous system."

This is how our days go by, storytelling and adventures and more storytelling. Before I'm aware of it, a week has passed and I've not seen a phone, running water, or electricity. I keep meaning to call Tex and check in with her.

One night, we drum in the teepee until I can't drum any more. I have the exact sensations I had in the hospital in Seattle.

I lean back against a bale of hay and recall a dream that accompanied my death.

"This is life," Palqtlo says. "This is the way of the heart."

"Rhythm starts in the mother's womb." Adltleena speaks quietly — her soft voice carrying across the room as she holds Aramara in her lap. "It's a heartbeat, a primal sensation. When you get back there through the drum, the rhythm talks to you in a basic and very familiar language of life."

"Well it works for me," I say stretching out onto the ground and the bright blankets that are strewn all around.

Adltleena continues, "The steady rhythm of a mother's heartbeat tells the child, you're safe, you're alive, you're not alone. Now that rhythm reaches down through the layers of your social chaos and establishes a harmony again. This is why children love rhythm and why you feel the way you do right now. This is why we love your music . . . your music has the heartbeat rhythms."

"These are the ways we spent our time growing up," Palqtlo says. "Our community is set in deep nature where no one comes, no one disrupts and there are always events of the heart taking place. The only thing that brings us back to the world of matter is the need to feed our body."

"Any chance of us going there for a visit?" I ask, sitting back up.

"That's a possibility we'd have to talk about," Palqtlo replies. "It's a long journey for just a short visit, but we can talk about it and then you'll decide."

We stay up late into the night, swapping stories of my life and the magic of their community in Mexica. As the sun rises on the teepee, I feel very whole.

Another week passes. At the end of a long night of drumming, playing my guitar, singing and talking, we walk out into the morning sun and agree to travel south to the Wirikuta.

"How long will it take us to go down and come back?" I ask.

"It will take as long as it takes," Palqtlo answers. "You won't want to go in a hurry. The drive will take about a week and then there's another four days on foot." He laughs and grabs my shoulder with a squeeze. "This is not a to-do list item."

"That phone call I spoke about . . ." I say to him.

"You mean the one you mentioned two weeks ago?" he chuckles.

I laugh too. "Well, I'd better make it soon. I gotta see if Tex will come with me — we both need this medicine in a big way."

"Well this might be a longer trip than you've planned, so just keep an open heart," Palqtlo says with a strange knowing in his eyes.

Eighteen

REACHING BACK TO TEXAS

The next morning, I rush to the general store in the village of La Madera. Palqtlo lets me take the truck, a drive that's beyond a fantasy. I'm glad for the ruts in the road that keep this antique truck in line.

I motion toward the phone as I enter the store. "Gonna make a call — I'm with Palqtlo." My eyes scan the room filed with antiques and canned goods as the man at the counter nods his head. "Here's ten bucks." I send the ten-dollar bill sliding across the counter toward the clerk.

"That'll be fine," he says, looking surprised at the amount of money in front of him. "Where are you calling to, Europe?"

"San Francisco." I chuckle as I dial . . . Tex answers on the first ring.

"Yeah?" She says sleepily.

"Hey kid . . . it's me."

"Shit, I've been needing to talk for fucking days!" she screams.

"It's incredible out here . . . I lost track of time. I lost time all together."

"My shows have been over the top man," she says. "But I'm fucking dying, I'm dying! Do you hear me?"

Very gently I whisper. "It's the insanity, kid . . . it's not you."

"No man — this is real shit," she argues. "Even in the day I can't lose this fucking sensation."

"Are you using anything?" I ask flatly . . . my point obvious. "Are you using?"

"I've got to, Frog," she whines. "I can't take it but I also can't afford to quit right now."

"No Tex, the only time you have is right now," I answer slowly. "This – will – kill – you. All this shit inside your body — no wonder you're filled with fear. What do you expect?"

"Let's not talk about this . . . not now," she says in a soft child-like voice.

"What does that mean?" I'm furious. "You mean let's not talk about this at all . . . right?"

Ignoring my comment she continues to speak in that little girl voice that completely pisses me off. "Bill's been calling every day. He really believes in you, but everyone wonders what's up."

"Tell him I'm doing my job," I say. "He will understand. Now, can you hear me out for a moment? I have an offer for you."

"Hit me, Frog," she says with a laugh. "I love offers and this is the first one I've had today."

"Take some time off," I say bluntly. "Come to Mexico with me, build your strength, then we'll come back and we'll do our music from strength."

"Mexico?" Tex asks. "What the fuck — are you mad?"

"Let's just do it to get really clear and really strong," I say.

"I may be exhausted, but I'm not fucking crazy, man," she continues with her attitude. "I'm just getting started buddy, my career is about to take off and I'm not going to walk away for some stupid trip to the desert."

"This is an opportunity . . . hard — no, impossible — to explain," I press on. "Just consider it — I'll be home tomorrow."

With that she changes her tone to one of concern and asks, "Are you okay man? This really sounds weird."

"Yes, I'm really okay. But where are you going with all this shit you're taking?" I ask, almost pleading. "This isn't okay."

"Who made you the fucking doctor all of a sudden?" she shoots back. "This shit is the only thing that is keeping me sane. Without it, I'll crack, it's just that simple."

"I'm going to Mexico . . . don't really know what I'll find there, but you should come — that's all."

"You do that my friend and you can kiss your career good-bye," she says, almost laughing at what sounds so ridiculous. "Your team is gonna shit, Frog. They're already asking me to talk sense into you . . . me, of all fucking people."

I can see this will go nowhere on the phone. "We both need to get our heads straight."

"Nope, not this chick!" she says with determination. "I'm on to something now . . . no turning back for me."

"You're asleep at the wheel Tex," I respond in total frustration. "I'm going to do it anyway, because life's too short to fucking sleep through it."

"You're too much Frog. You work hard to get somewhere and when you've almost got it, you bail. And you promised me you'd stick it out you son of a bitch."

"I'm not bailing," I defend myself. "I need more, that's all."

"Does Bob know about all this?" she asks. "Cause you know he's pissed anyway."

"Not yet," I reply. "I'm gonna do all that in person."

"Good luck, Frog, you're gonna need it man. I'll see you when you get back."

What a difference, I think, after talking to Tex. I'm right back in the chaos. The calm peace I've experienced over the past two weeks doesn't compare to the mess I've got to face back home.

"It's actually all your own doing," Palqtlo tells me. "Now you must undo it, or it'll undo you."

It couldn't be clearer. I'm going back to face my demons. My record company, my management team and the FBI all want me to change my ways — and all for different reasons. The FBI wants me out of the picture, and Bob Phillips wants me in Las Vegas, singing cute songs in some club. The record label just wants me to behave nice and to keep selling records.

I make sure no one picks me up at the San Francisco airport by not announcing when I'm coming. This way I can deal with everyone at a single meeting. When I arrive home, my key no longer works, but I see deep gouges all around the keyhole . . . someone picked this lock and not very well . . . the thing is destroyed. I go back downstairs, up the fire escape and in through the kitchen window. It all appears well orchestrated — they want me to know they've broken in, and when I get inside I find the place has been very meticulously gone through. Nothing missing, as far as I can see, but most of my things are oddly rearranged . . . this appears to be a message — we can fuck with you at any time. Chairs have been moved and the couch is shifted. Either Julia's been bitten by the decorating bug, or the cops are fucking with my mind. The job's been well done. They definitely want me to be paranoid — it's a power game. After I look through everything, I fix the front lock from the inside and grab a cab and head for the office.

"Why didn't you have me pick you up?" Julia asks when I arrive. "How was it?"

"Great," I reply. "But it's not quite over yet." This comes out to my surprise, I didn't really intend to just drop this on her, but there it is, sitting right in front of me now.

"What's that supposed to mean?" Bob questions, walking over to us.

"I'm still not ready to go back into this," I respond calmly. "I'll be ready soon, but it isn't right now."

"OK, what's it gonna take to be ready?" Bob asks in a bit of disbelief.

"Some time and some strategy . . . some time, mostly. I'm pretty clear on strategy, but I need to be stronger to pull it off. I know where I want to go with this now . . . I need to make it all happen."

"Shit!" he screams. "What is it with you? We have a lunatic on our hands. It's one thing after another."

"No, Bob, it's always been the same thing," I reply. "It's always been the same thing — you just always wanted a different thing."

Throwing a stack of papers, he walks for the door. "You're throwing away a career."

Trying to keep things calm, Julia grabs Bob's arm — looks straight in my eyes and says. "Stay in town, at least for a few days, please. We need to go over some ground here."

I nod my head at both of them. I feel compassion and confusion at this point — certain I'm doing the right thing, but totally uncertain of what the future will bring.

When I get back to my apartment, Tex is pissed and ready to beat the shit out of me for what she calls a betrayal. It's hard to tell what's more challenging, trying to express the reasoning for my decision, or the thought of living without a purpose.

"You have purpose, man," Tex shouts. "This fucking life is what we've always dreamed of. You say it yourself. The music is your dream."

"Music's my dream alright, but on my terms, that's my dream." It feels like I'm pleading my case. It was so much cleaner and clearer when I was in New Mexico.

"What are your terms then, asshole?" she yells with tears filling her eyes.

"To do it the way you and I do it," I explain. "Not to have someone looking over my material, choosing what I can say or not say, to have my team support me the way the audiences do."

"So how you gonna do this?"

"I don't know exactly. I wrote a new song in New Mexico. It was so fucking clear when I was out there." I pick up my guitar and play.

Come carry us over don't let us fall under
Please carry us over life's garden
We're on our way to stardom
Love's got our course charted
All you gotta do is get started

Fa la la la la la la la low your love
Fa la la la la la la la low your love
Fa la la la la la la la low your love

Miles south of heaven's reach
Here upon this Earthly beach where
All lovely Souls have flown
Resting in the womb — waiting to be born

Everything dying to be born
You know the infant day is an early morn
It's dark as night when day shall end
Into the light we are born again

Early morning sunrise caller
Found the prize a round sound dollar
It'll buy you gleam for in your eyes
I see reflected from those skies

Bellies of the birds so blink
And catch one there within your wink oh
Open up — let's be free
Looking after you can see
Love dancing endlessly
Your love dancing endlessly

Fa la la la la la la la low your love
Fa la la la la la la la low your love
Fa la la la la la la la low your love
Follow your love Follow your love

Love's the song bin sung the long
While we been sittin here
Looking for love the stone — heaven's thrown
Hold it to your ear

Sing along with love the song and
See so very clear

Pure child's play
Is your life when loves your game
Love's a gentle wave
Washing you my way
Hey hey

Fa la la la la la la low your love
All you gotta do
Fa la la la la la la low your love
Follow your love
Fa la la la la la la low your love
All you gotta do
Fa la la la la la la low your love
All you gotta do
Fa la la la la la la low your love
Follow your love
Fa la la la la la la low your love
All you gotta do
Fa la la la la la la low your love

As the song ends, Tex grabs my hair and shakes my head. "What are you doing man? Do you have any idea how good your songs are? Do you want to walk away from this?"

"No, but Bill's right and Bob doesn't get it. None of these people have a clue what to do with me. Now I have to get clear so that at least I know what to do with me. Look at me! I don't fit anywhere — I don't do drugs so I don't hang out with all the rest of the bands; I don't sing simple love songs so I don't fit with what Bob wants me to be. This is so stuck — this is so nuts."

"Then change management, change companies," she says coldly. "Don't quit."

"There's a contract," I reply. "I wish it were that simple."

"You're in charge here, not them," she says. "It's your music."

"Yeah, that's exactly the confidence I have when I'm around you and when I'm around Adltleena and Palqtlo."

"You don't even know these weird fucking people with their weird fucking names," Tex says with frustration. "And you're willing to throw away those really huge plans and go running off with them? This is so crazy. What the hell do you really know about them?"

"I know how clear and committed I am when I'm around them."

"That's bullshit, Frog! You're just scared like all the rest of us, but you're running away instead of fighting."

"So — I should drink like you and break through this bullshit fear . . . right?"

"Now you sound totally nuts," she laughs.

"When Palqtlo describes the experiences they've been through, where they come from, this is what excites me." I grab Tex's hand. "He tells of the walk to get to his village — there are no roads and it takes four days on foot."

"Big fucking deal," she replies. "What the hell is this supposed to mean to us?"

"Don't you understand kid?" I ask. "Please just understand, because there are no words to describe what this does to me."

"How could that possibly interest me?" she asks.

"Are you saying your career can't wait for a few weeks?" I ask back.

"No, that's not it at all — and you know what Frog?" Her tone suddenly turns icy calm. "This is not going to be a few weeks for you; I can feel it in my bones." There's a chill in her voice that sends the same up my spine. "And you're bullshitting yourself if that's what you think. This is the end of your life as you know it and the end of your promise to me. I can hear it in your voice as you describe all this fantasy. All I can say after that song you just sang is that you have no idea what kind of talent you have and what this all means to you." She starts to cry without caring that I see it.

With that the room goes quiet. Words don't work anymore as we blankly stare into space, tears forming in our eyes. The sun's setting over the city, turning the apartment into the rich tones of a day's end. No one gets up to turn on the lights and no one says another word. It all fades into shadows, then to dark with the old man's words in my head: *"Remember it's you who feels your feelings — choose how you feel. Remember it's you who views your vision — choose what you view."*

Nineteen

Playing for Keeps

Over the next week, Julia works frantically to change my mind by arranging meetings. She brings in several influential players, hoping someone will convince me to stay. Tex, on the other hand, is pissed, silent, and absent. Bob is just out of control and mad.

During the time I was in New Mexico, a good friend and fellow activist was found dead, his body turned up floating in the Bay. An autopsy established the cause of death as "heroin overdose followed by drowning." There's a problem with this story, however, because Dan was a completely sober person. Never in all of his life had he ever used drugs. This doesn't raise even an iota of suspicion for the police however. Just another dead activist — the hippies and their addictions — is the way the official story was reported. The peace community had a different response and began feeling a bit paranoid — we know it was murder. Dan played a big part in assisting AWOL soldiers traveling into Canada.

This bolsters my position of unwillingness to put up with bullshit — having come so close to death myself. Over these many months, Julia has mastered my weaknesses and can usually apply her pressure to work me, but this time she simply can't get through. God bless her, I know she's scared, but I'm armed with super determination.

As the anxious meetings roll on, one after another, I assure people of my simple intentions. I want a life and a career, but will not sacrifice one for the other. I try to explain in terms that everyone can understand. An artist must be encouraged to write from their truth. "From where I stand, it appears that you've caved into a government attitude gone very badly. And, if you bend to this censorship, you'll destroy the creative process and many careers in the process." They listen and agree in principle . . . I'm relieved at this progress, but I'm still going on my adventure.

Julia drives me home from our final round of meetings. My record company and management team, even Bob, have finally agreed that what I'm about to do is right. At the house, there's a long moment of very awkward silence . . . the kind that has absolutely no escaping except through the center of the heart. That's exactly where we go and the longest silent hug that I've ever experienced takes place.

I want to take a thoughtful walk down Haight Street. Palqtlo will be picking me up in the morning and I feel compelled to pay my respects to this street that has been creating so many revelations. I walk and absorb the sights and smells for over an hour when a man about forty puts his hand on my shoulder from behind. "Hey Bro," he says as if he knows me.

"Hey," I reply and keep moving at my pace.

"Pity what happened to Dan," he continues. "You know that could probably happen to anybody these days with all the shit floating around here."

"Excuse me," I stop. "Do you know me?"

"Never met you, but I bumped into Dan just before he died."

"Did you know him for long?" I ask.

"No," he replies. "Never met him before either."

I stand there looking at this man who stares back with a straight face except for the occasional shrug of his shoulders.

"What are you saying here?" I ask.

"Good," he replies. "Now you're finally paying attention. So what the fuck could I possibly be saying here?"

This is completely creepy and though this could just be a drug crazy, he looks too clean cut for that to be the case. "Are you saying that you're trying to get my attention?" I ask. "Is that what we are doing here?"

"I'm saying that you have been ignoring all of our warnings and now, with Dan's death, it seems you might be listening."

"This is fucking creepy." I turn and continue walking.

"I hope for your sake that Dan's death has caught your attention," he calls after me. "As I said before, this could happen to anybody with all the shit that's floating around. It could even happen to you."

I don't turn around and I don't say a word. I'm not feeling threatened, but it's a strange sensation. Definitely a confirmation that my confusion has validity and my commitment has power, it appears that my adventure has come just in time. This guy is definitely cold-blooded.

When I get home I call everyone I know to tell them of this. I hardly sleep during the night. I can think of all sorts of conspiracy answers to the unanswered questions, but decide instead to play my guitar since I can't take it with me. Four days walking through mountains and caves won't let me pack it. I'll drop it off at Dave's place in the morning.

Morning arrives with the sun shining into my eastern windows. It's time . . . I pack my 1957 Gibson J-45 in its case and look outside. There sits that old "loyal-dog" of a pickup truck. I walk downstairs with a mix of fear and excitement to greet Palqtlo with a warm hug and again I catch the irony. He's parked this earth covered truck in the very spot where I am always picked up in the company Rolls.

Palqtlo and I spend breakfast talking about the trip ahead, planning where we're going to cross into Mexico and calculating the amount of driving we can do each day. Palqtlo makes it clear that the longer we're able to drive on the American roads, the faster and smoother the trip will go. We agree to go all the way into Texas before crossing.

"If we share the driving and only stop for short naps we'll arrive where we are to leave the truck in five days." Palqtlo explains.

I feel like we are going on safari and even though there's a lot of sadness in me, I'm also excited.

"The Mexican desert can be hard on the truck." Palqtlo says. "We should rest in the shade during the heat of the day and do a lot of the driving at night. I know all the trees in that desert, I've made this trip so often."

I really want Tex to come with us, but she's nowhere. I've called all over and haven't seen her in days. She's hiding and feels betrayed, but there's nothing to be done. I know, once she thinks she's been abandoned, all her memories come rushing back to haunt her. Nothing but time will change that. I leave a note on her door.

> *Tex,*
> *You're upset and I understand your reasons. My decision wanted to include you, but here we are. When I come back, we'll continue our quest. I'm a strength in you and you've been one for me.*
> *Love you, Frog*

We drop off my guitar and extra belongings with Dave and are on the road by noon driving across California and into Nevada before turning south toward Arizona. Two days on the highway and we're crossing into Texas at El Paso. We follow the Rio Grande River along the border of Texas and Mexico passing through historic locations. It's like a western movie playing out in front of the truck.

"You can see how this land was taken from the originals," Palqtlo exclaims. "The same thing happened in Mexico. This is why we're going to such a remote location where my people have never connected with the thieves of the lands."

The flat of Texas seems to roll on forever — we reach the border at Ojinaga, Mexico in the middle of the night. Changing drivers every couple of hours, I take my shifts driving through the pitch-black night of Mexico where all you can see are the headlights carving a path through nothing. It reminds me a bit of death.

When the daytime sun arrives, the little villages disappear; no one's outside except for the occasional dog rustling through debris looking for a meal. The desert roads in Mexico are so desolate that I'm sure we're all they've seen in weeks. We nap under whatever trees we find, and Palqtlo was right, he knows exactly where to stop and how far to drive until the next shady spot on highway #16 to Chihuahua. In the heat of the day we often wake-up more exhausted than before, but our bodies needs the rest.

As we arrive in one of the tiny towns in the middle of this endless desert Palqtlo says, "Let's get some restaurant food before we push on beyond civilization."

"Beyond civilization," I laugh. We've been beyond civilization for several hundred miles."

"Not actually," he responds. "You haven't seen anything that's beyond civilization yet."

For the most part we're eating from our own supplies, a mix of bread, nuts and fruit. For some reason he wants to stop here. Palqtlo grins as he turns the truck into a small cafe. The screen door is sagging so badly it's worn a groove across the front porch. Pulling it open is really tough and I see that a little boy finds it nearly impossible. It has to have been this way for years judging by the depth of the groove. I remembered seeing a tool bag in the truck, so I fetch it and there's one oversized screw with the screwdriver. A quick fix and the screen actually works. It took me only a matter of minutes to fix it, but the owners act as if I'm God . . . the little boy can't believe the ease with which he opens it now. Energy and intention are sacred commodities here I discover. When you have it, you can do anything, when you don't, life struggles on. Even the three dogs on the front porch seem to appreciate my work.

"I want to explain more to you now," Palqtlo says as we sit on the patio of the little café. "I haven't said this yet because it would've changed your mind about continuing."

"Is this the part where you scare me?" I ask with a big grin.

"Not at all," he responds. "This isn't going to scare you. It'll just let you know where you're going."

Caught by this moment and very curious, I know Palqtlo's always teaching so I sit back and enjoy the Mexican morning, leaving my mind open for the lesson.

"Where we are going is kind of like the other side of the universe," Palqtlo begins. "There's nothing that will remind you of home and nothing that will resemble 1966. Even a little place like where we are right now has no comparison to where we are going." He adjusts himself in his chair as if settling in for a long talk. "There's absolutely no relationship to the outside world and as a matter of fact the 'out-world' doesn't even know we exist. It will be extremely important to keep it that way." He looks for an acknowledgement here.

"What should I tell people when they ask me where I've been?" I ask.

"We'll come up with something truthful without revealing our location," he says.

I smile as he continues. "In three more days of driving we'll leave the truck and continue on foot. We'll hike for another four days."

"That's incredible!" I whisper.

"Like I said," he answers with a grin. "I didn't want you to become discouraged by all these little details."

"Little details," I reply. "These are not such little details."

"Well they are," he says. "Compared to the whole experience. This was your idea to come and now it'll be yours to enjoy."

"Okay," I sigh with some acceptance. "Keep talking. Do you have any photographs of these people?"

"They don't photograph very well," he laughs. "Actually they've never seen a camera."

I remember there were no photographs anywhere in Palqtlo's house.

"Now listen," he continues. "I'm explaining what you'll need to understand about what you're getting into and I'll tell you more over these next days." This conversation goes on for the rest of the morning, keeping us out of the highway sun. The café owners and others from this little village obviously know Palqtlo as they come by and pay their respects. I use my high school Spanish with great enthusiasm.

"This will come in handy when we're at your village," I say proudly.

"What for?" Palqtlo asks. "No one there speaks Spanish . . . I'll interpret when I'm there."

"What do you mean, when you're there?" I ask, suddenly uncomfortable.

"It all depends on how long you want to stay," he answers quickly. "Going all this way, I can't say that you'll turn around and go right back. It'll be up to you."

"I can't stay for longer than I said I would," I say, feeling strangely insecure. "I got to get back to my life."

"That's not a problem," he replies. "But, even then, I won't be by your side every moment, so my sister will also help."

For the next day and a half, we drive with two-hour shifts and rest stops every six hours. We cover several hundred miles of old Mexican highways that couldn't pass for highways except on the map. The holes in the road are sometimes big enough to drop this truck into and much of the time we spend on the dirt of the shoulder because it's smoother. I've got a knot in my stomach ever since he spoke of how much time I'd spend there and how remote this place was. He's right, if he'd mentioned it before, I probably never would have come. I find myself feeling tricked so I struggle to remember that I'm here by choice. It's not about anyone else.

Palqtlo's lessons continue for hours as we drive and suddenly, for the first time since my death experience, I go into a full-blown panic. When I say to Palqtlo that we should turn back he simply says, "You want to see where we are from. That's all you have to do . . . just go there and see it."

"You're joking?" I exclaim as the panic gushes into my gut.

"Not at all," he answers calmly. "The world is asleep because there's nothing to wake up for except vast amounts of fear. When you're a slave to that fear, you grow old and your heart fills with sadness for a life you never lived."

"Just stop for a moment so I can catch my breath," I ask. "That's all I need."

Palqtlo pulls the truck over to the side of the rough pavement and stops. I jump out and run out into the desert. I can't catch my breath as mad angry and confused thoughts race through my head. It's all I can do to not run away, but where would I go? My heart's racing, my head's spinning, I'm pouring sweat. I walk for hours around in huge circles, glancing at the truck then back into the desert and the highway we have come on. The whole time Palqtlo waits in the truck as the sun lowers toward the horizon. At first, the truck and Palqtlo are definitely the enemy — then after a long sustained battle inside my emotions the panic slightly subsides and my thoughts become innocent once again. The colors in the desert around me turn richer and fade into the dim light of dusk. As I approach the truck it's lost its cute look. Palqtlo, either asleep or meditating, doesn't move. Exhausted, I crawl silently into the back, curl into a tight ball and fall asleep. I've never felt so naive in my life.

Twenty

Mexica Bound

I awaken to the end of a desert night, flat on my back in the bed of this old "dog-loyal" pickup, dreaming the chorus to one of my songs.

> ***Great day in the morning glory — hall-lay-luu***
> ***Days breaking that's its story — How about you?***

I've obviously had some emotional relief in my sleep . . . I'm no longer in a fetal curl. Looking at stars with the moon shining bright as daylight just begins to sink in . . . I sing it again — this time out loud.

> ***Great day in the morning glory — hall-lay-luu***
> ***Days breaking that's its story — How about you?***

But within moments of this calm, my emotions kick in and turn ugly again. My head fills with doubts. Thoughts swirl — what the hell am I doing? — I'm in the middle of the Mexican desert with someone I hardly know. — This could end up being dangerous. — What have I done to my music and my dream? — I'm wasting time — Tex was right!

I stumble, head spinning, out of the back end and up to the front of the truck where Palqtlo, already awake and meditating, sits on a blanket on the earth. He opens his eyes and smiles into my emotions as if they're not even here.

"I need to know why I'm good in one moment and completely terrified in the next. This feels almost as chaotic as my death."

"You're weaning yourself of the familiar," he says. "The only way we maintain our identity is through our relationship with things familiar. When we lose this, deep down in the mind, it feels like we are dying. Our identity is dying and the mind interprets this as death. It then goes into hyper-survival mode and you are definitely moving into absolutely unfamiliar territory here. When you experienced it last night, you panicked. I know all about that from my days when I was a child going through the life-passages, the vision-quests back home."

"Back home . . . you mean where we are heading to?"

"Yes. Our elders know that as long as a child holds onto the familiar, they can't grow into adulthood. Not the adulthood that your world recognizes, but a truly mature, highly aware and compassionate human being."

"Why does it have to be so unknown?" I ask.

"The absolute unknown is the most fertile land for real growth," he says. "The only way to grow is to become the unknown — then the moment will have the freedom to mold you into a known. This process will be fun and then horrible and then fun and horrible again. Your culture calls this a rollercoaster."

"Will I get used to it, or will this whole trip be a rollercoaster?"

"Life relies on identity to feel safe," Palqtlo continues. "You will go through many moments of feeling completely unsafe because nothing in the world we are going to will remind you of the world we are coming from."

"Nothing?" I question.

"Please understand — and this is what I wasn't able to explain before we left — where I come from is vastly different than any personal or collective memory you have."

I'm sitting close to him on the ground now and feel like a little child at the feet of a wise grandfather, but one that I'm not sure I want to follow. As far as my emotions are concerned, we have traveled far enough and I don't really feel the desire to drive any further than this.

"Your upcoming experiences, no matter how long you stay there, will cause tremendous insecurity and tremendous growth," he continues. "This has already begun. Your panic last night was emotions grappling with what appeared to be your death. It was the death of the identity that you are familiar with."

"There is no way I could have done this while in San Francisco, right?" I ask. "I was correct to decide to come with you, yes?"

Palqtlo smiles.

"And the government shit was really in the way?" I reassure myself.

"There are, in fact, only about 3% of the global population that is reachable and teachable. All the rest are deeply insecure and only involved in survival," he explains. "Many of the government and corporate leaders have gotten to their positions because they were the most insecure and therefore the most motivated and driven to achieve the power that makes them feel safe again. The majority of people in power are in power, not because of their awareness, but because of their insecurity."

"Their world feels like shit when it touches you," I say.

"Yes. These people become potent and also very dangerous because they weaponize this insecurity. When insecurity achieves power, then the subjects of that power live in repression."

"That's the whole world I have been fighting with," I sigh. "This answers one of my questions."

"Until they come up again," he laughs. "And they will."

"In the Wirikuta," Palqtlo explains, "children go through rites of passage in order to form a formless identity that is able to completely adapt to any unknown situation they face. Each of these passages has particular qualities that it teaches to the child. There's nothing learned in the schools of your world that compares to this. This is not intellectual learning, but a deep cellular education that the child has access to for the rest of their life."

"It sounds like what happened to me in the Seattle hospital," I tell him.

"Yes, looking through a window that makes sense out of all this is the ultimate goal, to discover your cause and the course of that cause." He pauses. "When big events take place for what seems like no reason, like you dying and coming back. I'm talking about making sense of the real mysteries."

"That all seems like a dream right now," I reply. "So much has taken place since then."

"Let me tell you a story about a dream that'll bring you up to date on our journey here," he says pulling a blanket up over his shoulders. He begins to talk in a soft reassuring voice. "Let's start at the beginning, the very beginning. You must understand, our people go back for thousands of years on this land we're travelling to. A lot has happened over time, some of it wonderful, some of it ugly. Over the last two thousand years, my ancestors lived in the vast area we now call the American Southwest, Mexico and Central America combined."

He sits up against the side of the truck as he continues. "You'll see peyote cactus all over the ground as we make our way into the Wirikuta. Unlike the other tribes in the Americas, we never lost the path to our human power. We've never resorted to these abundant hallucinogenic plants for our power and here's the story that'll explain why."

I make myself comfortable and wrap a blanket around my shoulders.

"For the most part we were farmers," he continues. "We built our communities and lived peacefully. The only time we'd ask for the life of an animal was when our crops failed. Then, in a ceremony we'd ask for the grace of a particular animal and promise that in the following seasons there would be extra crops planted for its family. The sacrifice of these animals was done in such a way that the animals were in charge of the entire process. Our community would survive and return the favor in the years to come."

"You weren't eating any flesh even then?" I ask.

"That's right, and we were healthy and peaceful," he replies. "Then within a short period, things began to change. One or two of the communities began to expand their territory by waging war on their neighbors. It's not totally clear how these wars started, but over time, nearly all the communities developed a more aggressive way of life. If you're living in a war mentality, you're not inclined to be tending to the fields."

The air gets colder. The sun moves lower in time with the stories Palqtlo tells. We have been talking all day. "Along with war came hunting," he continues. "Agriculture faded and the sacredness of the occasional sacrifice was replaced by hunting and killing as the source of food. A man's bravery was soon determined by his ability to wage war and hunt . . . awareness was replaced by aggression."

Palqtlo's look — made visible by the light of dusk— tells me to be very quiet; to be very patient and this story will unfold exactly as it's to be told. I've become much calmer from the story telling. The sounds of night and the absence of the heat begin in earnest in the desert.

"Along with the wars came prisoners," he continues. "And since prisoners needed to be fed, it was decided that killing them was more efficient. Killing had become a ceremonial art with the hunting. Animal sacrifices showed the priests that a creature dies and gives off power. They called this power the 'ghost' and devised methods to capture and use it. With human sacrifice the amount of energy was huge and the power and control unequaled. This completely corrupted the priests with obsession. They called it 'redeeming the ghost' and the priests required that only they could participate. They'd reward the warriors for bringing live prisoners." Palqtlo takes a deep breath and with some discomfort continues. "Wars were inspired by the priests just for this purpose, but soon the need to have even greater power created the sacrifices of non-prisoners. As the greed for power increased, young girls and boys became the victims of choice. They felt that their energy was more pure."

"What was actually happening?" I ask.

"The ability to see through the wall of life increases with a birth or a death close at hand. In death, when the consciousness releases from the body, it scrambles for safety. Like a prisoner befriending its captors, the consciousness clings to the killer. This creates an alliance and a power."

Palqtlo looks straight at me and says. "This is why we live where we do. This practice was corrupt and my ancestors left the region. They sought the isolation of the location we're traveling to and have held this sacred land without visitors for hundreds of years." He looks back into the horizon. "The warring priests became lazy. They lost their sacred visions so they began eating the hallucinogenic plants that grow in this region to attempt to regain them. This was another tragedy, for when the Spirit goes lazy, the entire life becomes lost."

"So your people have never used hallucinogens for their visions?" I ask.

"Never," he answers bluntly. "Before this corruption took place, all people of this region were masters of walking through the wall of life and death. When the psychotropic plants became their medium, they lost this power. It's like your televisions, you might see it all and think you're having an experience, but it's just a deception. This vicarious journey is not a spiritual crossing at all. It's just a TV show in the brain because it's easy and it seems so compelling. This imitation has fooled cultures for thousands of years. Even your culture is in this illusion right now."

"I've never been into that at all." I respond almost defending myself. "When I died my lesson was clear. It made me an outsider in the music scene."

"That's why Adltleena and I were attracted to you and your music in the first place," Palqtlo says. "For centuries our community has walked a different path through time. We maintained our purity at a great sacrifice. This determination has preserved a very sacred teaching system."

He stretches and talks at the same time. "Children are our wealth because of their innocence. My community never lost this innocence or enthusiasm for life. The way we treat our children is the way we treat our future. There's no fighting for position and no speaking harshly. We teach them that life is to break the chains of emotional slavery."

"Is that what makes your home I visited so incredibly calm and cozy?" I ask.

"Absolutely," he replies. "My people have a clear vision of this life and beyond. That's why Adltleena and I were sent to live in New Mexico. We've created a sort of keyhole into the modern world."

"Why do you need a keyhole into the modern world?" I ask noticing that my anxiety has completely left and I'm comfortable with Palqtlo's stories.

"Our community has lived in isolation for hundreds of years," Palqtlo explains. "We've become a dying people. It's time for this knowledge to reach the outside world or it'll disappear with us."

"But you have a baby, what do you mean you're a dying people?" I sit up, concerned.

"A few babies are not enough to save our culture, or affect this world," he replies.

"Affect this world . . . are you serious?" I question. "Your people really want to affect this world?" The thought of an ideal community wanting to affect the insanity of this world is strange to me at this moment. "You seem to have everything. What's the purpose of getting into the insanity of my world?"

"You want to bring peace, don't you?" he answers with a question. "What's the difference between you and us?"

"That's completely different," I respond. "I grew up amongst the crazy. I have a reason to change it. It's either that, or it'll eat me up."

"Well, there you are," he says calmly. "We live in that same world and we recognize that our isolation will not be able to go on forever. The world is becoming smaller every day. We can't take the risk of losing this knowledge."

He sits up and crosses his legs — I move into a deep yoga stretch. I relish this day spent considering our options in the universe, away from the constant concern over a song verse . . . an entire day sitting and doing some yoga on a blanket in the middle of nowhere. The desert's as enchanting as it was in the weeks I was in New Mexico. Coyotes in the distance begin calling for the night — twigs crackle close by from the nocturnal activities of small creatures. Too smart to be out during the heat of the day — they rustle up their lives in the coolness that is settling in on us all.

"You never actually told me about the rest of your family," I say. "What are they like?"

"Are you still coming there with me?" he asks bluntly.

"Yeah, why?" I ask, wondering where this question's coming from. I've almost forgotten my earlier freak out with the deep relaxation that we are in.

"I'm checking your commitment," he answers. "If you're coming I will talk — if not then there's no reason to describe them."

"I'm coming," I reassure him. "I know I freaked out, but that seems to be over now."

"It will happen again and again," he promises.

"I can't really say what got me, but you have to admit this is one hell of an adventure for me . . . only a couple of weeks ago I was in front of thousands of people, making records . . . now I am in the middle of the Mexican desert with you and an old pickup truck and though I barely know you, you read my mind like I read the newspaper." I laugh and say, "Maybe, in light of all that, it's okay that I freaked out a little bit."

"This is delicate, I know," his voice loses its edge. "This is going to be a bigger stretch for you than you ever thought."

"What do you mean, a bigger stretch?" I ask.

"When you live with my people, my world is full of what the out-world calls magic and we just live our life," he answers. "This will freak out the logic in your brain and make you silly — there's no way around it. Your body will react in a way at first that might make you feel sick all the time. There's no way to tell if your mind will comprehend what you see."

"I will be okay," I tell him. "And if I'm not at first, then at some point I will be . . . I adapt, that's what I do."

"This will go far beyond what you call your imagination," he cautions. "Things disappear and appear and reality as you know it will be gone. This is not understood by the rational mind. I'm just letting you know to expect this."

"Remember . . . I died," I say.

He smiles and says, "But when you see the same things and you're alive, it's different."

"Like what?" I ask,

"They're masters in the Maraakame — what your yoga refers to as Ether," he says. "They appear in front of your eyes as if they're there."

"And they're not?"

"Right, or who knows," he replies casually. "Often, they just prefer to move about in the Maraakame. It's much easier when you are older." He leans back and closes his eyes. "We call it the awakening . . . it's just the maturing of life for us."

"Can you do this? I mean no offense, but can you?"

He completely ignores my question. "That's what I mean," he says. "This is the most delicate time in our journey, and we haven't even turned off the main highway."

"No offense," I laugh. "This is not a main highway. We've been weaving all over this road just to keep from disappearing into one of those gigantic pot holes."

"No offense taken," he counters with a big grin. "We didn't build these roads, we just use them."

"Are you saying that when we get there I'm going to be in this twilight zone?" I ask.

"What's the twilight zone?" he asks.

"Oh . . . kind of a joke . . . it's just a TV show, about the supernatural," I reply.

"No, not at all. This will definitely not be like the twilight zone. This is the real thing . . . the real thing," he repeats for emphasis. "If my father will agree, I want you to go through some of the passages that all of us go through."

"I don't know." Fear appears again . . . crawling over me like a spider. "The passages sound a little crazy."

"Allowing a person to grow up without knowing who they are is condemning that person to slavery. That is crazy! Allowing your children to be sent into war. That is crazy! Crazy is not being able to find that sacred space inside of you where you can experience security no matter what's going on around you."

"Yeah, you're right," I answer. "I come from a crazy world."

"Our ways give you the opportunity to see you and be you," he says. "And when you can see yourself, you realize that everything is a part of you . . . that's it." He lays his head back and is immediately asleep, leaving me tormented with the thoughts of my dilemma . . . should I or shouldn't I . . . as I fall asleep also.

The old one and young woman are with me again, but this time they are completely silent . . . smiling and silent. In the dream we just stand there in the middle of what appears to be where I actually am . . . in the middle of this Mexican wilderness. We look at each other without a single word. When I wake, the dawn-light has everything glowing.

"Great day in the morning glory," Palqtlo mimics my song. "They're great songs to teach with."

After some stretching and deep breathing we hop into the truck. Water, bread, and dried fruit are breakfast while we drive through the early hours before the sun heats the desert to a sizzle. At a non-descript point in the highway, Palqtlo turns to me and says, "We're here."

"Where?" I ask, seeing nothing but the vast desert and the straight little road we are traveling.

"This is our turn off point," he says.

"How can you tell?" I ask, looking for some marker. "There's nothing here."

We turn off the highway on a couple of very faint tire tracks in the desert floor that never turns into a road at all. Palqtlo does all the driving now. We're following what may have been ruts at one time, but now they've faded into nothing but the memory in Palqtlo's mind. We just wander across the hard desert swerving on occasion to avoid a cactus. We spend the entire day and an extra inner tube traveling deeper and deeper into the desolation of nowhere. In the evening, we come to a simple mound of earth, but as we drive around to the other side it reveals itself as an adobe hut, half buried underground. Palqtlo drives the truck inside one half of the hut and turns off the engine.

"This is where we spend the night." Palqtlo says as he jumps out. "From here on, we're on foot."

"We'll sleep in the back of the truck so the snakes won't bother us," he says.

"How are the snakes?" I ask, not real comfortable with his comment.

"They're aware of our presence right now," he answers. "We're in their territory and they're curious, but we definitely won't see them with this city smell in us."

This answer offers no comfort to me, but I'm tired and drift in and out of sleep while the surrounding shadows creep in. Very early the next morning I awake to the howls of coyotes right next to us. Palqtlo's standing next to the truck.

"They're welcoming me back. I can tell by the tone of their calls," he says proudly.

I crawl to the edge of the truck bed, watching them dart back and forth amongst the sage and juniper. Morning has come too soon, but I'm happy. In this morning light I explore the adobe structure we've parked under. It resembles a small hacienda with a big open face and only partly above ground. It's been dug into the side of a fairly steep hill and the roof is completely covered with earth.

"This is where we'll clean up," Palqtlo says. "We're polluted from the chaos of the out-world and our cleansing process begins here."

The inside of the hacienda is one large room where the air is thick with a rich smell of nature.

"What's that great smell?" I ask.

"The juniper logs that we built the roof with," he answers. "And the sage you see in all those clay pots — the sun has been baking it into the air for months."

"How old is this place?" I ask. "It looks ancient."

Palqtlo turns in a circle. "Not that old. It just sits here in the desert and absorbs the heat every day — that makes it look old. We built it when I first left home five years ago."

In the kitchen area there are clay pots full of beans and corn meal and in the main part of the room sit two neatly placed piles of clothing.

"Those are the clothes we'll wear from here on," he says.

"What do we do with our own?" I ask.

"Burn them in the fire pit," he replies. "What you'd call a sweat lodge. We'll use it to purify our bodies also."

We walk out of the hut to a large pit, right next to another mound of earth. "That's the aneepee — the mound there. Our people have used these for thousands of years. The extreme heat works both for cleansing and for reaching out into the spirit world with prayer and vision."

"Where do we get the water?" I ask.

"There's a tiny spring over there." Palqtlo points in the direction where the coyotes are now gathered. "That's why we built this hut here. Are you ready for the water now?"

"Actually, I'm about ready for breakfast." I answer.

"Good," Palqtlo replies. "That's the way we'll do the sweat, being hungry and empty."

He grabs two clay pots, hands one to me and walks down the hill. About twenty feet away the coyotes run along side with their piercing eyes darting across our path. They look at me, then over to Palqtlo and back again. They seem to be running in a planned formation.

"Coyotes are the most intelligent of all dogs," Palqtlo tells me. "They consider us under their control right now so they're at ease."

"This is at ease?" I ask.

We reach the spring, a small stream of water falling ten feet from a formation of rocks. It's like a shower and once it hits the ground it gets absorbed back into the Earth. Palqtlo takes off his clothing and steps under it, fills his clay pot and washes himself.

"Drink all you can." Palqtlo says to me as he picks up his clothing. "This is what we'll fill up on this morning."

I strip and drink a huge amount of the water. It's sweet and cold. "If this is all I'm having for breakfast, I'd better have a lot!" I shout from the water refreshing my body.

By the time I get back to the hut, Palqtlo has started a fire. He gathers rocks to place into the fire and sits silently watching them heat up. We just sit there for a while with the coyotes gathering behind us.

"We're ready to have our sweat now," he says, breaking the silence. "Put your clothing into the fire."

"Why do we want to burn our clothing?"

"Nothing from the out-world is brought in," he replies.

"Yeah, but can't we just leave them here?" I can hear the tone of my voice and it sounds a bit wimpy. "Forget what I asked, but what about my wallet?"

"Leave it here in the hut."

I throw my wallet toward the house and the coyotes immediately run to sniff it back and forth. We bring about 20 stones into the adobe sweat lodge and the temperature rises — then Palqtlo carefully pours water onto the rocks and steam makes the heat unbearable.

"We'll go slowly," he assures me. "But this will get a lot hotter before we're done."

I nod and sink toward the earthen floor, trying to get as low as possible. I notice it's cooler from this position. The rest of the morning is more of the same, drinking water and sweating in the blistering heat of the little hut — rubbing adobe clay all over our bodies. I use wet sage and cedar bows to breathe through — it seems to cool the air ever so slightly. Every little bit helps, but it still burns into my throat and lungs.

"We're pulling as much of your civilization out of our bodies and minds as possible," he chuckles. "That's what this heat does for you."

We look like animated clumps of earth by now as the clay hangs from our faces and bodies. "I'm beginning to get used to it." I admit.

"Fire is 'Tal' in our language and a great teacher," he says, taking my mind off the heat as he pours more water on the rocks. "Tao Jreeku is the Sun and the father of fire. All things receive physical energy from the Father Sun. Fire is a piece of that sun and it's putting us through the Sun's medicine right now."

We remain silent from that moment on. The heat's so overwhelming I find it difficult to sit still. At some point as heat rises, I rest my face on the ground in front of me and nearly go unconscious. When I come to, the steam's gone, everything has cooled down and Palqtlo is not around. All the clay has baked dry on my body and it cracks and pinches as I lift myself from the floor. Just beyond the door of the hut Palqtlo sits in the same condition. Next to him are two neat piles of white homespun clothing. My mouth is so dried shut that I can't even open it to speak.

He motions me to follow and we walk painfully to the spring and stand under the waterfall. The clay dissolves from our bodies and the skin underneath feels soft and new. I drink as much as I can, my mouth open to the sky with the water cascading into it.

As we walk back to the lodge, he motions to one of the two piles of clothing.

"You brought these clothes with you?" I ask.

"No, they were here," he answers. "Whenever I return from the out-world I use this sweat lodge and the fresh clothing."

We set about cooking some of the beans and corn from the storage pots. As the evening turns to night, Palqtlo continues with his stories. He says they are preparing me for the rest of the journey into Wirikuta. "From here on we walk. At times our path will seem so treacherous that you'll doubt it's passable." He pauses to look for my reaction. "The deep seclusion behind this treacherous path is how my village has successfully lived for centuries without interference from the out-world. We are so deep in the Canyons that no one's ever found us, but this won't last forever and we know it."

We eat slowly while the stories continue.

"Caves and caverns are a big part of our lives," he says. "These mountains are riddled with them. We're gonna walk two days from here and come to one of the largest caverns on Earth. It cuts through the center of the entire range. We'll use it to get into my village."

"Do we go underground?" I ask.

"Absolutely," he replies. "These mountains are way too steep and rocky to climb. The caverns are tricky, like a labyrinth, but they're our only way in."

"Have you ever been lost in there?" I ask, intimidated by the thought.

"A couple of times," he responds rather proudly.

"How long will we be in the underground?"

"It'll take a full day depending on how steady we move," he says. "I've been through them so many times, I know my way by heart, but the darkness can paralyze you, so our speed will be up to you."

"That's not so comforting," I say.

"This is the training we've all gone through as children," he tells me. "Just remember one thing. The total blackness plays tricks on your eyes, some of them pleasant and some of them very fierce. We'll be in absolute silence to reduce the confusion."

"Really?"

"In the dark you are in an altered state and in this state, the only thing maintaining your stability will be your faith and determination."

"What if I need to know something when we're in the silence?" I ask.

"Endless questions will arise in a frantic mind," he answers. "But silence is the only way to penetrate the blindness of the caverns. They're so vast that even I'd get lost in the echoes of sound." He looks at me directly and says, "Our minds must be tuned together and acting as one at all times."

At bedtime, I'm on the roof of the truck, filled with the energy of the sweat and Palqtlo's stories racing through my mind. Thinking of the walk we face over the next days makes it difficult to sleep. I lie awake for at least half the night. When we wake up before the rise of the morning sun, I throw away as much anxiety as I can with a big dose of determination, quickly tie on my new cotton moccasins and walk down the adobe stairs to the ground.

"They feel comfortable," I say to Palqtlo, who's already up and building the fire out of the dried sage and juniper. "They're the right size too."

"Yes, of course they are," he says with a smile. "They've been made this way for centuries."

I look at him with a funny grin and chuckle as I admire their comfort and simple beauty. We cook up some more of the beans and corn and eat breakfast without much talking.

The following days are all spent at this enchanted location weaving seamlessly through a million questions. Wondrous stories flow along with the ritual cleansing of our bodies and minds with the fire, the steam, the adobe clay earth and the shimmering waterfall all blending into one. If we turned back now I would be completely satisfied, but I'm starting to trust a larger picture here. There have been so many synchronicities on this journey since first meeting Palqtlo that it feels like I'm surrendering to something important.

But surrendering is tough I'm discovering, and then this chorus shows up to a song not yet written. It hovers around and sings in my head as we do our daily rituals. I repeat it constantly to remember the melody, words and rhythm. I have no paper . . . nothing to write it down . . . my instrument is just sticks to accompany my voice. It lifts my spirit when I doubt what I'm doing here and then keeps me up in between doubts. When I'm not singing the words I hum the tune. "To be confident — that the Infinite — will take care of it — we're so fortunate." Becoming a friend, this has shown up at the perfect time . . . songs can do that when you need them.

Twenty One

THE TREK

After days of cleansing, the moment arrives for us to leave the relative security of our camp and climb on toward Wirikuta. We begin our journey at midnight, with a bright moon overhead allowing us to travel as far as possible on the first leg, without the heat of day. Each carrying a small food bag and dressed in our new homespun, we begin the trek. Quite innocent at first, the flat ground soon gives way to steeper hillsides, as the scrub trees become taller. The heat of the desert floor turns into strong cool winds. We're able to drink at the springs bubbling from the ground nearly every hour. We scale what appears to be a range of mountains, and as we reach the summit, it's obvious that they're merely the foothills of the larger climb ahead. After reaching into the thicker forest, we climb above the tree line. The mounds of boulders we climb over at this elevation consume my energy. Palqtlo, walking with ease, explains that his energy comes from moving without thought. My body, on the other hand, aches with exhaustion as my mind continues to steal precious vitality with endless chatter.

"Are you able to go on or do you want to rest?" Palqtlo asks, seeing my confusion and complete exhaustion.

I'm so out of breath that I haven't spoken for miles. "I need to stop," I tell him.

We sit on rocks near a tiny spring. "The elders come to these hills to heal them," Palqtlo says.

"To heal?" I ask.

"No, to heal the springs, the rivers, the mountains and forests. They all need our attention from time to time."

"How can you heal a mountain?"

"By seeing it without mistakes," he answers calmly. "And by forgiving your mistakes without conditions in the process."

This passes right over my head, adding to my high altitude confusion. By the evening of our second day of climbing, I'm again wrapped in fear. At one point I can't breathe and the ever-increasing remoteness produces a tremendous sense of danger. I have blisters on my feet, my fingers are cut from the rocks and cactus and there are blisters on my nose from the relentless sun. My legs are unwilling to take another step and San Francisco, with all its insanity, starts looking good to me again.

"Any chance we're lost?" I ask, having seen no sign of a trail or path. Much of our walk has been done at night, so I've barely seen the ground. I actually feel a faint hope at the thought that we are lost and can stop.

"Not even the slightest," Palqtlo guarantees.

"This is such a long way from everything," I say, with a timid voice. "No one even knows we are here if we were lost or something."

"We know we're here," he replies honestly. "God knows we're here . . . and everyone in my village knows."

"How can your people know?" I ask, somewhat disrespectfully.

"All they have to do is listen and they know," he says.

"Listen?" I laugh. "Listen to what?"

"We know everything," he continues. "We are created in the image of what you call GOD."

"Yes, but that's just religion," I say in defense of the myth.

"If we as humans are created in the image of God, like all religions say we are," he states this as if enjoying the play, "then we have to be in touch with everything also, right? Just like GOD." His eyes sparkle. "It doesn't take a genius to figure out that we're actually able to know everything. We do know it all." He stops and looks to see if I'm with him, then starts on again. "It's just a matter of mastering the ways that allow this to take place." He motions for me to sit a little closer. "First of all, my ancestors figured out that if we slow down the emotions and quiet the mind, then the information that we need comes through. It comes through our thoughts, our dreams, our visions and our will, but mainly it comes through our dreams. The only thing they had left to figure out was how to integrate all this information into daily life." He puts his arm on my shoulder as he says, "When you get to my village you'll see how this is all possible and why it's not at all possible in the bustle of your modern world."

"How much longer to your village?" I ask to ground the conversation in something measureable.

"Another day up here and a day getting through the cavern," he answers. "However, I have to add that it'll become steeper tomorrow, and our speed will depend on what shape we're in."

"Do you see that ridge along there? That's what we have to climb and cross tomorrow. It leads to the cavern entrance, which is the only way through those mountains. You can't go around them, no one has because of the sheer nature of the rocks."

We sleep through the night and begin trekking early in the morning. For the first few miles I have a hard time with the blisters on my feet. We're now crossing the rocks and sand, which give a moonscape appearance to the area. Acknowledging my pain, Palqtlo moves a bit slower this morning.

We're among hills, ridges, mountains and valleys that seem to continue on forever. The enormity of this topography is breathtaking. Every time we approach the top of a hill, I pray we're at the ridge. As we crest each summit, there's a larger one beyond.

Time after time, this goes on until I give up hope and just concentrate on walking one step at a time.

We've been walking in silence but as we near the top of one of the many hills, Palqtlo turns to me. "There is the one you've been looking for all day."

Far larger than I imagined, the cliffs appear to be several thousand feet straight up and down and from this distance they look smooth as glass.

"That's what I mean by our protection," Palqtlo brags, waving his hand at the ridge. "That's a total wall."

I'm standing and staring, without words, at the magnitude of what I'm seeing. I just stare at it, but the eyes find no power to comprehend its size.

"See that tiny point in the middle?" he asks, pointing to a dark spot on the wall. "That's where we enter the cavern. That's where we walk through the entire ridge."

I can't imagine what he means so I simply stare at the ridge and hold the bottom of my feet to give them some relief.

"From here we are two hours from that entrance."

"I know you've been through this all before," I say. "I mean that looks like a wall of glass."

"That's right," he replies. "There's a rope I've used forever." His voice is exact and confident, but this actually appears impossible to me. "We'll rest a little bit and arrive there by dark," he adds. "You're about to undo one of the greatest mysteries of your society."

"What's that?"

"The mystery of whether or not there's a vast power right inside you." He stops for a moment and takes a long drink of water. "You set up your lives to be so entertained that you are never below the surface. You're completely oblivious to your real power."

"Why are you saying that will change right now? I ask.

"Because to walk that cavern to Wirikuta, we will have to go through the black," he explains. "This is very much like one of our 'rites of passage'. This expression means you have the 'right' to 'pass' through the illusion."

"What do you mean by the black?"

"That's the total absence of light. After you've been in it for a while it reveals the illusion of fear and the illusion of doubt and all the other illusions that keeps a person from delivering on their biggest dreams."

"Do you think I can do this?"

"I hope so," he says half-jokingly. "I've never taken anyone other than my family, so we'll have to see, but I think so."

"Shit," I react. "You never thought of this?"

Palqtlo unties his moccasins and sets them neatly to the side, rubs his feet and proceeds more softly. "With our experiences in the passages, emotions like fear become our friends; the kind of friends that give us the confidence and strength to face life's difficulties. We rely on them in a way that's tangible; they're a tool."

This is more than I want to deal with right now. My feet are as sore as I can remember and I never expected Palqtlo to make such an oversight. I rest deeply and dream of what we're going to go through. In my dream, we make it.

Twenty Two

THE BLACK

A light rain falling on my face awakens me. Palqtlo's preparing to move again, tying on his cotton moccasins and stretching the fabric with his toes. Every time we stop walking, even when just for a few minutes, my blisters become more painful when we start again. Right now every step is a challenge. This is the steepest part and the thinner air at this altitude makes breathing harder.

Palqtlo tries to accommodate me by traveling slowly, but there's only so much that can be done. We have no first aid supplies to cover my blisters and I'm in far worse shape than I thought. My mind wanders doubtfully toward an old National Geographic story of people perishing in the wilderness. Thinking this, I take one more step and the blisters shift. The side of the mountain jumps into my face as I scramble onto all fours and tumble to the side as the wet ground gives way, I instantly slide thirty feet straight down the muddy incline and come to a stop against a boulder with a thud.

"You got to stay focused," Palqtlo cautions me as he comes to my aid. "That ridge is just as steep as it looks and if you start to slide, there's nothing but air to hold on to."

The actual goal of reaching that ridge is comforting to me. At least we have a purpose I can measure now. Walking for days has a confusing effect when there's no set goal. I have no idea where we are on a map, or how far we have to go. My thoughts have been exhausting me, but when we finally reach the top of the ridge, the view is beyond anything I could have imagined. The mountains, hills, deep endless canyons and desert far below us go on forever.

"This is fucking crazy," I say lying on my belly and looking off the edge of probably fifteen hundred feet straight down. Again, my eyes refuse to comprehend the lack of perspective.

We make our way toward the location where Palqtlo knows the rope is stashed. To think of dropping over the side of this ridge is making my tailbone twitch and I'm gripping the ground with every step for a sense of safety.

"Where we drop from isn't as sheer," Palqtlo assures me. "There are some gouges we can use as foot holds and hand grips so you really don't require a rope at all."

I've actually resigned myself to the inevitable reality of my circumstance. This journey that I'm on is absolutely insane, but I chose it and I am becoming accustomed to the insanity.

"I'll go first and you lie down on your belly to watch me," Palqtlo tells me as he tests a homemade rope that brings me absolutely no comfort. Confident with the rope, he motions where I'm to lie down and he proceeds to walk to the edge and over the face of the ridge.

He holds tightly to the rope and descends while I'm lying on my belly with my head hanging in space. I gaze through the distance below me and really want to puke. As I watch the top of his head travel down the thirty or so feet to the cavern ledge, I feel as if I'm sliding off, but it's just the blood running to my head.

Now it's my turn. I pull the rope back up and come to the edge. My stomach churns, my throat locks, I can't breathe and start feeling dizzy. Seeing what's happening, Palqtlo yells, "Scream at the top of your lungs, hurry, do it!"

I try but nothing comes out and Palqtlo continues to yell at me. Finally, my voice shoots out of my mouth like a cannon. "GOD . . . I NEED . . . SOME . . . FUCKING HELP!" I'm screaming at the top of my voice and my breathing starts up again. Finally, my lungs relax and a wave of warmth rolls over my back.

I lower myself down with a totally false sense of confidence and within a few seconds I've reached the ledge of the cavern. I sink to my knees with a combination of tears and laughter. I bury my forehead into the sandy ledge. "My God," I exclaim, "I don't know why I'm laughing, but it sure feels great."

"You're laughing because you survived a moment that was ruled by fear, the fear that you wouldn't survive," he tells me. "You're laughing because you now see that your fear was bullshit . . . important to keep you alert, but bullshit nonetheless. This is how the body and mind react. It's what we all go through in our passages. It teaches us to fear less, to fear with accuracy and enjoy more of the moments as we live."

I've heard words like these before, but now they're making more sense. A real experience gives them life. I want to live what he's talking about, now with my newfound courage. "I think I want to do more than just visit Wirikuta," I tell him.

"We'll see," he replies. "We have a ways to go here."

The sun's setting over the distant mountains and the last light gives everything an iridescent glow. The whole place comes to life when the sun goes down.

We walk toward the entrance of the cavern, when the soft sound of our moccasins on the sand is shattered. The loudest crackling and rattling I've ever heard comes from everywhere at once. It's the sound of total confusion. Palqtlo freezes his step mid-stride and motions with his arm for me to do the same. He doesn't even turn his head to look back at me, but keeps his eyes fixed on a spot a few feet in front of him. Then, in the dim light, with both of us frozen in time, the creature reveals itself. It's a rattlesnake coiled with its head waving slightly back and forth and the tail standing straight echoing its warning against the cavern walls. Palqtlo remains motionless for at least 15 minutes until the snake slowly moves off the path and into a small burrow at the side.

"That's unreal," I exclaim.

"This is their territory," Palqtlo reminds me. "We're the guests here. He's just reminding us to take care."

"What if he comes back?"

"He won't," Palqtlo says with confidence.

As we step inside the entrance of the cavern, there's a fire pit rimmed with round stones and a small stack of wood. Palqtlo pulls a small fire-bow from beneath the firewood and begins to set dried grass with smaller pieces of wood into the pit. He sets the fire-bow up and begins to work it on the grass and some shavings of furry bark. "I've never seen this before," I tell him.

"This is the only way we've ever done it," he says as he keeps the saw motion going back and forth. "When this fire goes out we'll be in silence till the end of the cavern."

I can already feel my blood freaking out at the idea of going into this pitch-blackness in total silence. "What is the purpose of the silence again?"

"This cavern will help you become a master of your emotions, not a slave to them," he answers.

I'm still looking for measurables and ask, "Exactly how long will it take?"

"It will take us a day to get through," he replies. "But you must stay close to me, not just physically but mentally and emotionally as well."

"Don't worry about that," I assure him. "I'm going to be stuck to you."

"In order to do this, you've got to know that I am to be trusted absolutely." He pauses for a moment to let it sink in and then continues. "There are no distractions in this total darkness and total silence. The only stimulation will come from inside. You will hear the pounding of your heart and your thoughts will scream.

Trusting me will make it possible to get through. Without this, we don't stand a chance."

The little spark of our fire grows as we sit and Palqtlo continues to tell me what to expect in the cavern and what he expects of me. As the sun's light completely disappears, the light of the fire plays with the cavern walls. They begin to close in on our campsite as if to turn off the day. We continue to talk throughout the evening. I see images in the dancing firelight, mostly imaginary ones from my recent dreams.

"Caves are one of the most sacred gifts from the universe," Palqtlo explains, stretching back to a more comfortable position in the sand. "This particular cavern is known as Taquatsi, or 'medicine basket' and the river that comes out the other side is considered one of the many rivers feeding the underworld."

"Is this the river that flows through your village?"

"Yes," he replies with tremendous respect. "These are the rivers that flow through the Earth and feed the mother so that she can continue to give birth to the humans, the animals, the plants and the rocks of the surface-world."

"Where does this water come from?"

"This particular river comes out of the ground inside this cavern," he says. "It runs for several miles through the middle of our valley and returns to the ground at the entrance to the largest cavern on the other side of the valley."

"You're excited about being back here aren't you?"

"These places are magical, but the real magic lives in the people," he says with his eyes glowing in the firelight. "I'm always inspired when I'm around my people . . . it recharges me."

"Do you ever plan on living here for good?"

"Someday . . . someday perhaps soon," he answers and continues to explain his point about the river, drawing in the sand with a stick. "These two caverns are our medicine baskets and the river joining them is the handle. The river is also known to my people as Taquatsi because our greatest medicine, our food, is cleansed and nourished by these waters."

"What happens in the other cavern?"

"That's the location of our highest passage. Where the river returns to the ground we enter the Earth and follow it through to the other side of our life."

"This is what all the young adults go through?"

"Absolutely!" he exclaims. "This starts our awakening into real humans. Without the courage and character that this brings out we would be just like everyone else in this world, scared and struggling to survive."

I think about what he's saying, my fear quieting down for a moment.

"During the journey you must stay in what we call the presence of the presence, absolutely in the moment, or you'll go mad," he says firmly. "Your contact with me will become a sense beyond your senses. You can't hold on to me because this will cause me to lose concentration. I need total concentration to know the path through the black."

"Holy shit," I blurt out. "Now I'm scared. This is like horror stories when I was a kid out camping, but it's real."

"You'll have to experience our connection. I can't explain it, but you'll actually feel it strongly," he assures me. "Our silence will enable us to go through our mental garbage."

"That could take a while," I say. "My brain's been talking up a storm all day."

He just smiles and closes his eyes to sleep. I lay awake. I was tired before this conversation, but now my mind is running. Dawn comes all too soon and the embers of the fire are still glowing in the first light.

"Before the fire's out, and we go silent, I need to tell you this," Palqtlo instructs me. "Move your bowels and toss over the edge, we leave no trace."

I promptly do just that and fling it over the edge of the ridge. Watching it sail through the air gives me a smile and I take a last look at the beauty of this place. By the time I get back to the fire pit, the fire embers are completely out and Palqtlo motions for me to be in silence now. We walk into the coolness of the cavern's entrance and walk two hundred yards in a straight line. It remains light all the way until we turn sharply to the right and begin descending slowly into total darkness, that same inky blackness I remember when I died. I want to wipe the blackness off my face and eyes, but it doesn't wipe. I feel it choking off my breath, but I force my breathing. My blood turns cold as ice as I lose contact with Palqtlo's sounds for a moment and I want to speak. I'm deathly afraid but I control myself and with this moment I immediately sense the presence that Palqtlo spoke of. I work hard to retain it as it comes and goes over the next steps. This is the only thing that's guiding me at this moment and it's a full time job to maintain the contact. My mind thinks of nothing else . . . thank God.

Hour after hour we step through the black and the sound of my heart becomes quite comforting in the silence. It's like a giant womb, our footsteps nearly silent on the soft sand.

Then suddenly and without warning the sense vanishes and I panic. I struggle, but can't retrieve it and by the time I realize what's happening I've completely lost contact with Palqtlo. I freeze. "Don't stop!" a voice shouts inside me. "I can't go on", I cry back silently. I grab at the space in front of me, hoping to find Palqtlo there, but I find nothing but air. I lunge forward to again search for him and fall flat on my face in the soft sand. I begin to sob without sound. Tears pouring from my eyes because I know that he's going on without me and there's nothing I can do. Though I want to call out, there's no sound coming from my desperate breath. Then, just as quickly as it started, it ends. With the touch of Palqtlo's hand on my back, the warmth in my body returns and hope re-enters my heart. Like someone else crawling inside my skin, I feel the most outstanding joy I can ever remember. I stand back up and start walking again, following the sense of his presence.

Deeply exhausted from the constant focus to maintain my sense of connection, we round a corner that I only sense.

Standing before us is a deer silhouetted in the light of the moon beyond her. "This is the Mahjrah," Palqtlo says breaking the silence for the first time. "She's considered a most sacred creature." His voice comes as a shock to my quiet ears. "This is a great sign for you. Welcome to the Wirikuta."

There's tangible inspiration in both of us as we walk out of the total darkness into the moonlit night. I feel a deep connection with this place that I've never been in before . . . a connection from the experience of these past days.

I try to respond, but can't clear my throat from the silence, so I cough a little. "You startled me with words," I whisper and kneel down to touch the ground.

He nods and smiles and again says, "Welcome to the Wirikuta."

I return the smile with so much relief, "Welcome home," I answer back.

As we exit the cavern and look across the moonlit valley I see what appears to be a small fire in the distance. "This is exactly the image in my death in Seattle," I exclaim. "It's not just similar, it's identical." I stand here in complete awe.

"Welcome home to you then also," Palqtlo responds with such compassion.

"Thanks," I say.

"I look forward to seeing family," Palqtlo says with a smile. "It's been two years since I've been home."

"Why are you away from them for so long?" I ask.

"Looking for you little brother . . . I guess," he responds with a chuckle.

This catches my attention, but I let it go.

"My little sister is an incredible gemstone. Xochina Kuikameh is her name." He says all this with such great love and then carefully tells me, "It's pronounced Zah-chin Ku-ee-ka-may which means 'the flower that's singing." He stretches with a huge reach, as if to gather her in and then continues. "Both of us are the children of Ilnamikiz Ezkayo." Again, Palqtlo carefully spells it out for my benefit. "That's pronounced Il-namih-keez Is-kai-oh and

192

this means 'A Memory left on Earth'. He's the eldest Maraakame in the Wirikuta now. His name comes from an ancient poem that's been passed orally from generation to generation for thousands of years.

Having never heard him speak of his father before, I'm acutely interested as he continues.

"My father's a poet and often speaks in poems. All our names come from these ancient poems passed on in the oral tradition. We recite them throughout our lives, in good times and hard. They give us strength because it takes us back to the core of our identity."

The poem of my father's name goes:

> *A memory that I left*
> *What will I take with me when I go?*
> *Will I have something to leave on this earth?*
> *How will my heart act?*
> *Let it not be useless to have come to life*
> *To this world*
> *Let's leave at least flowers,*
> *Let's leave at least songs.*

"And this is also how my little sister received her name," he explains. Xochina is a young woman now, about sixteen years old and going through the quest passages herself. There's a poem about this time in a young person's life. It's what we relate to when we're going through the passages."

"Everyone goes through this?" I ask.

"Yes," he replies. "The poem is called 'Buried Treasures'."

> *Being in dreaming*
> *Is to live forever, but not in this world*
> *By receiving the Buried Treasure*
> *Only in a moment only*

Recognize this treasure
Only in a moment only
Accept this treasure
Only in a moment only
Live this treasure
Only in a moment only
Not forever in this world
Being in dreaming
Being in the Buried Treasures

"In the darkest hours of our challenges, it reminds us of purpose, the love of those that care for us and how to deeply care for ourselves." Palqtlo turns to me and says, "They know we're here now. We'll rest till morning and then they'll be here to welcome us home."

"How do they know we're here?" I ask. "We're miles away from the camp light."

"We've broken the silence," Palqtlo says, "And they've heard every word we've said. When your ears are clear and your mind is quiet, you can hear for miles. All of Earth's peoples used to be like this."

"That's hard to believe."

"Even after what you've been through," he replies. "You're going to find some things hard to believe here."

"Yeah," I say dryly, "Sometimes I like proof."

"Listen," he says quite assertively. "We speak a language that's not made up of feelings. We use language to develop insight, not to communicate gossip. We spend our days speaking of realities, not opinions. Under the power of this trance, anything becomes possible and nothing's considered impossible. We're not limited by doubt."

"I understand, but isn't there a limit?" I ask.

"In this language there are no limits," he explains. "No matter what is happening to us, this is just life."

"And this is with everyone here?" I ask.

"Everyone," he answers. "Remember there's no contact with the outside world with all of its misdirected doubt and fear polluting the psyche. If you don't know that you can't do something then you'll succeed. That's the way the human psyche works."

"Where can this all go?" I ask.

"Into the rest of your life," he says with a smile. "The only question is, are you willing to go with it?"

"Yes," I respond instantly. I surprise myself in answering so fast, without pausing or thinking about what all this could possibly include.

Twenty Three

HOME AGAIN

Morning arrives, much cooler than it was on the other side of this mountain valley. I'm awakened by the greetings of a group of starry-eyed people so unbelievably joyous that I'd swear they walk on the air around them. Outwardly and openly gracious, their eyes sparkle and pierce through me even with their casual glances. These people are far different from what I expected. Palqtlo's father has remained at the village, but his sister Xochina is among the welcoming committee. She's every bit the flower song that Palqtlo described, she has long black hair and deep brown eyes that never seem to blink.

I'm inundated with affection as they hug and kiss us both. I'm completely unable to understand a word anyone is saying until Xochina walks up and says so clearly, "My brother teach me little English."

"What a relief," I express with great joy. She looks so familiar; perhaps it's family resemblance but the tone of her voice and the softness in her eyes…I feel that we have met before.

She obviously doesn't speak a lot of English however as she has nothing to say after that and shyly retreats back to her brother's side.

They've brought us heaps of food and a corn tea, so we sit and feast in the shade of several pinion trees.

"Don't stuff yourself," Palqtlo cautions me. "Even though the food's terrific, we've had very little for days and have to start back slowly."

The food's beyond delicious and it is all I can do to control my desire to eat it all. Xochina watches her brother intensely and the deep love between the two of them is a pleasure to experience. This is like no other sibling relation I've ever seen. It reminds me of my early relationship with Tex and for the rest of the meal I'm missing her.

As we get up to walk to the village, Palqtlo says to me, "She isn't ready for this and you know it." He turns away and says no more.

I'm intrigued by the comment, but I've spent the majority of this last week being intrigued. I look at Xochina and she too seems to know exactly what and whom he's talking about. There are no boundaries between these people; they all seem to know everything that everyone else knows.

As we approach the village, the crops surround us. All that Palqtlo has been telling me is true. This village is pristine, with lush fields against the natural vegetation and the river flowing through the center of the valley. There are wiggly rows of cotton amongst the food crops and food is growing everywhere abundantly.

The children are deeply respectful of Palqtlo's presence and they are intensely curious as to who I am, but keep their distance and only talk among themselves. In the shaded entrances to many of the dwellings you can see women cooking and men working on their looms or spinning cotton. Palqtlo told me they never cut their hair and everyone has bright swatches of cotton cloth woven into their dark braids which many of them tie together on top of their head.

Most of the indoor living is done underground and as we approach a group of kiva mounds, Palqtlo breaks rank and runs to greet an older man rising out of one of the underground dwellings.

It's Illanamiqt, Palqtlo's father and he's everything Palqtlo told me except, to my shock, he's the exact man from my dreams. He's the one who was there when I died and I now realize that Xochina is precisely the young woman of my dreams too. This is so bizarre . . . I keep it to myself.

This man of ninety years or so looks to be no more than sixty and it's obvious from his eyes and manners that he's very magical. I don't know what he possesses, but he moves and speaks with a gentle power. Everyone in our group reveres him and treats him with deep adoration and respect. He and Palqtlo spend several minutes away from the group talking among themselves. He motions for his daughter to join them and as they all stand together the similarity to my dreams and death is so clear that my heart races. I'm not sure what to say, or if I should even say anything about this, but tears pour from my eyes and I'm unable to stop them.

A few of the villagers see this and begin to nod toward me as if acknowledging my realization. Am I paranoid, or is this all real? Occasionally Palqtlo looks over at me from their conversation and then turns back to his father and sister. Then Xochina leaves the discussion and comes to me. I try to wipe away the tears.

"Come, join to us," she says.

I enjoy her musical accent.

"My father says he's met you before in your time of crisis," Palqtlo says as I reach where they stand.

I nod toward Illanamiqt and he catches my eyes with his eyes . . . they are endless. They go in so deep that I don't know how long I've been in them when I regain the awareness of my surroundings.

"I was just realizing the same thing," I say without looking away from Illanamiqt. Again tears flow down my face. Still looking into his eyes, I reach out to shake his hand and from the periphery I see his arm disappear up to his elbow. He never so much as acknowledges my reaching and does not leave our gaze.

Then, just as Palqtlo said it would, my body begins to cold sweat. I move away to the bushes and vomit all the fresh food. I stand there for a moment feeling very embarrassed. As I emerge from the bush, no one's laughing as I'd expected. Palqtlo comes to my aid and whispers, "He considers shaking hands a practice of fear. Hugs are far more appropriate."

"I thought that'd be presumptuous," I answer, wiping off my mouth with the back of my sleeve.

"That's where your timid nature gets to you."

"Is he in the Maraakame?" I ask as we walk back to join him.

"Most of the time," Palqtlo answers. "He's older now and it's so much easier to be in dreamtime throughout the day."

With a twinkle in his eye, Illanamiqt bows slightly as if to welcome me back. I walk straight up to him and hug him for all the times we've met and all the help he's been, though I know I've not totally accepted all of it.

From this point forward Palqtlo interprets everything that Illanamiqt says. "You've been expected for some years now," Illanamiqt looks at me and says in Azteca.

"Yes sir," I reply. "I heard of you a few day ago and only realized just now who you are."

Many of the villagers have gathered around us now and these are genuinely the most beautiful people I've ever met.

"You're curious about where we all come from," Illanamiqt says, knowing exactly what I'm thinking. "So many cultures over the centuries have risen to great power throughout these parts of the world. Your world believes they all just vanished without a trace." He pauses for the translation. "Where do you think these people vanished to?" As he says this, he smiles and laughs at the implications of what he's saying. When he laughs it's almost as big as the mountains.

"You're here for a good reason," Palqtlo says.

"Don't try make sense," Xochina cautions me.

"It will become clear with time," Illanamiqt assures me and goes to greet some of the other villagers.

Palqtlo takes me through some of the parts of his home. "You'll discover a lot here in your neutral time," he explains. "The time you spend doing nothing but observing and absorbing."

My amazement turns into pure logic as I ask, "So what we're all saying here is that your father knows all about me . . . right?"

"Yes," Palqtlo replies. "That is what we're all saying."

"This is completely outrageous."

"He tells me of you," Xochina softly joins our tour. "My father — I look forward to this day."

"Our world will soon be consumed by the out-world," Palqtlo says with a true voice of sadness. "We won't be isolated for much longer. It's essential that our wisdom becomes part of the world before the out-world becomes everything around here."

"What of me?"

"You'll reach thousands of people," he answers bluntly.

"Our bloodlines reach back to the origins of the Americas," Xochina explains — this time with Palqtlo interpreting. "We've completely isolated ourselves for centuries."

"We did this to preserve what would be destroyed by the civilizations of the time," he reminds me.

Quickly and without any sound several elders of the community join us. They move so gracefully and easily that it's hard to tell they're arriving. Then again, I think, maybe they're not even here.

Palqtlo interprets for me as one of them speaks. "We're the seed of human nature and glad you're with us."

I look over at Palqtlo who smiles at me.

"I've visited your cities in my dreaming," he continues. "They're extremely chaotic and toxic. It's becoming more and more difficult for the Soul to remain in the physical body with all this physical and emotional pollution. This is why your world is having so much difficulty with disease."

"What he is saying is that something has to be done," Palqtlo emphasizes.

I look around and see that at least thirty or so more have collected around us.

I look over at Xochina as I ask, "Why was the FBI able to be all over me?"

"Who?" she asks.

"The trouble that was always around my music. Was that also part of this?"

"No," she answers, "that was just the laws of fate, it was bound to happen that way."

Palqtlo adds, "Great intentions always encounter great reactions — it's the law of nature."

"Don't you recall the warning in your dreams?" Xochina asks, "About knowing the people who touch your vision?"

I feel a sense of comfort. Is this falling in love with my captors? I think to myself.

"Right," Palqtlo laughs. "Let's get you settled in your kiva and rest for the afternoon. There's a celebration tonight for the young ones who have almost finished their passages."

"That is my group," Xochina speaks proudly.

We walk down a path between the sage and the pine trees to a mound of earth.

"This will be your home while you're here," he says, pointing to the door in the mound.

The sun's heat reaches through what little shade the trees provided, but as soon as we enter the underground kiva the temperature is extremely pleasant. We eat some hard corn rolls and drink the tea that Palqtlo quickly heats up on the embers left over from the morning fire. The pots are the most exquisite pieces of pottery, all different shapes, some like animals with mouths as the spouts. With a full stomach, I curl myself amongst a pile of blankets on the floor and sleep.

"Wake up from the depths," comes a voice above my head as Xochina calls to me. "It's time for the celebration — Palqtlo just taught these new words."

"Wow, that was the deepest I've slept in months," I respond without opening my eyes.

"You needed that — you need more," she says.

Multi colored blankets are all wrapped around me now. Palqtlo's told me about all the cotton and wool they weave. This is the first soft bed I've had for over a week — like clouds in heaven to my body. I stretch to get up from the pile I've been wrapped in like a knot.

We arrive at the celebration after it has started and as we're making our way into the underground area the music has already begun. The sound is luxurious and rich. It reminds me of the music I've always heard in my dreams and wanted to play on stage. Seductive rhythms from mostly wooden drums fill the forest. The firelight dances with the melodies, the voices, and their harmonies as if the whole thing was exquisitely composed.

"Music is a large part of our life in the Wirikuta," Palqtlo explains.

The wooden drums are tuned to various pitches, there are clay and wooden flutes, and shakers made of various gourds and lots of singing. Their singing voices are much different from those they speak with. The language of their songs is filled with unique sounds of clicking, squeaking and breathing in ways that are not really words.

"We only use the animal skin when the animal dies naturally," he tells me. "This way the animal can sing with us long after it's gone from the Earth."

As if he was waiting for us, Illanamiqt gets up to address the gathering as soon as we arrive. He walks with great nobility, as do all of the people here. It's as if their heads are attached to the sky. As he addresses the small group of youth who are going through their passages, Xochina joins them. They all look incredibly wise for their age. There's a boy who's fourteen, Xochina at sixteen and another boy of about fifteen and they're all at different levels in the passages.

His talk is also delivered for my benefit and Palqtlo interprets for me. Illanamiqt begins by saying, "Children are the wealth of life and as adults we never lose our innocence or enthusiasm for their life. When we've learned to acknowledge the power within us we're able to use it. These powers become our friends after we've faced the full force of our emotions."

As I sit there in the dark with the fire reflecting on the trees and people it is hard to tell the difference between them . . . trees and people all being one with nature. As I look around at the faces not one person is curious or staring at me. It's as if I've always been here and it gives me a sense of self.

I tune back into Illanamiqt's words as he continues to address the youngsters. "The way we treat our children is the way we treat our future. Remember your first obligation in life is to break the chains of your emotional prison. Use them for their power and you will pass through the mystery of this world on your path to freedom."

He stops and looks across the fire at me and continues speaking, but now directly to me. "There's also a dark world inside each person, a world of slavery and pain. This world's attached to our senses, creates our feelings, but does not let us live. In order to be alive, we need to see beyond this darkness each day." He turns back to the three children. "That's what you're doing here. Learning to become your masters."

My eyes are drawn to the images of the fire dancing on the faces. It reminds me of ancient mythology and the power that their characters contain. Palqtlo leans over to me and explains what his sister is about to do.

"She'll spend the next months memorizing a map of Taquatsi, the largest cavern and then navigate it from beginning to end."

"In the total dark?"

"Yes."

"By herself?"

"By herself."

Having just come through the smaller one with Palqtlo, I can't imagine doing this alone. The only thought that comes to my mind is that she's brave or crazy."

"How's that possible?" I ask anyway.

"These emotions my father speaks of, they are tools, but if we have not learned to master them, they control us," he answers. "They overpower life and set our limits." He pauses for a moment as the elders play the gentle rhythms again and then talks into my ear over the sound. "When you feel lost down in the Taquatsi, you're believing the limits. You learn over the time that you practice that this is an illusion that the emotions create . . . you learn to be their master not their slave."

These words stick in my mind as we enjoy the music that's becoming more and more energetic. The drumming is truly the most hypnotic I've ever experienced. This is exactly the way I need to play, I think to myself as it echoes out into the night. We listen and dance into the night, partnered by the fire dancing off the trees.

I'm exhilarated by the end of the evening. As we walk back to the kivas, I say, "Even playing my songs has never been this powerful and believe me, I've had some great times."

"That's how we spend most evenings," Palqtlo replies.

We walk among the delightful villagers, all going home. We are with the shadowy trees under the lights of the Milky Way and the intoxicating smells of the cedar and sage. I climb down into my kiva to curl up with my pile of blankets. In the mystery of the pitch darkness I think, is this really happening? Have I actually been through all that I've witnessed? I push my face against the sweet smelling cotton and sleep without answers and without time.

Twenty Four

HEAVEN ON EARTH

I'm fully rested for the first time in days as I climb out of my blankets and up out of the kiva to find a paradise. The morning sun shines down on the village as I walk through the land. Again, people pay no special attention to me other than being extremely loving and polite. This makes me feel right at home as I wander through this exquisite world. Eventually I run into Palqtlo, he's catching up with all the news from the villagers.

"Are you ready for food?" he asks.

"Hadn't thought about it," I reply, but I am hungry for something. Right now I'm just taking in this paradise."

He laughs, "Illanamiqt wants to meet with us in a couple of days, so the between time is ours."

We have a breakfast of corn, vegetables and tea prepared by Palqtlo's mother, Ezkaya, a woman of exceptional beauty. She is in her mid-seventies but looks fifty. She has wisdom, perhaps even beyond that of her husband though she'd never admit to it. She stands out with a simple radiance. Without Palqtlo's translation for everyone, my world here would be a bunch of hand signals.

"Corn's the main food here," she says. "We have it with every meal in one form or another. We call it the mother's food. "It's cooked in many ways, but the best is baked in our ovens."

Palqtlo's mother is beyond what you would imagine even if you stretched your mind to its maximum. "She loves to scry with an obsidian mirror," Palqtlo says as her eyes sparkle, knowing we are talking about her. "That's when you gaze into an object until the object dissolves into its molecules and then into its atoms and on into the subatomic parts. It allows you to see behind the mirror of this illusion to where everything comes from."

"How does that work?" I ask. "My promoter in Seattle, Jimmy Green, had a friend who would do that with a crystal ball."

"She creates a continuous loop with her gaze and the information just pours through her," he says. "She can tell exactly what the weather is going to be months in advance and right to the day."

"What if I asked her a question?" I ask, getting excited, "about something I want to know."

"She'd look for the reflection of it in that black mirror and go into a dream state while still conscious. When she comes back she tells you what she saw."

"I'd like to know how Tex is doing," I tell Palqtlo. "Do you think she would answer that?"

"I'm sure she'd look for you."

She hands me some of her fresh baked corn bread and speaks some beautiful words in her language. Then Palqtlo laughs because she knew what I was saying all along. "My mother says that your concern for your friend is real."

"She didn't even use the obsidian."

"She doesn't really have to," Palqtlo says. "It's easier sometimes without it."

"What does she say?"

"Tex is in great confusion. Her doubt is getting greater as her success becomes greater. This is the nature of nature and so you need to have a way of balancing this"

"I didn't say a word to your mother."

"She doesn't need you to," he says. "She's just like my father, often in the dream state— the Maraakame."

We go back to eating breakfast with my mind on Tex. "This is delicious," I say, distracting myself.

"Don't mix eating with worrying," she tells me in her language. "It's very bad for your health. Your friend's not going to improve no matter how much you worry for her, so it is best to live your life and be healthy."

There is such a compelling power in her words that they set my mind at rest. At the moment I even try to worry, just for a test, I can't. I decide to enjoy releasing this habit.

"Your mom could make a mint in America," I say as a joke. "You know with all the crazies there." I laugh again.

Palqtlo doesn't laugh. He looks at me without any emotion, like I need to be real. After our breakfast we continue our tour of the village.

"The Wirikuta is a unique ecosystem," he says. "It allows us to have the best of all worlds by providing us with all the climates. We have the barren desert and lush fertile valleys," he says. "We also have mountain forests with a bit of snowy ice at the very tops in the winter. Off to the west there is tropical jungle."

We walk down to the river and take off our moccasins to wade across. The river here is only a couple of feet deep and the black obsidian on the river bottom causes the water to glisten with a deep reddish-blue hue.

Everywhere we go in the village, people greet us as best friends. We have tea and food with them all till I'm stuffed to the gills. It's a must to sit with everyone and visit. In between, Palqtlo continues to explain life here. "We grow everything from the cotton for our clothing, to the foods we eat, to the hemp used for the ropes and the blankets we use on our horses. Then, we gather the wild fruits and nuts from all the other crops that God grows."

"How much natural food?" I ask.

"Just about everything you can imagine grows in the Wirikuta," he answers. "River cabbage, a root potato like a yam, banana, cactus apples, pine nuts, wild asparagus, wild chiltapeens (a hot chili) and several other kinds of nuts."

It's a world within a world existing right here, with nearly all the climates that exist on the Earth.

"Great storms come to this land from time to time," Palqtlo continues, "especially in the rainy season and when there's ceremony taking place."

"Do you eat like this every day?" I ask. "This seems like feasting to me."

"We eat meals that deeply feed the spirit and the body every day," he replies. "Incredibly wholesome, absolutely vegetarian, and grown with love and attention in the richness of the soil of the mother."

As we move about the village, everyone smiles and bows to each other with respect. When they turn and look at me, their dark eyes sparkle and dance as if telling me a thousand year old story. All the babies I see are attached to papoose boards, calm and observing the ways of the adults.

"The main duties in our community are to provide love, shelter, food and clothing for everybody," Palqtlo continues. "Everything's done as a village. There's really nothing belonging to any one person. We feel abundant, we've all got the land as far as the eye can see."

By now the sun is baking the valley as the horizon ridges shimmer in the heat. The people who were working the fields have all sought shelter from the sun under the shade of the pine trees. The dogs and horses have also found their shade and the children are in the river, jumping and splashing to their heart's delight. The weavers have moved inside their kivas.

As we continue on our way Palqtlo mentions, "It's the simple things in life here which are most extraordinary. Our village life is all about simplicity and clarity."

We go on exploring the entire village and the one person we don't see is Palqtlo's sister who's noticeably absent.

"Where's Xochina this morning?" I ask.

"Preparing for her final passage," he says, "of the underground cavern I told you about. Those preparations take many intense months of study. We do it out beyond the end of this valley in a dry lake."

"Do they live out there while they prepare?"

"Some of the time." he says.

"A dry lake?"

"It's dry except in the rainy season. It's where the first and last passages take place."

"What's she doing to prepare?"

"She's learning the map of the underground Taquatsi," he answers. "It entails memorizing every step, each turn, each distance so you can make your way through the black on your own."

"You did this . . . right?"

"I remember mine as if it was yesterday."

There must be a few hundred people here and everyone's deeply connected to Palqtlo. He's like a favorite son, but as he explains to me no one's interested in the world he's just come from. They're just glad to have him back and express hope that his wife and daughter will be there soon.

"What happened to the advanced technologies of the cultures that your father said you all descended from?" I ask. "All that you have here is so basic."

"It was during great chaos that our ancestors walked away. They walked and walked, returning everything back to the earth except for their understanding of the rules of nature."

"No one wants to build this all back?" I ask.

"We came here hundreds of years ago to maintain the seeds of wisdom, understanding these rigorous ways to protect them. Nothing has changed over these many centuries."

Late the next afternoon, we come upon an elderly man. He is sitting among many blankets at the entrance to a kiva nestled against the side of some cliffs, "This is my grandfather," Palqtlo says. "The father of my mother. He's what you would call retired. He and my father are the eldest Maraakame in the village, but my grandfather is not strong enough anymore to carry on the ceremonies."

We sit down together with him and he is so incredibly quiet. Just being near him makes you hear things that you'd never hear otherwise, just because he's so quiet.

"Now his task is to just remember and tell the old myths and stories over and over," Palqtlo says. Grandfather nods his acknowledgement. "He's our historian and we all go to him for the stories about our people." He continues with a laugh, "This is what we do instead of the movies."

We sit next to him in the shade of the kiva and wait for him to speak. After a time of staring off into the distance, he turns to Palqtlo and holds out his frail, almost transparent hand. Palqtlo leans forward and his grandfather holds Palqtlo's shoulder.

"We've come to hear the stories of how our village was born," Palqtlo explains in words I can't understand. "My friend here is from the land near the ice."

As he says that, the grandfather turns his gaze into my eyes and says something softly to me. "Warm greetings to your ice," Palqtlo translates.

I smile and nod my head, transfixed with the transparent nature of this man's presence. He's in the Maraakame, I tell myself.

"No," he answers through Palqtlo's translation. "I am resting in the physical body and enjoying the sun's warmth immensely."

I'm impressed by how fast he read my thought and I remain as silent in my mind as possible.

"Long ago, we worked with the spirits of the weather through our devotion to the science of the Earth," he begins. "We've become very lazy now," he pokes at his grandson.

"He means thousands of years ago," Palqtlo adds. "I think he's going to tell you some of what I've already told, but he'll tell it much better."

"That's right," Grandpa reads our conversation. "I'll tell it better," he laughs. "We've maintained the knowledge of the rain dance and the sun dance," Grandpa tells us. "This brings the elements to grow our crops. Since I was born we've always been provided with the food we require. I've never known us to sacrifice our brothers and sisters of the four legs, the wings, or the fins."

I've never seen Palqtlo in this little boy mode before, but it's very charming, showing tremendous respect.

"When he really gets rolling it'll be hard for me to keep the translation up to speed, but I'll make every effort. When I hear the stories I've not heard before, I too get lost in them."

Grandpa motions for Palqtlo to stop talking so much, he's ready to continue. "Many hundreds of years ago our people were a very large community. We lived from Great Water to Great Water."

"Ocean to Ocean," Palqtlo explains.

"We had leaders who were wise and we built great buildings." He pauses, gazing off into the mountains and then continues. "We had human nature and we sometimes used it too much to protect ourselves from Mother Nature." He looks straight at me as he says this, as if telling me something that I really need to remember. "Human nature ultimately produces territorial disputes, an inherent problem. This comes from fear and anger."

He reaches for a clay pot, taking a large drink of water that trickles down his chin. "Our natural ways began to crumble as our leaders began to scramble for more power. Before this time, we farmed and we rarely had to eat a living brother or sister, the animals of the land were our friends, not our food. When our crops would fail however, we'd be forced to ask for a sacrifice from the air, the water or the land. We would ask for these brothers and sisters to help our people."

He takes his transparent hands and rubs his face deeply as if to remember something buried deep in his memory. "We did this with great prayer and reverence. We learned to store our crops from one year to another and the sacrifices of our brothers and sister animals were very seldom. Only when we were forced to, we would hold counsel with the birds and the fish and the earthly animals and ask them, 'If you can help us through this time right now, we'll repay you in the coming seasons.'"

Again, he looks over at me directly. "They would always tell us where they had abundance and we would go there to receive them for our survival. Over the following years, we would plant extra crops for them to harvest and live on."

Palqtlo goes to fetch him some more water in his jug. Everything goes slowly here . . . it's the only natural pace. When I think of San Francisco and all that goes on in our world, it seems unnecessary from this view. After he takes another long drink, he continues.

"When our ancestors became lazy, the sacrifices increased until a man was judged by his ability to kill. These greedy sacrifices eventually led to human sacrifices because after many generations even the leaders became lazy." He pauses as if to remember exactly how he is going to tell it. "In the dissatisfaction which followed, people competed for the leadership. This was unheard of before this time. Leaders had always been obvious by their wisdom, not their ability to compete. Now leaders were chosen by their power to kill and they killed the sacred nature of the people. To control this competition, the priests and leaders began to sacrifice prisoners. Ultimately, this too became even more deeply corrupted."

This point is emphasized by a clap of thunder from an afternoon storm that comes rolling in over the mountains.

"The connection with mother had now been lost," he continues, paying little attention to the noise outside. "As they killed her children in her name, they could no longer understand her nature."

The rain begins to pour down outside the kiva. "They could no longer recognize this Great Reflection, so they found herbs to help them obtain their visions. Tobacco, peyote and others were used to re-capture their spiritual powers, but it was not a solution. Actually, it created more chaos."

He turns to Palqtlo with a huge grin as if to say here's the good part as he continues. "It was during this great chaos that the ancestors of this community walked away. They returned everything back to the Earth, except for their understanding of Mother Nature in the Great Reflection."

He knows I have a question even before I do, so he stops talking and raises his eyebrows as if to say well, go ahead, ask it if you please.

I look over to Palqtlo and he says, "He wants to know if you have a question. He's wanting you to ask it if you do."

"I keep hearing the expression, 'the Great Reflection'," I say. "What does this mean?"

"The Great Reflection is the name we have for all creation," he says. "We know that everything we perceive is just a reflection of what we are." Grandpa looks at the both of us to see if we are with him and then continues. "We came to this place here and no one over all the hundreds of years has ever found us." He beams even brighter at this point of the story as if to celebrate the fact.

"We have always known we must maintain the seeds of understanding and these rigorous ways to protect these seeds within the human psyche." Again he looks at me to make his point more clear. "Nothing for us has changed over these many centuries. The whole purpose of our community revolves around the passages. The most important thing to everyone is raising the children to be truly awakened humans."

He leans back against his blankets with a smile spread all over his face, his hands resting calmly in his lap as he begins to stare off into the distance. He closes his eyes and we sit in total silence. Just the rain is talking now. We wait for the sun to come back out and leave the kiva with Grandfather still resting.

"He's fast," I marvel. "That was impressive."

"He reads it from attitude," Palqtlo explains. "From your face, your eyes, from the way you hold your body and the energy all around you. You have to remember that, to his eyes, all of history is written clearly in every moment if you know how to see it." Palqtlo smiles.

On the third day, we set out to explore the surrounding wilderness of the Wirikuta. We climb one of the smaller hills just beyond the valley and see what I call cougar tracks in the dirt. "The Puma, as it's called in Mexico," Palqtlo says with great respect. "We call it Mayetze. He's common in this area and lives near humans only because he chooses to. He could live anywhere he wants. They're powerful and versatile. Our dogs are in large part coyote. They are called the Kumukite and they're nearly as wild as the Mayetze. The Kumukite dogs protect our horses by keeping the Mayetze honest. Otherwise, they'd become thieves and just live off our animals."

The few adobe structures above the ground here are all nestled amongst the trees and very hard to see. They are round just like the kivas. Palqtlo points out, "These buildings are used primarily for protecting the gardeners from the sun and our animals from the predators."

As we make our way back to the main part of the village we cross the Taquatsi River. The black obsidian in the riverbed is worn smooth and slippery by the waters of time and it's nearly impossible to stand on. "These pieces are used for our mirrors," Palqtlo tells me. "And the mirrors are used in scrying when the Maraakame look through time."

"What exactly do you mean by looking through the mirror?" I ask.

"Looking through the mirror into the next world," he replies very matter of factly.

"How's that possible?" I ask again hoping for something more than an answer.

"We parallel our eyes and the physical perspective of the three dimensions is broken," he says.

"Okay, I hear your words . . . what does that mean?"

"Your eyes go parallel every time you sleep," he replies. "When you dream, you see inside the reality of life on Earth, but it's all jumbled up because you are unconscious. It can happen consciously into a mirror if you train yourself and what you need to learn is to hold the gaze. This is why we call it the dream or dreamtime. Where the conscious mind's ability to see beyond the physical senses is ignited."

He winks as I try to comprehend. I look down into one of the pieces at the river's edge and actually see my reflection for the first time in over a week. My curly hair is flying straight out from my head and down on my shoulders.

"Can I tie my hair up with some of your cotton braid?"

"Sure," Palqtlo replies gracefully.

And so, just like this, the few days pass as we walk the village, talking with the elders, exploring the countryside and eating the best food I have ever had. Illanamiqt meets with us on the fifth day of my stay. The three of us sit together in an underground kiva room. There's a fire in the center to give us light and it gives our faces a surreal look. Illanamiqt examines me with his gaze over and over without saying a word. As this goes on, I feel heat rising with each heartbeat.

"You will need to wake up," he finally speaks through Palqtlo. Illanamiqt's voice is like music, but I can tell he's quite serious. "Your connection with the spirit is not fully awake. You're very much awake to the needs of your body, thoughts and emotions and this is a good start."

I feel a bit slighted as I think how different my life's been since dying in Seattle. I wonder why he doesn't see this.

"I do see this," he responds immediately, knowing exactly what I'm thinking. "Doubt, fear and anger were gifts from God to help us focus the mind, but we're only supposed to use them sparingly. I'm showing you where you are to grow, not complementing you on how much you have grown already." He's staring so sternly into my eyes that I find it difficult to look at him. As I sit there, all I want to do is ask him about my death.

"There's an intuition in each human, which separates us from the other animals," he explains. "This is available at all times, but when we don't use it, we lose this guidance in our life."

Unable to contain myself any longer I just speak out. "I've been through so many changes over the past year. Something must be going right."

"When you blame, you dissolve your strength. Your connection to life is lost."

"You were there, what happened to me in Seattle? Why did I have to go through that?"

"Misfortune is only equal to the amount of power you've given away and or the amount of power you will need to build to fulfill your destiny," Illanamiqt tells me.

"And why is this all so familiar, you, this place and everyone else?"

"Death took you outside time," he answers calmly. "When you leave the physical body, you go beyond all physical limitation. Without the restrictions of time you're able to be in any time."

"When I died," I ask, "Where did I go?"

"You didn't go anywhere," he answers. "Your awareness of what exists, without your body to hold it back, expanded into the time you hadn't yet lived."

"It was terrifying," I exclaim.

"You were losing identity," he replies. "You had no base left. In life, your identity is based in the body, the mind and the emotions. When they start to disappear, there seems to be nothing left, but nothing has actually changed, only perspective."

"I was here instantly."

"You were able to participate in the future at that moment. Your awareness came right here to Wirikuta, though you didn't actually go anywhere."

"Why here?"

"Destiny," he says candidly. "Wirikuta was a potential future."

"In my death experience, when Xochina asked me — Are you You, or an imposter — what did she mean?"

"Are you?" he asks smiling. "When you stop laughing, God finds someone else to have fun with." At this moment his huge smile breaks into laughter.

"I am who I believe is me."

"No, you're partly that, but you're also controlled by who you are with at the time; what you want at the time; what you fear at the time, and that's not being you. That gives away a lot of power."

"I thought I left all that in Seattle."

"Some of it was left. The indoctrination goes deeper however and it takes a lot of practice to release such habits. You, like everyone else, learned this as a small child, insecure about your survival long before you could talk. When you don't have a system to release this, it stays with you for the rest of your life."

"I had a lot to release this with growing up in a spiritual household."

"That was your home, which was wonderful, but you were also living in a world filled with a chaos that is considered normal."

"What can I use to release it?" I ask.

"This is why we have the passages," he declares. "We all use these as children to release our insecurities and their accompanying obsessions. It's through this that we're able to grow into excellence — into human nature."

"Is that possible for me?"

"All our children go through these passages. You could choose to go through these too. You'll be one of our children." His eyes look through me with a slight glint and he turns to walk away.

"To try the passages?" I question as he leaves the cavern.

"The passages are not for trying," he calls back. "They're for accomplishing."

I turn to Palqtlo as Illanamiqt leaves the kiva. "Did I insult him?" I ask.

"I'll agree to the passages," I call out to Illanamiqt as I hurriedly emerge from the kiva.

He turns and smiles very brightly saying, "I know . . . you have already gone through them. You need to sing your songs with truth and be strong to do this."

I walk toward the sun setting over the ridge. I've only been here a few days and already what's real and what's not is becoming less clear by the moment. These are medicine people way beyond the world I come from; I've just committed to another step in my dance with them.

Twenty Five

COMMITMENT

On the very next day my commitment is tested; I'm thrust amongst the three village teenagers going through their own passages. Palqtlo's sister is one of them, but as it turns out I'm not actually going to be with any of them. They're all months ahead of me in this process.

Though I'm 21 and older than them, I actually feel considerably younger. One thing is immediately clear. I have more fear. These children seem dauntless, truly disciplined and never fearful. They are respected and never punished when they get out of line. If they ever have to be corrected, it is done simply, with compassion and with no shaming.

Beyond all my expectations, the magnitude of what I've agreed to appears rather quickly and Palqtlo sees my dismay. "Remember, there's no decision that is of itself, right or wrong," he tells me. "You make a decision and then you either cause it to become right, or you let it go wrong."

"How do you know that for sure?" I ask.

"We live our lives by it and have for centuries," he answers. "Our people have experienced far greater consequences than this."

The first part of the passage begins several days later in the early hours of the morning when I'm brought into a kiva to meet with a gathering of villagers. These men and women look as if they're barely on the planet and Illanamiqt is noticeably absent. Palqtlo stands with me, but I feel absolutely alone. Within the rhythm of a very deep drum, they begin to talk to me in slow and hypnotic voices. Their tones are melodic and pleasant.

"Relax with their words as I translate," Palqtlo advises me.

I don't actually understand their words, but in a strange way I get the gist of nearly everything they say. Palqtlo continues to translate; yet in all the sound of drums and voices, most of his translation is lost. Often their words don't seem to be spoken at all, but transmitted somehow directly into my mind. I keep checking my ears, stretching my lower jaw to see if they're plugged, but this changes nothing so I just go with it. There are statements of what I'm to face and questions I have to answer. I ask about my life and the future of my vision. This goes on for the rest of the morning.

One point they make extremely clear. There are countless ways to visit the other side of this reality and they all produce answers to live by. The physical shock of my death experience is the most brutal way, but there are other less ferocious methods. Many of them are equally fruitful and more affordable. Some of these are embedded in the passages that I can go through.

After several hours we break for water and food. From what Palqtlo explains, they're preparing me to commit to the task at hand. They have all passed through these in their youth. Many of them are related by blood to the three youngsters crossing through the passages right now.

We step outside the kiva for a moment. The sky is gray with thickening rain clouds, as if it's sending me the message that this is not the brightest morning of my life. I sit by myself to eat cornbread and fruit. I'm not in the mood for conversation and I'm almost ready to run. I look around with a deep sense of being among the enemy. The others are so carefree in their nature that I wonder why they don't have healthy concerns.

"What are healthy concerns?" Xochina asks me, approaching unnoticed.

Her question startles me, but I better get used to this. I clear my throat of the food and say, "Concerns about my well-being for one thing."

"Everyone loves your well-being," she replies.

She obviously does not understand what my needs are. Palqtlo comes to her rescue to translate.

"What she's telling you," he says, "is that your well-being is why we are offering you the opportunity to participate in these passages. No one outside this community has ever had this chance."

"The dangers you face in these passages aren't really necessary are they?" I ask both of them.

"We face the dangers on the outside to take excess fear out of our inside," she says frankly. "Palqtlo tells me that in your villages, everyone hides the fact that they are filled with fears inside. This makes everything on the outside false."

This is so true, I think to myself as we are called back to the kiva. I notice, in the flicker of the firelight, a small coyote dog resting among the villagers. She doesn't move, but simply lies there watching and listening to everything. As we continue the work, one of the elders speaks barely above a whisper. "We are the seed that disappears into the soil of time." I strain to understand these words. "Our time is almost over," he continues. "The time for you is just beginning. Yours is the future and your presence is your key to open the gate."

Palqtlo illustrates this very clearly when he says. "The present moment is the only living moment. Remaining conscious of this present presence is extremely important for life to exist. Don't become lost in the memory of the past, but use this past as a tool to build the present. Don't be fearful of the future, but use your present presence to build your future. This will keep you growing powerfully."

Several of the elders begin to speak. "It's up to each and every one of us to overcome the hypnotic spell of this physical world.

We must work to see beyond the belief of limitations to understand the larger picture of reality. This is the sole purpose of our passages. You'll need to use this power in your life if you are to make any difference in this world."

This catches my attention. 'If I am going to make any difference in the world' echoes in my head, their voices like an orchestra. Each one knows when to speak and what to say, when to start, and when to stop.

"It is very simple," Ezkaya emphasizes. "We must commit every breath we take to being in our present presence. We must do this in order to be truly alive. How can you possibly stop the killing in your wars, if you're not fully living yourself? If you're not alive, your voice cannot be effective and it will be stopped by the stronger force of the opposition."

"This is a very clever trick," another adds with laughter, the first laughter I've heard all morning and it breaks the heaviness I feel. I'm so glad to hear from Ezkaya. As Palqtlo's mother, she feels like family to me. With the rhythm of the very deep drums, their voices remain bouncy and hypnotic; they are speaking ever so slowly.

"We're on Earth to learn how to fully engage each moment. We're here to then fully release that same moment to make room for the next. This is called momentum and it's a very powerful tool that saves effort and energy. We live life fully through momentum."

Palqtlo's having one heck of a time translating this for me, the first time it's ever been done. I'm sure I should feel honored, but there are too many other conflicting feelings for that one to fit in right now. "The opposite of this momentum is stagnation," they continue. "And stagnation produces all of the negating emotions as a warning that stagnation is present instead of presence. Among these are fear, guilt, and other emotions that warn us that we are out of our power."

The rhythm continues while the fire dances and the little Kumukite, the sweet-faced dog, rests near the edge of our circle.

Outside, thunder and rain begin to pour. The little dog stretches her legs for a moment as the thunder crashes and echoes through our gathering. The fire warms us all.

"What's guilt?" I ask. "We feel it all the time."

"Guilt is the emotion that forces us into the past where life does not exist. The past is dead and therefore you're not alive in this emotion. Guilt will make you ineffective in your efforts. You're unable to give yourself forward to this moment."

"What does it mean, giving yourself forward?" I continue to question.

"It means to forgive," Palqtlo explains.

"Forgiving what?"

"Yourself."

"For what?" I ask.

"For any moment in the past . . . it's the ability to give yourself forward to the present moment from a past moment so that you can fully live in time . . . to be present in your presence."

My head is spinning. "Why is guilt so strong?" I ask again, wanting to completely understand.

"Because we think it's an answer. Because we think feeling bad will lead to feeling good, but it never can. You must give up your guilt and forgive yourself."

"You must also give up that twisted satisfaction, the satisfaction you get from holding someone else guilty. Either you hold someone in that moment of memory, or you hold yourself. One way it's blame and the other way it's shame. Both are toxic to your connection with spirit."

I turn to Palqtlo's mother. "Help me here. Help make it a little clearer."

"When a moment's over and yet you don't give it up," she says, "then you remain attached to that moment. You stay there while time proceeds forward and leaves you behind. That part of you that's left behind is the part of you that is not alive, because it's consciously involved with a time that no longer exists." She pauses to see if I'm still with her and seeing that I am, she continues.

"You jeopardize your connection with spirit this way because spirit is presence in the present. In the out-world it's a miracle that anything goes right."

"So, this is the reason for the passages?" I ask. "To place you in charge of your time?"

"The path of your demons is always as strong as the path of your light," she explains to me. "The passages prove to you that there is a choice at all times of which way you go and you end up with commitment."

"Commitment to what?" I question this word with some obvious passion.

"Commitment is not to anything, commitment is a choice." She sees that I'm making progress and I'm comforted by her style. "When you're ruled by your feelings, you are not making choices. It takes discipline to maintain your authority to choose."

One of the older men must sense that it's his turn and he interjects, "When you choose your fear over your faith, then you're led down the path of your doubt."

Another draws a picture in the dirt with a stick and in the flickering firelight I see the characters. Palqtlo then explains what this all means in English terms.

$$(\text{Intention} \times \text{Focus}) \times (\text{Time}) - (\text{Habit of Fear} + \text{Doubt}) = \text{OUTCOME}$$

"This is the equation of life and the sum of all attitudes," he tells me. "If the focus of your intention is held over a period of time and this is longer than the time that you give to your fear, then you accomplish your desire."

"It's a constant battle between the new discipline and the old habit," Ezkaya adds to the round. "Our passages are set up to overcome this old habit pattern built into your life from generations before your childhood. The habits and feelings speak a language that reports the condition of the illusion. This is not truth, but a product of your experiences."

"Aren't my experiences real?" I ask her.

"That's hard to say," she replies. "They've been filtered through your emotions and thoughts and they may not always be telling you the truth. There is no guarantee."

"How can anyone be sure then?"

"Make it your habit to be sure and test the results over time."

"How much time does that take?"

"More than you have."

"So how's that possible then?"

"Nearly impossible," she replies. "So we intensify the equation, and accelerate time. That's what the passages are."

Just then, Illanamiqt enters the kiva and says. "In the vastness of the mind, beyond the portions you are conscious of — live the images of every fear and every doubt. These images are accessed by your life when you're unable to be disciplined."

"When they act like this, they're like your demons, but they are just you," Ezkaya adds.

"On the other hand," he continues, "in the higher frequencies of the vast mind — there resides the images and energies of your heroes and guides, your joys and loves. With great discipline you are able to use these strong images to override your demons. This is what your religions work with. This is what our disciplines work with. This is the purpose of the passage."

This proceeds for the next three full days with time out for food and sleep. At the end of these days I'm asked. "Are you truly willing to go through to the edges of perception and beyond? Are you willing to define the purpose of your life, step by step?"

This sounds exciting to me after all I've been through, and I answer, "Yes, I am."

Twenty Six

MISSION AND VISION

For the next few days, I am taken, without breakfast, to the base of a nearby mountain. I am met by a group of the elders I've seen around the Wirikuta. We begin a climb to the mountain's summit. Every morning, I reach the top in about two hours and every morning the elders are already there. These eighty-year old men all get to the top in about half my time.

Day after day I work on my speed and my breathing. I even try running for the first bit which is a complete disaster . . . I almost can't make it to the top. I request of Palqtlo to ask the elders their secret. How do they beat a man sixty years their junior every single day? The answer comes back immediately. Palqtlo explains what they said, "The only difference is that when we climb the mountain, our bodies and minds and emotions are only climbing the mountain and nothing else."

This answer is surprisingly simple and yet totally clear, what a perfect formula for success. It seems that this has been my official introduction to the passages and it certainly captures my attention. A person of any age can accomplish almost anything with a simple focus, an attitude of silence and consistent discipline of the body, mind and emotions.

On the morning of the fourth day, I'm awakened before sunrise and told to remain silent. I'm taken on horseback half a day's journey from the village and left alone with my horse in the desert after receiving a few brief instructions for my first passage.

The instructions are: I'm fasting on water only; I'm to talk to no one, not even my horse; I'm to inscribe the reason I'm alive on the Earth around me so it can be understood from the highest point nearby. This would be the mountain some five thousand feet high near the edge of this flat desert location.

The final instruction is that the dirt from my carving has to be dropped into the waters where the Taquatsi River flows back into the Earth. And I'm to sleep on the lakebed or the mountaintop every night. I have one horse — I call Horse, two clay pots, four cloth bags, a blanket and a fire bow. Using the fire bow will be exciting. I watched Palqtlo use it on the way in and I've seen it used several times in the village, but I've never done it myself.

Sensing my concern before he left me, Palqtlo told me that no one knows how to do anything until they have to. This comforted me immensely and as soon as they leave me here, the daily storm begins and I'm thoroughly drenched within minutes. The thought of learning this primitive fire process in the middle of freezing my ass off, hungry, and soaking wet is hilarious as well as outrageous.

"That's it, God!" I scream at the top of my lungs. "You're playing with me again." Horse's ears perk up for a moment, and then he returns to grazing on the scrub grass and not minding the rain. I realize that I just spoke, but it was to God. I'm sure that doesn't count.

"Food! Hungry!" I call into thin air. You've got to maintain your sense of humor out here, I'm sure of it already. I'd better stop using my voice, I think, or I'll flunk this first passage. "That was meant to be a joke," I respond to the horse with a smile. "I'll shut up now. I promise. I won't say another word till this job is done."

I've been told to drink lots of water I recall as the rain pours down. I catch the streams running down my face as I move to the shelter of a juniper tree. Perhaps I should have asked how long this would take. I consider asking Horse, but am determined to maintain the silence now. I wonder how long it usually takes. The mountain's quite tall, but the sides look easy enough to climb, nothing like the hike into the Wirikuta, or the one that the elders beat me on every single day. The trees start just above the base of the mountain and become taller as it goes up. At the top of the mountain there are no trees at all, just what appear to be fields of rocks. The lakebed is huge; it must be miles in all directions and the surface is covered in cracked lines that are now filling with water from the rain. I look around, wondering what I am to use to carve the letters. There are several possibilities in the branches lying about, but wow, this is going to be an immense job.

I get up and test a few of the branches for strength. They all seem to pass the test as I scratch into the earth. The lakebed is soft, which is good news and I spend a little time just drawing circles and doodles in the moist dust.

I spend the rest of the day planning my project until the rain stops and the sun reappears just enough to dry me off before it goes down behind the mountain. I start looking for a good campsite. My stomach's growling with hunger and I think of the food back in the village and imagine all kinds of meals in the States. The growing darkness and the silence fuel the fantasy that builds over the time it takes the sun to set and I'm left in the dark of the evening, chilled, empty, hungry, and without a plan.

This isn't much fun, I think to myself. It was a great fantasy, but the reality is that I've got no firewood and now it's dark. I gather the blanket around me and lean up against the base of the tree and try to block everything from my mind and fall asleep. It must be the middle of the night, or perhaps early the next morning when I awaken shivering in the dark. I have one blanket to keep out the chill and it isn't enough. I take up the fire bow, determined to create some warmth and light. I gather a few pieces of the abundant dead fall and set my bow to action. The movement of bowing the wood warms my body quickly. After several minutes of intense stroking, exactly as I've observed others do, a small glow and then a flame appears in the smoking chips of wood. The trees and branches in the dark surroundings appear to close in on the tiny flickering just as they did on the hike in with Palqtlo.

The stars barely show above the thick tree branches around me. A small sliver of moon rises in the distance beneath them, but there's no real light. Only my fire creates a tiny visibility in this darkness. By finally getting warm I realize that all it took was the effort and determination to build this fire. I had no idea how to use this bow before. Palqtlo's words resound in my mind. "No one knows how to do anything until they have to." I'll remember this, because I love the warmth.

As the night continues, I hear voices emerging from the crackling fire and the gentle wind rustling in the bushes. Images join the voices as the shrubs and firelight dance. I can turn this movie in my mind friendly or scary with just the slightest twist of my thoughts. I occasionally jump up and down for intermission, to break up the physical monotony. My mind, however, is fully entertained with the abundance of being totally alone. I don't think I've ever been this isolated in my life. It's a strange sensation. I can imagine all sorts of scenarios if I allow myself to. I keep the fire well stoked as I scour the nearby ground for fallen branches and this keeps my mind busy. I'm wide-awake until the early sunlight slowly changes the shadows in the woods around me — then I fall asleep to nap in the warmth of the morning sun.

As soon as it's completely light, I get up to look for water. Mounting Horse isn't easy. I cinch my blanket around his belly with two soft cotton straps and gently fit cotton bridle around his head. I jump high enough onto his back to land on my belly. After some careful negotiating, I rotate my body until I straddle him with my legs. The moment I'm in place, he knows precisely what to do and takes off trotting. I learn to quickly ease the pounding of my butt out of necessity. I tuck my knees under me a bit to find some relief and this works well until we make turns. With no stirrups for my feet to grip, I feel a bit helpless, but eventually we manage. I've got no real sense of this animal yet, but it will be important, I'm certain of that. Right now it's all I can do to stay on board and I'm learning as we go. Not really a learning curve — more like a learning wall. My water jugs bounce behind me. They have straps woven tightly to them and they ride on the back of my horse fixed to one of the blanket straps. They have wooden stoppers and seem sturdy enough to withstand the bouncing ride as I recognize how important they'll be for my assignment ahead.

We finally reach the river where the water soon changes my mood. I strip off my clothing and jump into the current. It is surprising how deep the moods cut through everything when you're this isolated. At this place in the river, the water is pooling in gentle eddies and it's deep enough to swim quite comfortably. The obsidian river bottom glows blood red as it shines from under the water in the morning sun.

I untie my saddle blanket and pull off the jugs. The stoppers are tight but eventually come out with coaxing. As I push them under the gently pooling waters, I hold them tightly. With every move I make right now, I'm tending to imagine disaster. I wonder if this is always going on in my mind and there's just too much distraction to notice it. Here there are no distractions and this tendency is glaring and blunt.

The trip back to camp takes about three times longer. I'm careful not to trot, concerned of breaking or spilling the jugs. Taking the blanket off of Horse, I lay down and drift off into sleep as I contemplate the task ahead. I end up sleeping most of this first day. I must be avoiding something because I never sleep like this, but there's nothing to do. I can't eat, there's no one to talk with, my task sits before me and I'm not ready to start.

As the evening shadows lengthen, I gather wood for the night fire. Off in the corner of my eye, I see a small animal dart through the shadows. I hold still and look more closely . . . Choti, one of the Kumukite dogs has joined me for my passage. Friends, I think to myself, it's really great to have friends. Once again I work hard over the fire bow and in time, a small flame comes to life. With these tiny flames, a sense of calm rushes over me. Each time I use this fire bow I marvel at the miracle of the fire and am grateful. The nights would be nearly unbearable without it.

I'm filled with many ideas of this mission that I can write into the desert floor, but I'm not ready to start. The next morning, I take a ride with the animals. My sense of liberty is unique. I've never felt it this deeply before. I'm on planet Earth, but I might as well be on Mars. No one who knows me knows where I am. I could die here and there's not a soul who'd ever notify my parents or friends. These are odd thoughts, yet they give me a sense of freedom. In addition to freedom, there's a constant insecurity as well and the mixture is electrifying. We ride to the top of the mountain this morning. The trail is far steeper than it looks from the lakebed, but Horse knows exactly where to go and Choti walks in the lead.

As we make our way back, the sun is setting over the last hills in the horizon; the voices of a coyote pack break the quiet rustle of our movement. Choti's ears and stance immediately come to attention. The skin on Horse quivers in a wave. He stops dead in his tracks. Their response, more than the coyote's sound, cause chills to run the length of my spine. Choti quickly moves between the legs of Horse, not looking afraid, but appearing extremely alert. The number of coyote voices increases. I slowly dismount and pick Choti up placing her into one of the empty bags slung over Horse's back. Her head moves back and forth securing every square inch of the valley at once for any possible sign of movement. I jump up on the cinched blanket once again and inform him with a slight tap of my moccasins that I'm ready to move.

234

He turns his head toward me. With his eyes and breath I clearly feel him say, "I've got this. You never have to kick me."

I'm delighted with the communication. Just as soon as this thought goes through my head, he turns around again, shaking the reins and snorting. I lean forward and scratch his forehead. "I got it," I think silently and let out a loud coyote whoop of my own.

The pack's voices sound like hundreds. They're growing louder and coming from everywhere around us. They're playing with my mind and waiting for a mistake, I think. I feel like a guest in the enemy's house, excited by the drama and completely alert. The bond between the three of us is fundamental. By the time we arrive at camp, we are 10 legs on a single creature.

After two days of playing on the desert floor, I decide to begin my passage duties and I write.

> *I will share healing and love through music, words and consciousness. I will bring a peace and calm — prosperity and joy, to the life of this planet.*

This is why I live, I think to myself. I quickly complete a few letters and the soil removal is a huge task. The letters are five feet tall and dug a half-foot or so into the flat of the desert. This produces a lot of sandy soil and we have to make several trips to the Taquatsi River several miles away. The entrance to the cavern where the river plunges into the Earth is breathtaking. The water flowing over the black riverbed just disappears into the ground through a hole about fifteen feet by five feet across. You can see nothing of the bottom of this hole. The fact that you enter the Earth on the final passage here is beyond comprehension. I spot a tiny salamander on the river's edge. Palqtlo told me that salamanders were the power animals of the rainmaker. His mother is also a rainmaker. She can dance in the spirit world of the salamander and bring back clouds to fill the sky, he's told me. She could even do this on the hottest day of summer if necessary.

Right now it's the beginning of the rainy season and this afternoon as the clouds roll in, I experience the passion of the storm. Lightning strikes just a hundred yards away from me. I'm lying on the ground and I've pulled Horse and Choti next to me for safety. We're getting soaked, but the energy's exhilarating. When lightning strikes it sends off a blue light and the instant thunder shakes the earth like a quake. Neither Horse nor Choti are bothered by the intensity of this sound and we must make a noble sight, all heaped in a pile. I'm laughing with the electricity it's so intense.

Then it's over as soon as it began. The last rays of the evening sun make a valiant effort to dry my soaked shirt, pants and moccasins. I take them all off and hang each piece carefully from the branches of the juniper trees. There, I think silently to my friends, now I'm just like you, naked as God made me.

In the rainy season the dry lakebeds of this area fill with frogs. They hibernate in the earth when it's dry and come out when the rain turns the hard packed earth into mud. They make a tremendous sound with mating calls. Together with the coyotes, the wolves and the owls, our camp has turned into a concert hall this evening. I wish I had my guitar, the first time I've felt this in weeks. I build a tremendous fire from sage branches and dry my clothing and blanket and more wood. I sit there in the firelight, naked with my animals and the fire. I remember the mythology of the Wirikuta, the origins of this region when the angels settled it. Tonight, I feel like an Angel . . . I'm free.

Twenty Seven

THE EAGLE'S EYE

I wake up several times in the night to stoke the fire. By morning I'm totally ready to finish the project. I blanket Horse and ride to the center of the lakebed to see if my writing has survived the storm. It's worn from the rain, but readable. I turn Horse to the mountain, he knows exactly what to do and up we go with Choti leading the way. After about two hours, we reach the top. I turn to look at my words in the desert below and I can't believe it. I can't read a thing. The letters are so small that I can't even find them at all, let alone read them. I sit there smiling, three days wasted I think. Horse snorts and shakes his body.

"Not so, is that what you're saying?" I think silently. "Okay then, we're going to plan this. I'll make one letter ten feet tall and another twenty feet tall and we'll come back to see which one we can read." I laugh at the thought of a horse and a dog reading my letters, then stop myself and change my laughter to respect.

I reach over and stroke both of them. "Sorry there. I'll get used to this." Silently spoken.

By the end of the day, we have our two letters and head back up the mountain. Near the top I try to see the letters, but need to clear the tree line. The sun's getting low in the sky and

I'm concerned about getting back down by dark. I didn't think of spending the night here and my fire bow is at the bottom. Sensing my concern, Horse moves quicker through the trees. We emerge into the rock fields. I turn and see the larger of our two letters plainly legible. "This means that all my writing has to be twenty feet tall." I think to the animals. "This is not very practical if I want to finish the project soon."

The fasting has made me physically weak, and it's at this time of day that I'm the weakest. I didn't bring any water with me when we rushed to get up the mountain so we have to go back. We reach the bottom long after dark, and Horse knows exactly where the camp is. I go to work on the fire bow as soon as we arrive, with the desert chill in full force. Horse and Choti enjoy the night fires as much as I do. They're as human as anyone I've known. I depend on them; I trust them; they take care of me.

As the days go by I learn how to communicate without words. I have a mutual respect for the mountain lions, wolves and coyotes, all the creatures of the Wirikuta. Horse and Choti drink water from the rain puddles in the desert. Horse grazes on dried grass and sprouts and Choti disappears every evening for about an hour and returns looking very satisfied. Each evening, once the fire's going, I drink as much water as possible to stop the hunger and that's my dinner. I then curl up with my friends and sleep. It's the same ritual every night. I get up several times to re-stoke the fire. I've lost track of the days. I think we're at day seven right now, but it doesn't matter or make any sense anymore. I estimate that with the digging and carrying, I have a couple more weeks to go.

Morning comes quickly and by now I love these surroundings and the vastness of my life. I already can't imagine living in a city, so rigid in comparison. Sometimes it feels like this task could take a very long time to complete, but just as Palqtlo said, time is releasing its furious grip, and whatever time this takes seems surprisingly acceptable. This morning however, I wake up with an enormous idea. Sitting in the dirt, with Horse and Choti,

I'm okay. Writing the purpose of my life on a dry lakebed in the middle of nowhere without anything to eat, I'm okay. Horse and Choti smile back at me as we head off to work. And today my task has shifted. I have a brand new idea.

The letters would carve rapidly this morning, but I am not going to carve letters anymore. I am going to carve a gigantic symbol — a huge circle, around the vast desert that begins with my last letter written and encloses all the words already done and means — everything I haven't written — everything I could possibly think of — and even those things that I might never think of. We make several trips to the river and my circle takes shape. I have to stop every so often to keep balanced — the lack of food is making me very light headed. We make our way up the mountain to view our work for the afternoon. The mountain is always far cooler, so it's become our daily routine.

At the top of the mountain, I sit with my two friends. Out of the corner of my eye I see an angel-like figure dance across my symbol. I look more closely, but by the time my eyes focus, it's gone. I think very little about it, because the heat and lack of food makes a lot of things appear and disappear.

Later on when we're ready to return down to camp, it appears again. In the light of dusk, the figure appears to shimmer in the middle of my letters. It stops every so often, as if looking them over or trying to read them. It looks like a young woman dressed in white and floating back and forth over the deep ruts that I've dug.

I'm so caught up and spaced out with hunger that I just sit staring while the light fades to total blackness and I can see nothing at all. I can't stay on the mountain all night so I mount Horse, place Choti in the bag and begin the treacherous descent in the dark. I hear a puma several times, and wolves and coyotes gather around me. I've never been so indebted to my friends as I am now. At times, the bright strips of cotton cloth braided in my hair catch some branches that I cannot see in the dark so I lay my body on the back of Horse and let him take me home. The wild animals around us seem like sentries to the darkness.

Morning arrives quicker than usual. I'm barely able to get up and I'm determined to finish the circle today. Palqtlo said that when you feel all of your emotions dedicated to your chosen actions, then your life's 'on purpose'. This is a power of commitment. "We have no idea," he would tell me, "how much doubt plays in our lives."

This morning it's as if there is no such thing as doubt — not a drop. I'm just digging and measuring and bagging as the final part of the circle takes shape.

As I'm bending down to pour my last bag of soil into the water, I catch my reflection in the pool. This is the first I've seen of myself in days and it's a shock. The strips of bright colored cotton braided into my hair make me look like a native. I'm left feeling that I'm someone I don't know, but someone I admire.

When I return to the desert floor there are several hours of sunlight left and I'm anxious to view my finished work. I'm tired and lay down on Horse, holding his neck for the entire climb. At the top, I can read my message clearly.

I will share healing and love through music, words and consciousness . . . then it wanders into a gigantic circle, clearly visible from the mountaintop.

I'm elated at having finished and look forward to returning to the village as I notice a large eagle, circling overhead. Being this high in elevation myself, the eagle's only a few feet away, looking and sounding very strong. I must be too close to the nest so I mount Horse and prepare to leave as her call pierces my ears. She swoops down and spreads her wings into my face as if she would hit me and though she does not, the intensity knocks me off Horse onto the steep slope. I tumble a few feet down the mountain against the base of a large boulder. My ears are ringing. A coyote scampers across the rim and looks right through me. It's dream-like as I lay there.

"I'm your death angel," a voice in my head tells me. "When I arrive, your time is done. Right now I'm close — I will always be close — but this is to advise you of this time."

I lay back and close my eyes. "Look," the voice says pointing to what appears as an aerial view of San Francisco. The picture changes and I see several musicians on a stage including Tex, Hendrix, Garcia and Morrison.

"Why are you showing me this?" I ask without daring to open my eyes.

"It's not difficult to figure this out," it answers.

"Is this their time? They've had so little!"

"There's never much time, and always less than expected. What you want to be must be every moment, or it'll never happen. To make a dream come true, you've got to serve it to yourself and appreciate each day."

"The time is closing," death says calmly, "and sleepwalking will make the dream end as fast as it began. Until you've come here to live, you'll never learn a thing. Until you've come here to prevail and use fear and other emotions as tools, you'll only survive the ordeal of life . . . surviving is not living."

I shake my head, open my eyes and look around me. It's as if nothing happened. Horse and Choti are right there, Choti in the bag and Horse standing perfectly still, waiting for me. I look down the mountain to see if my letters are still there. I read them clearly all enclosed in the huge circle. The figure in white is also back and floats across the desert below me so I hurriedly mount Horse and this time I'm determined to catch up with it. I race down the mountain trail nearly falling off several times. As I approach, the angelic figure turns out to be Xochina.

I point at her as if to say, "So you're the one whose been walking on my letters." It's very strange to be in someone's presence and not talking.

Xochina nods yes knowingly, and responds with the words, "and you're the one who rides through my map."

I shrug my shoulders as if to ask what she means.

"Yes . . . this is near where I memorized my map."

I indicate with my arms and hands that I'm done now and they should be coming for me soon.

"I'll take you back," she replies.

We ride through the darkness. She's skilled at navigating the dark woods and desert. I follow her closely with Horse and Choti. Again, I think of Tex and what a great time we would have here together.

"She's troubled," Xochina says, turning to me on her horse. By now it comes as no surprise when they read my thoughts.

Palqtlo meets us as we arrive at the village. "Great job," he says with his usual smile. "You actually did well. You can speak now."

"Wow," I reply and whisper out the faint words. "No one tells you how. You figure it out for yourself in the middle of chaos."

Palqtlo laughs and gives his sister a big hug. "Thanks for bringing him home. I was beginning to miss him and all his questions."

I continue to whisper. "Sometimes there was so much fear out there and at other times the joy was so large it was not possible to fully experience . . . it just overflowed."

"That's the beauty of it, little brother," he says. "That's the absolute beauty. Pity we don't get to have that in the out-world. It so strengthens the nerves."

Exhausted, I quickly fall asleep. I miss Horse and Choti. They're out there somewhere in the night. It's as if two parts of me are missing.

Twenty Eight

A DESPERADO REFOCUSES

Before the sun rises, the charm is gone again and I don't want to be here. Still desperately hungry, my mind races through every justification of why I should not be here. Maybe it's the feeling that I need to go back and warn Tex but I've had enough. I want to get back to my music. I just want the hell out of being in the middle of nowhere.

I jump from my blankets and run to the top of the kiva entrance. I stand there holding onto the earthen walls, dizzy from the lack of food. There's the slightest hint of morning light on the far mountaintops. I resolve to leave the Wirikuta today and decide to leave on my own. I make a bundle of my blankets and fill a large sack with pine nuts. As I cautiously emerge from my kiva, I can faintly see the entrance of the cavern we came in through on the far side of the valley. I take a deep breath and start walking slowly and quietly, to avoid drawing the attention of the villagers doing their morning ceremonies.

After two hours of walking, I'm at the cavern entrance and sit to have some pine nuts before continuing. After eating, which helps a lot, I walk a few feet into the cavern when reality strikes. "Shit", I think as I stop dead in my tracks. "I'm not thinking here . . . without Palqtlo, without any light, without a map, this can't happen."

I step back outside and sit down to collect my thoughts. If I just feel my way along the walls I'll make it out. I take a deep breath and enter again. I walk about a thousand feet, hugging close to the wall and after turning the first corner, all available light leaves my eyes. The pitch-blackness does strange things to the mind and I'm in the middle of it. I try to grip the wall tighter but I drop to the ground. Within a few moments of sitting I'm unable to determine which way I just came in from. As confusion surrounds me I'm absolutely still with every sense heightened. I breathe deeply and steadily as the elders have taught me. I wait for the mind to calm and keep pace with my breath. I crawl a little distance in each direction in search of the slightest trace of light. After three directions of failure I breathe again, slowly moving the muscles around my lungs. I move in the fourth direction for a few feet and there is nothing but black. I lie down on my blankets and fall asleep. I dream I've made it back to San Francisco.

"Where the hell did you blow from?" Tex questions belligerently without even extending her hand to greet me. "You look like total shit."

"Hey kid, it's great to see you too," I reply reaching out to give her a hug.

"You can kiss my butt with that kid shit!" she says, pulling away from me. "You're the kid, you ran — you ran scared, but I'm not the kid anymore. I'm all grown up now."

"That's great Tex," I say, trying to get through her guard, "but why so bitter . . . what's going on?"

She glares and walks away from me shutting the kitchen door behind her. "Let's talk," I say leaning against the door. "There's something you've got to hear."

"Say it quick then," she says sarcastically without opening the door. "I really don't have time for any of your shit."

"There's no time left for any of us," I tell her. "We have to be super conscious with what little we have left."

The door swings back open making a grand entrance as she shouts in my face. "So you been to Mexico and now you're the fucking prophet. Is that what you're telling me? Well congratulations, but I don't need any of your insight."

"I'm just trusting my teachers, Tex."

"Yeah right, like running off with some Indian chief. You abandoned your dreams man and abandoned me too. I used to know you, but I don't anymore, so cut the advice. It doesn't mean shit to me now."

I take her shoulders and look straight into her face as I say, "I never left you. I even offered to take you. I'm offering that again right now, I want you to come."

She reaches over and pushes my hands away from her shoulders.

The dream shifts back to the Wirikuta. Palqtlo sees the pain on my face and asks, "Would you like me to take you back to San Francisco?"

I pause for a moment then shake my head, "I don't think so, but I'm flipping out here."

"When you want to learn," Xochina says point blank, "there's always a sacrifice."

"Tex is so stubborn," I tell them, "Her addictions are talking for her."

"Death's on her doorstep," Illanamiqt says very quietly, "She's taunting it."

"What can I do?" I ask.

"Prayer, that's all there is right now," he answers. "We're in a time of no time and there's little you can do." He pauses for a moment, gazing off at the mountains. "A few years ago our community realized that our ways were important to the world, but we had no way of reaching out because of our isolation." He looks into the distance as he continues. "We decided that music and musicians were the messengers."

I look around at each of them, not entirely sure what he means. "Are you saying this was all planned?" I ask.

"You were noticed a few months before we met," Palqtlo steps in to answer for his father.

"Noticed me?" I ask.

"Yes," Xochina answers.

"Are you telling me that the experience I had in the hospital was real and I actually came here?"

"As real as you and I here," Illanamiqt replics.

"You recognized us right?" Xochina asks. "You even recognized me. How's that possible if we've never met?"

I lean back against a tree behind me and look at the three of them. I laugh and we all have a good laugh together. I ask questions about my death, the music I heard, the people I met, my relationship with Tex and more.

"We hear that music when we've been deep underground for long periods," Xochina tells me. "This is the music we play on our flutes and drums."

"Where did I go?" I ask. "What was all that?"

"In your death you visited the other side of time," Illanamiqt explains. "In the physical form, time is divided into three sequences. The present presence is where we live if we discipline ourselves to be present. The past presence is our foundation, and the future presence is our hope. When you focus on the negative of the past presence you shake your foundation and when you place fear into the future presence you destroy hope."

"This is where you and I met," Xochina adds. "In the hope, the future presence."

"In the dreamtime everything happens at once," Palqtlo says.

Illanamiqt smiles broadly at his two children with obvious satisfaction. "You can use the dreamtime to look at the total picture of all things, if you know how."

"Yeah, but how long does this take?" I ask, sounding very impatient.

Palqtlo takes hold of my shoulder, "Listen, little brother, you get it started and you can awaken through all the years to come."

"You're very impatient," Illanamiqt scolds me. "These teachings have existed for centuries. Our people have preserved this path through time, but we've never taken the easy way to this knowledge, never resorted to the herbs. We choose only to gain this ability through our music, our stories, and the meditative journeys of our passages."

He stops and looks at his children again and then continues, "We'll not be around many more years, but our ways must live on." He looks straight at me. "This is the reason you're here."

I look back with tears running from my eyes. "This seems hopeless when I look at the world."

"It could take years for the world to listen," Palqtlo says. "And until then your words will gather the few who are reachable and teachable. You will meet a great one who will teach you to hold your breath for a very long time so that this can happen in the world out there."

With these words a gentle wetness washes over my face. I reach out and feel the body of Choti in the darkness. She's licking my nose and very excited to roll her body against mine. I cuddle with her for a few minutes and then realize she is communicating for me to follow her, which I do just like her, on all fours. When we get to the entrance of the cavern, I gather by the position of the moon that it is close to morning. What a sensation, what a dream, what a turn of events.

As we walk back into the village, most of Palqtlo's family seems to be waiting for me on the path. They look at me and I can tell from their eyes that they were actually there in the cavern — maybe not physically, but they were there. With a sense of complete wellbeing I walk over and give them a group hug. When our bodies make contact I realize that we don't experience our power until we make the hard decisions to commit.

In the evening we celebrate as usual, with our voices echoing off the drums and flutes and shakers. Music is so important to these people and singing is the reason I'm popular with the children here. I start singing a song that is just coming as I sing. Though the little ones have no idea what the words are, they try to sing along.

All for one
One for all
The good Lord loves to see us that way, Yeah
All for one
One for all
The good Lord loves to see us that way, Yeah

Everybody really loves everybody
Sometimes in our rush we don't play our part
Slow your rhythm down
Gather all the folks around
Let the grace of God open up your heart

All for one
One for all
The good Lord loves to see us that way, Yeah
All for one
One for all
The good Lord loves to see us that way, Yeah

We've traveled quite a while
Everybody in their own style
Now we sit here and it's time to play
Although you have your choice
God loves to hear your voice
So won't you join this song
We'll walk all along His way

All for one
One for all
The good Lord loves to see us that way, Yeah
All for one
One for all
The good Lord loves to see us that way, Yeah

Everybody really loves everybody
Sometimes we just don't know how or where
Catch if catch you can right now
A hold of your neighbor's hand right now
Squeeze real tight
Show them you might care

All for one
One for all
The good Lord loves to see us that way

I welcome these gatherings and the dreams I receive after them. Tonight, I dream again of the Wirikuta and the challenges that lie ahead. The villagers in my dreams say that much of my time will be spent outside the sensations of my body.

"Your eyes and ears won't serve you much in the passages," they tell me. "They will deceive you."

"How can I work without my senses?" I ask. "What can I count on without my feelings?"

It's very cold tonight — too cold to sleep — so I build a fire in the pit of my kiva. If I trust my commitment beyond my senses, re-hashing what I've heard, and commitment creates trust, this runs in a circle.

"That's what makes it so powerful." Xochina says as she enters through the stairway down into my kiva. "I'm not able to sleep either and I saw your firelight."

"What's keeping you awake?" I ask, happy for the company.

"I go underground in the Taquatsi soon," she answers. "The final passage and the hardest one."

"I'm just starting my work and everything seems hard."

"I know," she says, her eyes in the light of my fire are calming. This is such a difference from the people in my life before. With the other musicians, once our careers started to take off, it was never calm and meditative.

"Rather than relying on your senses," Xochina continues, "It is better to just use your determination."

"That's comforting," I say, "I can do that, for sure."

"Yeah, you can," she smiles. "From what my brother tells me, in America people get very determined."

"It's a way of life," I add. "Without it everything becomes complex."

"That's usually when the events of your life become tangled with feelings. You're supposed to keep them separate so you can see each one for what it is."

"That makes sense."

"Many times feelings are lying, but you can't know when. They're mixed with everything you're experiencing."

"Back home people use feelings as the truth."

"That's what I mean," she says. "Feelings are very strange that way and if you use them as truth, without examining them carefully, they can cause trouble. That's the greatest part about these passages. They challenge you so deeply that they cut all that away."

In the morning, Illanamiqt greets me at breakfast with a big smile. He must see a change because for the first time he behaves like he's counting on me. What a relief, I think; he can be tough when he wants to be.

"We're going to work you," he says with a twinkle. "We're going to work your past presence, your present presence and your future presence, your history, your story and your mystery."

Ezkaya is preparing breakfast and laughing at her husband's intensity. Xochina and Palqtlo listen and have a great time with the interpretation. This is a warm and loving family that has taken me in.

Illanamiqt looks at me, "The present is the only living moment," he says. "It's the only event that contains your life, your love, your power, your wealth of time and your reality. Our passages force you to come back to the present moment as your home."

I smile with anticipation as he says, "It's going to be enormously confining once we continue so you'll have the next few days off."

It's been a delightful morning and I look forward to the vacation. These people are charming and easy to live with. Later on in the morning I go looking for Xochina. Before coming to this village all I heard from others was how ridiculous my questions about my death experience were. Now I can speak with a person who was there and who talks about it as if it's the morning paper. Choti finds me as I walk and follows close by.

"Xochina is studying the Taquatsi." A group of gardeners tell me in the best way they can with hand gestures and sounds. "She's at the lakebed."

I hike through the farmed fields and out into the more barren land toward the lakebed. The ground is filled with insects running among the perfume of sage and juniper. The smell is compelling and I pause over and over again to study their microscopic world on the ground. The sand catches bits of sunlight and casts tiny rainbows across this universe. A beetle walks through it as if on some stage. There's such passion and purpose in the simplicity of the insect world . . . how seldom we notice it.

Choti stays close but her wild instincts maintain her independence. The village children follow for a little while with carefree abandon. The richness of this delicious world is their playground.

I arrive at the lakebed with the noon rain coming in a thunderous cloudburst. I see Xochina walking with cloth tied around her eyes on a trail that's scraped so deep into the ground and now filled with water. Her bare feet step slowly through the mud. It takes her at least a minute to go only a few yards. Every so often she stops and seems to be counting as she nods her head. In parts the water is halfway to her knees. I sit and watch, both of us soaking up rain. After an hour or so of walking, she sits and takes off her blindfold. I walk over to her and she just smiles, clearly in a trance she doesn't speak and motions for me to sit. I gather that this is the same path that thousands before her have walked for hundreds of years.

It takes about half an hour before she breaks the silence. "You want to ask me about Seattle," she says.

"For you it was a strange way for us to meet," she continues, "But this is a vast universe and it was as real as you and I sitting right here."

"Yes," I reply, "But what was it exactly . . . my mind has to understand before it will rest."

"You stepped outside time," she replies.

Attempting to look like I understand, she smiles over at me knowing I'm dumbfounded.

"Right at this moment you sit here and this is where you were sitting back then," she explains. "The sequence of time makes it look like it took time from that moment to this one but that is pure illusion. It has power over confining us when we're dedicated to maintaining the fallacy. With your death you killed the illusion and you stepped out of the spell. The deception profoundly ceased in that moment. When that happens, your list of priorities changes. Your life after that moment has tried to put the illusion back together again."

"Do you have to die for this to happen?" I ask.

"Not at all," she answers. "This is why we use the passages. They produce the same intensity as death."

"Why death?"

"Death is a reality check between lifetimes," she replies. "It breaks the spell, but then every time you fall asleep, you break the spell. Because your world has such an intense agenda, as a child grows up the spell is re-established and the connection is lost."

"You are speaking English well now. Have you been practicing?" I ask.

"I have been sitting with Palqtlo as he explains all of this for me to learn it in the English ways."

I feel relief in these answers — my body is even lighter as we walk back to the village. Sun replaces rain and dries our clothing as we walk. When we arrive at the village, Palqtlo informs me that he's going back to New Mexico to bring Adltleena and the baby.

"Now that you're staying," he explains, "I'm going to give them the blessing of being here too. I'll be back quickly, in a couple weeks and while I'm gone, Xochina will translate."

For the first time since being here in the Wirikuta, a sudden adjustment doesn't freak me out. Everyone notices this and smiles and nods and we part with a warm embrace. "Travel well," I tell him. "Give the truck a big hug for me."

Twenty Nine

Cocoon

I miss having Palqtlo nearby. I ask Xochina if she misses him too and she tells me that he's always with her — why should there be a missing piece?

I hold this answer for a long time. I go and walk the lakebed where my words are carved. I walk to the mountaintop and read my sign again. I catch a glimpse of what she means. I can relate to this with my mind but that is no longer enough. I want to know in my guts and in my heart.

My 'vacation' time is brief but appreciated. The instructions for the next passage turn out to be far less confrontational than the previous one, perhaps because I'm committed now. I meet the elders at dusk in a cluster of pinion and cedar. Xochina isn't with us and trying to find out why turns silly. The elders chuckle as I struggle to communicate — it's hard for me to understand their answers — but they're reading my words from my mind.

I finally understand that she's under the ground. Palqtlo's gone to New Mexico, Xochina's in the Taquatsi cavern and I'm struggling with no one to translate. I remember the words of one of the elders that I deciphered with incredible effort. "In this moment, there is no question and nothing familiar because in now there is no time. If you can get to this level of awareness then the tools you have at your disposal are courage, confidence, faith, discipline, commitment, and trust. Nothing will serve your life if it does not serve your moment."

It took hours for this information to be communicated but it will take years for the real meaning to sink in. It's like a long game of charades and the difficulty obtaining the information makes it more precious and profound. This is serious shit, I'm in the middle of nowhere, these instructions are going to save my life and I can't understand a single word they're saying. My mind swings back and forth. I watch opinions come and go like clouds in the sky, not one of them any more valid than the next, each one campaigning for its cause. The only tool left is faith.

The details of my next passage are revealed through this tedious process. It takes half a day using sign language, facial expressions and a hell of a lot of laughing. "Allow yourself to understand," keeps resounding in my head. "Allow yourself to." I get the distinct feeling that the absence of a translator was planned. It certainly allows me to work for the knowledge, and once I get it, there is no way I'll forget it.

This passage is the cocoon. It reproduces the time we spent in the womb. I will go through it over and over in the weeks to come and it will prepare me for the next passage. The cocoon is at the bottom of the deepest and largest kiva in the village. I'll be rolled up in a long cloth, unable to move. I will be blindfolded and placed between two large stones so that I can't roll. Since I cannot move, I cannot unwrap myself and I'll be forced to lie there motionless and blind. There will be drummers surrounding me drumming a constant heartbeat rhythm. As I become more at ease with this condition, the time I'm wrapped will increase.

We go down into the kiva in the afternoon of the third day and I'm rolled up. I made sure to move both my bladder and my bowels before starting. I'm fine with the wrap for about an hour, all the time thinking that this is nothing . . . then it hits me. I want to move and I want it right now but it's not happening. After struggling and calling out until I'm drained, all I have left is the ability to think and think and think. God — how tireless the brain is — I literally think of every detail of my life, past, present and future.

As I go through these playful and painful memories of my life, I've been instructed to recapitulate them — to turn them inside out and upside down. I'm to dig into the tiniest and most intimate details. Whatever supports me I'm to hold and whatever disrupts me, I'm to recapitulate. I'm to deconstruct and reconstruct, redesign, reassess and reframe. I'm to render every moment harmless and God knows I have the time — I'm not going anywhere.

They keep drumming like a tag team in shifts. It becomes thunderous and unpleasant at times and then barely noticeable at others. It all depends on how my mind is occupied. If I focus on how disturbed I am then it becomes worse. If I focus on the task at hand, the discomfort fades. I remember how annoyed I became with some people around me in San Francisco. This could disturb me for days and disrupt my work. I look at the war in Vietnam and the way that disturbs me. I see a positive use of anger when it stimulates right action and a negative use when it disrupts your life.

It becomes obvious after being wrapped up for a while that the purpose behind a lot of movement is avoidance. I want to move to change my focus, to avoid certain thoughts, to avoid confronting certain issues. I want to move to move and therefore do something other than what I should be doing. It's a tool we use to avoid mental, emotional and physical discomfort. Now that I'm forced to be still, I'm forced to deal with all this. This opens a set of tools I've never used before and I witness the resourcefulness of the mind.

They finally unwrap me and I go back to my kiva. I am to report back in the morning without having breakfast. Choti greets me at the door and we walk home together. I eat some cornbread and fall asleep without building a fire.

The next morning everything is the same as the day before with the wrap and the drumming. It goes well for what feels like a long period of time when suddenly it becomes quite irritating. A mild annoyance, an itch here and there sharpens my desire to move. This builds to a point where I am angry. I must move! I witness my mind as it sends these impulses. Then it pulls out the heavy messaging, telling me — I'll die if I don't move — I need to pee — I need to do something — anything. Witnessing this is a real trip and while it's obvious that it's avoidance, I can't stop it. It builds and builds and nothing changes, no one unties me and I'm freaking out.

I don't know how long it's been but I'm done. There's nothing I can do to change anything. I've tried it all. I've never felt this powerless before. My mind goes ballistic. I scream for a while but my voice is drowned out by the steady drumbeat. I try to bounce but I can't. I cry. The tears wet my skin and it itches. I scream until I lose my voice and I'm still just wrapped and stuck. I have to deal with what's inside of me.

I've cried at the drummers, yelled at them and for all I know they'll leave me here until I die. That does it — when this thought hits my brain fear takes charge and changes the game. The pressure in my head goes through the roof and I black out. I come to after some time and the drumming is still going on. Not one muscle is able to move except my breath, my eyes and my mouth — I am going to suffocate — this I know for a fact — still no one comes to rescue me.

I'm out of control. I piss in my pants — no muscles left to stop it. I'm ready to vomit but I don't. Slowly, an acceptance emerges as the drums continue and even soothe me a bit except that I'm now wet and shivering. Fair is not a factor here. This is real, this is the wild and there's nothing fair about the wild. Nature is about life and death and your strength determines your survival.

Along with this surrender, I see all the times in my life when movement was just a way of getting away from, rather than confronting my discomfort. I'm really uncomfortable now and there is no way to escape. Within what seems like forever, the drumming softens and stops. I hear and feel them moving the large stones from around me. They unwrap my cloth, pay no attention to the fact that I've pissed all over myself and take me to eat a large meal. After this, without a word, I return to my kiva and sleep from dusk to dawn.

In the morning, I just lay on my blankets. My brain is blank. I hear the children running through the village on their way to the river, singing and playing, calling the sun to come out and shine. I remember when I asked Palqtlo if the children actually thought this worked. He replied to my question with total sincerity. "They've never missed a morning, so how could anyone know? Why would anyone want to know?" I know for a fact that it raises the sun in each child.

Xochina is still underground in her final passage. Everyone is focused on her and I'm told this is a day of rest for me. That comes as a blessing because I'm out of fuel. I eat breakfast in silence and the rest of the day is filled with walking amongst nods, smiles, and grunts.

I recall one of the statements Palqtlo said to me on the journey into the Wirikuta. "The more you take charge of your life, the more you live your destiny." I've spent so much time in silence over the past weeks that I've run into a part of me that is delightful to be around.

The break is only for a day and I'm back for a second stage of the cocoon passage. I bet I'm the only one in a thousand years who's pissed himself but I'm determined not to do it again. The drummers are so clear and calm that nothing seems to bother them. Once again, I'm rolled in the cloth like a corpse and lay there motionless. The drumming begins and after what seems like a couple of hours, the anxiety hits again. I'm actually suffocating this time. I was certain I was going to breeze through. I've got to think clearly, but the intensity increases and my will becomes weaker. I try focusing on the present moment and flex my muscles one fiber at a time. I do whatever I can to stay calm and then suddenly I'm gone.

My body floats and I disappear into a deep trance. This is a comforting relief and I follow this sensation, falling deeply asleep. In my dream I am told, "Enter the space not yet occupied and then glide into the space that does not yet exist." When I awaken, the drumming has stopped and they're unwrapping me. I have difficulty finding one muscle that will function properly but they leave me to figure this out for myself.

When I get out of the kiva it's completely dark and there's a celebration taking place in honor of Xochina. She's completed the final passage in the underground in a very short time. It only took her two and a half days to get through the maze. She's finished all her passages and is now an adult. This is a huge day in the life of the Wirikuta and the festivities go late into the night.

I'm ecstatic to see her. Finally, a person I can talk to without colossal effort. We talk for hours.

"I've been wrapped too many times," I complain.

"Do you want to be great or just okay?" she asks.

"I want to be great."

"Then you'll have to tie your psyche to the Soul," she says. "And this is not easy. The body and the mind always try to slip away and lose themselves in distraction." She tells me a lesson she learned in the underground that applies to my life in the outworld. "Ultimately, the map to safety is not in the mind or in the memory," she explains. "It's in the willingness of the heart because in the greatest of times the head has no power. The courage of the heart is the only savior."

"So why the months of memorizing?" I ask.

"Why all the years of memorizing our life's experiences?" she answers with a question. "The head needs the details but the heart is the ultimate will. When we don't give the head proper details it becomes overwhelmed with doubt and fear, and this will spread. You must learn to master the Taquatsi — the underground — of your psyche, that's the place that blocks you with

260

demons of fear and doubt. The heart allows you to know the unknown, a place of no memories. Keep the brain occupied with memorizing the path and then allow your heart to lead the way forward. That's what I learned under the ground."

"God, it's great to have you back." I say.

"How do you like the cocoon?" she asks.

"I feel like a beginner," I say. "How long till I'm where you are in the process?"

"You mean finished?" she asks.

"Yeah."

"Well, if you go at your current pace, it should take you a year."

"What?" I ask, stunned by the answer. "I can't imagine being here for that long. What about my music? I need to get back to tell people that I'm okay or they'll think I'm dead. I can't stay here that long."

"I didn't say you have to do anything," she responds. "I just answered your question."

It is obvious that she's in a different time zone than I am. She's not the slightest bit concerned about all the commitments that I have and the details of life back in 'civilization'. My fears are so blatant to me at this moment that I burst out laughing. She joins in and a great laugh puts the night to bed.

I'm given another day of rest and then it's back into the cocoon nearly every day. It's grueling and we're at it for a month. It's hard for me to keep track of time without a calendar but I'm counting.

Every time they wrap me I go longer and I get better. The wooden drums beating around me are the same drums we dance to at celebrations. They fill my memories and have become friends — each with a personality. I really have no idea how many people are playing at once because I can't see, but it's like rolling thunder over my entire body. Sometimes I shake from their force and the rhythms are the same each day, very clean, extremely hypnotic and steady as a heartbeat. I wish I had a drummer like this back in the States. It takes me right out of my thoughts, right out of my concerns and delivers me to a focus unlike anything I've known.

I work to recapitulate all the events and relieve the burdensome stories in my memory. I reframe each event carefully and look forward to these cocooning sessions.

"Change your past to support your present," they tell me over and over.

Day after day, my senses strip away as I lay in a deeply calm state. Without the interruptions and stimulation of the senses it becomes clearer and clearer what a huge role the stories held in memory play in life and attitude. No matter how pleasant or unpleasant they may seem, there's a reason for them all.

When the senses are in charge, the desire to feel good at all times wins but when the senses are stripped away, a larger purpose emerges. Feeling good has to align with the larger picture and with the purpose of one's life.

When I ask Xochina how it works, she says. "It literally burns a new outlook, a new attitude, and a new opinion into your physical cells. It's not enough to simply know a thing — it must become an intuitive instinct and this takes constant repetition."

"Can't we just do this in our lives while we live them?" I ask.

"You will always avoid dealing with issues because they're uncomfortable and the effects will build up," she answers. "Over time this buildup becomes so powerful that you're enslaved by it. In your world you go through life without even knowing that you're a slave. To all of you this is just normal, but to us it's ridiculous. Why would anyone want to live in such a state of slavery?"

"How to avoid this?" I asked.

"Clear yourself every day in some way," she replies. "As children, we grow up strapped to that board, then we're educated in the ways that matter. We're shown how to relate to each other, how to marry each other, how to support, not compete with one another. To become adults we go through the passages and defeat our worst demons and then life just opens up, but we keep it open by being with it every single day."

Thirty

BURIED ALIVE

*A*t the end of several exhausting weeks of being wrapped in the cocoon, I am introduced to my next passage. In the process of cocooning I've been re-framing the moments that have led to the present. The goal of this next passage is to face death before dying. This is to establish enough courage to actually be living while alive. This passage, known as the burial, is much like cocooning, but it requires even greater surrender and forgiveness.

Palqtlo hasn't returned from New Mexico yet, so Xochina is still translating for me. She tells me that the lessons of a person's life are buried inside their identity. She says that this definition lives for generations within the body and is passed from parent to child. This is what medical science would call genetics.

"Family is extremely important in this world," she says. "When you create family, you tap into a body of spirit — it's a tribe that travels together through time."

I think about my family for the first time in weeks. Early on I would think of them every day, but now they seem to be here with me.

"The breakup of family in modern culture is the disintegration of your tribe," she continues. "This has consequences beyond this Earth."

"What about other relationships?" I ask, thinking about everyone in San Francisco.

"All relationships are based on this," she replies, "And the Earth is made richer by them. When you go into the burial, you can visit the reasons why you're with the ones you have. You'll ride spirit from your grave — it will show you why you exist."

"What do I ride?" I ask.

"The body of the spirit," she answers. "It's one of your subtler bodies, it's outside time."

"How do I get there?"

"You already have," she replies. "In the hospital in Seattle, but now it's time to learn how you can ride it at will. We call it riding the stallion and it is quite a ride."

I think on this for the rest of the day and in the evening I'm brought to the sweat lodge and told to be in silence. After sweating and praying in the aneepee, one of them hands me a wooden shovel. Xochina tells me to go to my letters in the lakebed and dig a grave. It's to be large enough to lie beneath the horizon. This takes me several hours, I've missed dinner and it's getting dark. At the moment I finish the job, Illanamiqt and several villagers show up and lay fresh cut cedar bows on the bottom of this grave. He seems excited — the first time I've seen him like this.

"Now climb into the grave of life," Xochina tells me. "Death will have no power over you."

"Look for the stallion of your life beyond the fears of your death," Illanamiqt adds. "When you find it, ride him through your visions and don't get thrown off and do not jump."

"Why a horse?" I ask.

"Walking takes too long, the visions are very large and the horse is a straight line runner," he answers with a faint smile.

They place a blanket on the bottom of the grave just over the cedar bows. I look at Xochina for support and lower myself in about two feet deep. I lie there and see nothing but the stars above me. A highly polished piece of obsidian river stone is put in each of my hands, a blanket placed over my entire body except for my face. One scoop at a time they carefully pour earth over my legs and torso. I begin slowly panicking — the sensation of being unable to move is far worse than in the cocoon. Sweet smelling sage and cedar bows are placed over my face until I can see nothing. Drumming begins right over my head for a brief moment, and then it all comes to an abrupt end as I lose total control, pissing, vomiting, and gagging until I begin to choke. In a flash, the weight's gone from my chest as the blanket with the entire load of dirt and bows raises from my body, pulled up by about ten attendants. Illanamiqt looks down at me with a huge smile revealed by the firelight. He and the others then leave without a word.

I painfully struggle out of the grave and onto the ground. I'm ashamed and embarrassed. I ask myself if I have failed and wonder if I get another chance? I just lay there next to the fire and I don't move until the morning sun warms my face. I walk back into the village with the feeling that everyone's staring at me but in fact no one pays much attention as I pass. All except for Xochina, she runs up to me with a huge hug.

"Congratulations," she exclaims. "You should be very proud that you lasted so long."

Certainly she's joking, I think. "Yeah right, I was only there for a few seconds," I say. "This must be a low record."

"No, that was good," she claims. "This is what happens to all of us."

That makes me feel better, like I can show my face now without embarrassment.

"Everyone's on their own journey in these passages," she says firmly. "This is your journey."

"So at least I didn't fail. Is there anything I should do differently when we go back?"

"When you get through the initial shock, there will be a rush downward as you leave the world of the senses. Just like when you're going to sleep and it suddenly feels like you're falling. This means that the senses have shut down before the brain goes un- conscious. The only way your brain has to explain this sensation is to tell you that you're falling."

"And this happens to everyone?" I ask.

"Yes, this is fairly common," she answers, "But during the journey downward into the quiet world, you must hold firm to remain conscious and clear. If you let the pressure take over, it will literally knock you out and you will just go to sleep. You want to remain alert."

"I need to absorb this in silence for a moment," I say. "I'm also hungry."

"We'll go to our place. Mother will feed you and let you be quiet. You need this."

When we arrive, breakfast is ready. Ezkaya is the kindest woman I've ever met and her warmth is contagious. In her pres- ence, I feel completely accepted. In the deep silence I've learned to uncover rich moments tucked in the mind beyond the brain . . . moments that don't appear any other way. She sits with a smile of total peace, never changing her expression. She just lets me be as if she's not even there.

In the evening I'm called back to the gravesite and placed the same way as before, covered with earth, feeling nervous the whole time. This evening I last about twice as long before my body reacts beyond my control. This surprises me, after the co- cooning I thought I was over my fear, but fear goes very deep I'm told later. It takes a long time to untie the knot of fear.

Night after night we go through this process and each time I extend the time further by a few minutes. Xochina says I'm mak- ing progress. Illanamiqt has endless patience and barely says any- thing as we go through the ritual each night. Every few days we take a break and don't get back together for several nights. This comes with great relief. I take full advantage by taking Horse and Choti to ride out into the wilderness as far as I can in a half-day and we come back the same way. Horse doesn't require me to guide him and when I get completely lost, I just give him the freedom to lead us back. I find that what used to frighten me has absolutely no hold over me now, but I'm still working on the burial.

Choti sometimes prefers riding in the sack on top of Horse and then other times loves to chase alongside. Weeks pass, I stop keeping track, but I see the seasons changing. It's later in the summer now and the nights are becoming colder. The sun is lower in the sky at noon and the harvest will be soon. Every day we gather corn, melons and squash. The melons and squash are eaten right away, while the corn and the beans are dried in the sun. Huge quantities are then placed into the largest kivas for winter storage.

I'm getting better and better with each burial and I must be lasting fifteen minutes by now, but still haven't gone into the 'falling' on the stallion. The 'falling', that's what Xochina calls it. Instead of surrendering into the infinity of the universe she says I'm holding on to some of my fears. I get frustrated at times thinking I'm in control. That's a hoot, being in control of anything out in this wilderness. Tirelessly, with each session, Illanamiqt and others take up positions around my gravesite. They tend to the ritual of drumming and singing for as long as I last. The drumming now strikes through my body like a hammer. One night, I remember Palqtlo's words. "When all is taken away from you and you are zero, your infinite mind will resort to its infinite power and your vastness will show you eternity." He called this the immortal authority that is dormant in each of us until we awaken it. And with that thought, the 'falling' begins . . .

For the first time, no longer bound by fears, I move beyond the senses and am finally falling freely. There's a memory of Illanamiqt's words, "If you maintain consciousness during the falling, you know hope and it guides you beyond the cycle of birth, fear, pain and suffering." And with these words I'm gone while still here. I'm floating in a vastness, crushed into nothing. Anywhere my mind goes, I am. I'm the power of my thoughts without the throws of my emotions. It's happening so fast, I'm whatever I want to be at any moment. I have freedom as long as I hold the focus and at the same time let it all go. I quickly learn that when a thought is troubling me, if I don't attach to it in any way, it dissolves and resolves. It doesn't have to be with me, it's just there like a cloud in the sky.

I find myself in the womb with many voices talking at once. One voice breaks on top of all the rest. "In the ninth month there's no comfort here. When you're born from this womb it's the death of life, as you've known it. It's a freedom from the crushing pressure of the womb, which was once your domain of total freedom. From this death you're born into a larger world where you live until that crushing pressure is once again upon you. Forced into another death that takes you through yet another birth, until you're once again in the freedom of another world."

Once again the stifling pressure collapses in on my grave turning my vision into the unbearable inability to move. In the darkness I notice a young injured hawk. I carefully pick it up and carry it back to Illanamiqt who takes the young hawk and squeezes it so tightly I'm sure it will die. He throws it into the air and it flies. "That's me," I think, and I'm enlivened once again. This is me; I too can fly out of here. My energy returns and I breathe without panic. I become satisfied with the simple movement of the blood through my veins, the movement of thoughts through my nerves. I note all the ways I'm still completely free, free to move even now. Then the earth moves beneath my hand, it quivers for a moment, stops and then does it again. I stop my breath to investigate more closely. I feel it again ever so slightly, but when I focus on it, it stops. Then I accept it and it begins again and this time it takes on the definite appearance of a horse's back. I struggle to move even one finger but I can't. As frustration rises the whole scene disappears, leaving me with nothing.

Panic steps in to be my grave partner once again. I scream at the panic, my heart pounding in rhythm with the drumming above me. "Get the hell out of here." And just like that the panic vanishes and I feel the quiver and the hair under my hand once again. I'd know this hair anywhere. I've ridden Horse hundreds of times and this is definitely his back. Inspiration races in my blood as I experience every gland of my body reactivating. The stones in my hands disappear as I plunge through the Earth, holding Horse's mane in the locked grasp of my fingers. We race together through the black Earth up and down. The stones in the Earth smash against my body as we pass through them. All my blaming is being beaten from me as we ride. In the intensity of my anger I see its source. These seeds of anger sit in the brain of the universe, waiting to become active. I have a choice at every moment — I always have a choice. When the attitude of my thoughts changes, the entire outlook changes simultaneously — an identical scene can become glorious or hideous. With every moment a choice is born and with every choice a moment is born.

We ride upward and surface into the bright starry night. Riding up to Illanamiqt, I slide from Horse's back and down beside him. He sits by my grave with the others still drumming. Without thinking I say in a loud whisper, "It's time to dig me up now." He turns and nods with his usual bright smile but does nothing. They just keep drumming. Looking at my grave, I know my body is in there and I'm not. I look down at my hand and it looks real. I reach out to touch Illanamiqt on the back and my hand passes right through him.

"No fear," whispers in my head. "Get used to the dream, for it is always right here."

I look at my other hand, shimmering in the light of the stars. Somehow I know that the awareness of this moment is going to be the rule of my life forever. I place my hands together and they pass through one another, I do it again and they don't. This is my key. This is the awareness of the illusion.

"Live the dream," whispers into my head. "Dreams wake up."

"We should bring the body back now," I say again without speaking.

"This is a good time," Illanamiqt responds now. "I have been waiting for you."

I feel light, incredibly light and powerful as the attendants lift the blankets and the earth from my grave. There before me is my physical body. It's beautiful, like seeing a best friend after a long absence. The attraction is intense and I cannot resist being drawn back in. I'm looking out through my eyes once again and I feel heavy and exhausted and sore as hell. I reach up and struggle to the surface of the grave. Illanamiqt and the attendants quietly slip away through the darkened night. All that remains is Xochina, sitting by the fire, which seems to be the same as it was when I went in.

"How long was that?" I ask, feeling like I've been gone for hours.

"Just longer than before," she answers. "This is great, you're improving each time."

"My God," I sigh. "You're telling me that this was just a little longer than before?"

"Just longer than last night." she replies.

"Just longer," I say out loud without judgment. "Just longer has to be good."

This was the breakthrough we were all looking for. This was the 'falling' and we continue the process, perfecting the journey until I'm in the ground for hours at a time. Week after week — they drill consistency into my brain, discipline, and discipline over and over again. I get tired of the routine and exhausted from the challenge but day after day I go through it. Over the weeks Xochina explains that each burial clears away a tiny bit more of the emotional slavery. "Your very base emotions protected you as an animal, but they do nothing for you as a human," she says. "As a human you must perceive beyond the chaos the sensations create."

When buried in the ground I reach a point that, whatever I fear, I will instantly create. By the same power, whatever I truly love without doubt I instantly manifest.

Xochina explains it in this way. "In our lives our emotions manifest their likeness. Fear creates the fearful and anger creates the angry. It works in the same way that you've experienced underground."

I absorb her words with great purpose.

"At times you fear more powerfully than you love, or you mix your desires up with doubt. With this you create struggle. This struggle becomes normal and then it brings comfort. You look for the struggle because it makes you feel like you're accomplishing something. This is the way of the out-world today, but it was not always that way. Our world does not identify with this struggle. We are the masters not the slave. We manifest joy through our work, not challenge." She pauses for a moment and looks fondly into the distance. "My father always says, the universe controls our diet, but we control the flavor of the food with our attitude and with our outlook."

Thirty One

TRUE FRIENDS

The passages of burial have ended and I hardly recognize myself. Over six months have passed since I've seen the out-world. Palqtlo is back with Adltleena and their daughter. He says the war is getting worse and that they count bodies every day on the news. It's like football with the score measured by numbers of dead soldiers. Though he's not been with me every day, he's been with me. The simplicity of the conditions here builds relationships that are far deeper. So much so that sometimes when I think, it's his voice I hear in my head, or when I speak it's Xochina's words I'm speaking.

The goal in the cocoon was stillness for recapitulation. The goal in the burial was to face the terror of death and discover the treasures buried in life beyond these emotions. My next passage is the final one. It's about emerging exalted from the depths of your Earthly life with your powerful treasures still intact. Managing the power of these treasures releases you from the slavery of the emotions. With this freedom your purpose connects to the moments of your life — to every breath, they tell me.

Early morning one day, Palqtlo and Xochina bring our three horses and take me out into the wild. They say it's in celebration of my graduation to the final passage and I find we have far more in common now.

"You've clearly grown here," Palqtlo says as we ride. "The Taquatsi is a lesson earned through your faith and determination. Life is like a sharp obsidian blade, handy if you use it right and disruptive when you don't."

"I look forward to this," I tell them. "I can't imagine how there can be any test greater than what I've already experienced."

"That's what I thought too," Xochina admits. "But don't hold that thought too long, or it'll cause you serious trouble in the darkness. The quicker you realize the 'black' is to be deeply respected, not worshipped or feared, but respected as a teacher, the faster you'll find your way through it."

The 'black' is the nature inside the caverns. Without light you aren't able to see one inch from your eyes — it closes down so solidly around you that at times you feel you're being physically crushed. I remember both experiences I had of it— on the way into the Wirikuta and once when I tried to leave.

"This will bring out all the faith that guides you," Palqtlo says. "Your life will depend on this guidance every moment in there."

We ride to the top of the dry lake mountains to look over my preparation area for the passage. This is the same mountain I climbed during my first passage. I'm nostalgic on Horse with Choti in my bag seeing my pledge still carved into the desert below.

Xochina twists sideways on her horse and looks at me, "There were times when I wondered if you were going to make it," she confesses.

"Thanks for not telling me before," I reply.

She laughs. "You were so negative when you first arrived."

"And I'm not really a negative person," I tell them. "You should meet some of the people back home."

"No thanks," she says.

Palqtlo pulls to a stop, "That's the hardest thing to comprehend," he says. "When I first arrived in what you call civilization, I could not fathom that your elders were sending their children to kill and die. This is the reason our ancestors isolated our village."

"We would have been overrun too if they had found gold or silver near here," Xochina adds. "We have none of the fantasy wealth metals to attract the obsessed so we've been left alone so far."

"What's that supposed to mean?" I ask.

"Somebody's going to find us someday — you have planes now. You have cameras photographing the entire world for the oil under the ground."

"You amaze me," I say. "For people living in the middle of absolutely nowhere you certainly keep up to date."

"That's my job," Palqtlo reminds me. "We need to reach the world before the barbarians destroy it all. Many people have been lost over the decades searching for gold and silver back in these Copper Canyons, but they've never made it this far in."

I turn to Xochina and ask, "Do you think I'll have a problem getting through?"

"Not at all," she replies. "It will be very difficult, but you have a confidence that will keep you going."

"But even when your preparation is complete," Palqtlo tells me. "You'll come face to face with the raw terror that fills all of us in the Taquatsi."

Xochina looks at him very quickly, as if he's just spoiled the mood. I look at her and we're all quiet for a moment as our mood resets itself.

"Listen," he continues. "I have to tell you because I've lived in your world and now you've lived in mine. I know how you've been trained to think so in the middle of the Taquatsi you'll be certain God has abandoned you."

Xochina looks at him sternly again. "Palqtlo, why are you saying this? This does not have to happen."

"Xochina," he responds with gentle respect, "you've never lived in his world. This is the way they treat God there. They blame God for what they have or don't have in their lives."

"He's right," I tell her.

We go to silence, the mood softens and we share an unspoken awareness. We've come up the mountain today to prepare for something beyond anything and I disengage my confidence in order for new information to gather. This is good I've discovered — good to lose some confidence to get it back even stronger.

"Our father has also seen your world," Palqtlo says. "His visions show that we're fast approaching an end game." He dismounts and walks beneath a large pinion pine. "In order to avoid this, we need conscious people in large enough numbers to balance the huge greed and rage."

"That's what you're preparing for," Xochina adds.

"That's becoming clearer," I answer, "but I haven't thought about going back for a couple of months. At this moment there's no reason for me to go back there."

"Except we have a job to do," Palqtlo reminds me. "That was the reason for your coming here in the first place."

"Well, at least I have some months to prepare for this last passage. Just thinking about going back there brings up emotions."

"What emotions?" Xochina asks.

"The emotions of living in that culture," I tell her.

"That's the point," Palqtlo reminds me. "This is why the Taquatsi is so defiant and important. In your world there's far too much time studying logical ideas. Very little time is spent on the magical relations that allow a culture to prosper with successful families raising and loving children. Right now they only compete for money and send children to kill and die."

"That's why we have this job to do," Xochina says.

I smile and say, "There's massive prosperity here in this simplicity."

"That's how our community has lived and prospered for centuries. We need to take our place in this world and spread these teachings." Palqtlo reaches out and touches his sister's shoulder with reassurance. His consistent support for everyone is so incredible. I most admire that quality in him. "This is what is missing back in the States," I say pointing to the two of them.

"Yes," Xochina says.

"This is family," I hold out my arms.

"This is nature and we love being natural," Xochina chuckles as she speaks.

"The Taquatsi becomes very personal," Palqtlo reminds me. "Personal can become negative or positive however you respond."

"How long do I have to prepare?" I ask.

"As long as you want," Palqtlo says. "When you're ready to make the journey you will know."

"Knowing you, I'd say the preparation will take about two months," Palqtlo says. "It's a combination of physical, mental and emotional training."

"The length of time you are in the blackness is what gets to you," Xochina explains. "You and Palqtlo were only in it for a few hours coming in here. In the Taquatsi you'll be in it for a few days. It changes all your perspectives, distorts and unravels your identity, tests your strength and wants to throw you away."

"Great sales pitch," I respond laughing.

"What's a sales pitch?" Xochina asks.

Palqtlo looks at her and laughs. "He's making humor," he tells her.

How great it must be to be 16 years old and never been sold to and never needed to buy.

"Taquatsi requires more concentration than you've ever known," she exclaims as if the previous conversation wasn't important. "I know because I've just been in there and you'll need help too."

"What kind of help?"

"Guides from your faith," Palqtlo says. "You'll definitely meet your guides and animal helpers in there."

"I've met a few already," I say looking at Horse and Choti.

"When you memorize the map of the Taquatsi," Xochina says, "the head remembers the details and the heart remembers the will. Feathers are especially helpful for calling on guidance. They give you the wings of guidance; they are the witness of your higher guidance . . . like angels in your culture. They help you see like the eagles do."

"We'll get you some to work with," Palqtlo says. "The feathers of the Wealika — the eagle — will let you fly beyond time whenever you get stuck in the 'black'."

"Is this for real?" I ask.

"Completely," he answers. "They carry the memory of flight and carry you above wherever you are to see from a great elevation and know what's happening all around. We take them from a living bird to keep the life energy of the feather intact. The tracker has to approach the Eagle in full sight and slowly take just one feather from the tail. It's a gift from the Eagle and it then immediately takes flight to bless the action."

I've watched individuals come back from acquiring a feather. They have the most concentrated look I've ever seen.

We ride back from this mountaintop visit and play the whole way, allowing our horses to lead. They know exactly where to go and how fast they want to go. It's such a peaceful way to ride.

Illanamiqt has explained to me how to work with power animals in Taquatsi. He said it's moving into the treasures of your human power and your incarnate past. Asking for assistance from these creatures is asking to relive the lives when you were the same as they are now. These two animals I'm with, Horse and Choti, have given me tremendous power.

We ride near the lakebed where the village children are playing with the frogs, which are very sacred creatures. "Frogs represent the courage we all seek in this lifetime," Xochina explains. "They represent the courage to go through great change. The children become very excited when someone prepares for Taquatsi. They spent days with me and I remember when I was young and Palqtlo was preparing. We would meet him almost every day."

It's hard to imagine Palqtlo preparing for these passages. He seems as if he's always been who he is. I think of when we first met and that thought leads to thinking of Tex.

"She's getting famous now," Palqtlo tells me. "Her music is on the radio."

"Wow . . . she finally made it," I respond.

"She never dropped the addictions though," he adds.

All evening I review what's been told to me about Taquatsi and how it brings out the real treasures. The stars shine brighter tonight as I walk through the village, lost in my thoughts of being inside the 'black'.

The entrance to the Taquatsi is at the waterfall at the end of the river where I placed the earth from my desert carving. When it's time I'll float down the river and plunge into the cavern. I'll navigate for three days or so in the black. This is done from memory and intuitive trust. The memory is the mental map I'll learn over the months and the intuitive trust will come from the inside. I'll train with the same map carved into the lakebed, following the thousands who have walked this path for hundreds of years.

I'm anxious but comforted by the fact that Xochina has just gone through it. There are countless wrong turns available and if I become lost, I could never find my way out.

With the next morning daylight, I begin my months of total dedication. I spend a lot of it in silence except for questions and instructions. Xochina walks me through the cavern map and is available for all my questions as she watches me many of the days. The children are always near there. They're keenly interested in my study, knowing they'll do this someday.

I study the map from the top of the mountain, remembering when I met Xochina doing this all those months before. I sit in concentration with my eyes closed and review every possible turn over and over again. I walk the map with my eyes closed, sometimes blindfolded, and constantly installing the steps and turns into memory. I push myself to go further and further without looking.

This lakebed map has been prepared for centuries and thousands of youngsters have walked through these months of preparation. I measure the distances of each step with the sense of my predecessors. Over and over again I memorize the number and measurement of each footstep. I walk the lakebed day after day — memorizing the map — forgetting it all — memorizing it again.

I'm told that if I stumble and roll, it will misplace my position and I must retrace the stumble and begin from that exact point in my mind. If I sleep, I must awaken and remember the exact step I'm on. I move through with precise concentration — it must be like defusing a loaded bomb.

I'm taught movements of power to restore my energy and focus in the cavern — Illanamiqt teaches me the moves. "If you really want to achieve something — you must consider it deeply over time," he says. "Your out-world is scattered and you teach your children to be scattered. No one has the time to focus and allow themselves to have what they truly desire. In the Taquatsi, you'll be taught to receive what you so deeply desire." He laughs and his eyes always dance.

I train the pathway into my subconscious to react with instinct. I know if doubt comes up it can kill me, and other negative emotions will cloud my memory of the path. This is just like life, only we assume the stakes are not this high.

"The stakes are equally as high," Illanamiqt reminds me. "It disconnects your spirit when you sleepwalk through life."

Thirty Two

TAQUATSI

Two months of preparation go by, as Palqtlo predicted. I study every step with and without the blindfold. I count, measure and calculate and I'm now ready — a little scared — but ready. On the morning of my passage I prepare myself without anyone around, focusing on the memory map. I've notified the village of my decision to go under with complete confidence. I use the sweat lodge to clear any last debris from my body and feel light for the first time since I began the training.

It's the winter of 1968 and the water of the Taquatsi River is extremely cold. I go in naked with my clothes in a large water-tight gourd to keep them dry. Lowering myself into the river with the gourd tied around me with a rope, the cold water takes my breath away. This is similar to every other morning when I bathe, but at this moment it seems colder. I float down a few hundred feet looking around at the world — the last view of this place for a while when . . . wham! The bottom drops out of the river and I'm falling in a bubble of water. I dare not breathe, though I want to gasp. Then just that fast, I hit the pool at the bottom of the falls and sink under. Rising to the surface, I look up through the water at the blue sky and sunlight filtered through the falls. Wow, this is only the beginning.

My gourd is bobbing near the shore of the pool. I dry off as best as I can and get dressed. My hands are shaking so much from the cold tension that I can barely tie my pants. Now I'm dressed and a sense of euphoria comes over me. It's an excitement about the path ahead mixed with confidence from my training. This stays with me as I walk the few hundred yards to the end of the light. I'm counting the steps, remembering the map firmly in my mind. As I turn the first corner and enter the 'black', I get my first visit from panic. I stop and breathe deeply, confronting it slowly, relating to it as a friend though I know it can turn ugly on me at any moment. I start walking again and continue to count my steps, seeing nothing of what's in front of me, but seeing the map like a TV screen in my mind.

"Don't become overly confident or be seduced by doubt . . . walk in the middle," these words from Palqtlo echo in my mind. "When you walk the path in between you will walk your map with balance."

I have no idea of how much time is passing. All I do is walk and count, turn and calculate. When I get tired, I rest, but try not to sleep. I'm not ready to test that part of my training just yet. Deep inside the Earth in the pitch-black silence, my senses are beginning to tighten just so slightly.

I know I'm fully prepared. I heard Palqtlo and Xochina speak of the severity to be encountered and the need for constant balance. The demon of fear and doubt is just behind me now . . . it's very close. There are times when I feel its lukewarm breath brushing the hairs on the back of my neck. I continue with deep concentration, counting and stepping. It will cost me my life if I fall under the control of that demon . . . I work gently and consciously to slide through it.

I take out my eagle feathers to hold for strength. A serpent flies out of the feather's tip and winds its way through the 'blackness'. I was warned that the mind's hallucinations would come to me in the dark. It beckons me to follow and I do when I suddenly realize that with this distraction, I've stopped counting. I sit down to remember where I am in the map.

It's happening too fast —I've started counting breaths not footsteps. I drop to the ground and bury my face in the sandy earth wishing for Choti to come and find me. Slowly, I gather where I was in the count and the terror calms.

I hold the count firmly . . . I can no longer differentiate whether these images I'm seeing are real or head-trips. They have to be head-trips — there's no light to see. I'm also hearing sounds. I focus on the count and the map. The echoes of my breathing and moving seem to go on forever now. "Drop all your senses," Xochina warned me. "They'll distort your map." My body's sweating and shaking.

As I walk and count, beyond any sense of rational time, the mental vision of the map is disrupted by a figure in front of me. It's my mother and I feel comforted as I walk toward her. "Mom, can you help me?" I ask. "I'm glad to see you."

She turns to me without expression and says, "Don't forget where you are."

I realize it's a mind projection and I've gone some distance and lost count again. I try to reproduce the run in my mind when I see her again. "Can I do this Mom?" I ask. "The map is falling apart."

I kneel down and hold the ground for security — her image disappears. I feel the deep grooves of my memory fading. I carved them over all those months and now they're slipping from my grasp. Huddled in the total darkness, my map has all but disappeared. I'm alone and afraid to move for the first time in months.

I hear movement though I've lost all sense. I look through the 'black' and see Tex, walking away from me in the distance. I know I was warned to abandon my senses, but I have to rely on something . . . at this moment I have nothing else. I follow after her and begin feeling better about the journey, when suddenly she turns toward me with rage in her eyes.

"What the hell are you doing?" she screams out.

"Following you," I reply. "It's okay."

"Don't follow me . . . I'm lost," she warns. "You've got to get the fuck out of this place."

"I'm trying," I answer.

"You son of a bitch!" she yells. "What do you mean trying?"

"I mean I'm trying to get out of here."

"To hell with your trying, man. Are you worthless? You either do it or you die. Is that clear? You have a slight chance to make it if you don't give up. Are you willing to take that slight chance?"

Her words find a thread of connection here among my deep sense of loss. I've been diminished to the tiniest most insignificant piece of dust on the floor of an underground cavern in the middle of the Earth. I experience the sensation of a child in the womb as I start crawling without a thought of the map or my direction. The only thought I have is of safety, and crawling is safe . . . that is what I think.

As I move slowly along on all fours, I'm certain that this carefulness will be the answer. I'll crawl until I can't crawl any more, that's no problem. I'll just keep crawling I think as a silly fatalistic attitude slides over me like a blanket. There was no way I was going to make it through this cavern anyway so why should I even try. Who am I to do this anyway? Just some guy who can't make it out of the Earth . . . why try? I'll just keep crawling, that's good enough. I'll crawl till I die and that's all . . . I'll just die.

A rocky ledge gives way beneath me and I fall several feet to another floor below. As I hit, I hear a rib crack and my chest fills with fire as I lay with the wind knocked out of my lungs. Time stops and I merge into languish for a moment.

"Shit," I think very quietly to myself, "I blew the map, where's the fucking map?" My breathing is very shallow to decrease the pain and I am motionless and fall asleep. After some time I awaken to the sensation of hot moist breath on the back of my neck and then hear a voice. "You are pathetic," it says just like that. Clearly I know I heard this and it's not an illusion in my head.

I struggle with my breath and whisper. "Can you get me out of here?"

"Why should I do that?" the voice asks. "You've given up and expect to live from sympathy."

"What do you mean?" I ask.

"Emotions and senses have become your boss," it answers coldly. "This is evolution my friend and the survival of your pathetic nature does not serve the universe. It's as simple as that."

In pain and barely able to speak . . . blind, cornered and broken . . . I don't stand a chance against these odds. So what the hell . . . why hold back . . . let's go out on fire. "Fuck you!" I yell as it echoes over and over throughout the Taquatsi. "Come and get me, but I won't make it easy!"

My hands grip the sandy cavern floor in a state of rage — determined not to give up any of the dirt between my fingers. It's all I know and all I have, but I stretch to find the map — where's the memory? The emotions and hallucinations have erased it. My face presses into the sand that pushes between my teeth. "Fuck you," I spit and in this moment I hear the voice of Illanamiqt in front of me. With all this rage ravaging any image beyond its grasp a wisp of faith asks me to listen.

"Don't follow anyone now," Illanamiqt warns me. "This is your time and you'll prevail by faith. Know this in each step you take and the map will return one step at a time. Know this in each breath you take and the courage will carry you one breath at a time. You can't penetrate the moment until you know you can."

The fire in my ribs and lungs is excruciating as I roll over to find a more comfortable position . . . every move is rocked with pain. "Don't move until you know," he continues, "and don't stop moving once you start. Force all knowledge to come to you through your knowing. Faith moves this entire mountain, but without it even stones are far too heavy to lift."

My breath's barely coming back as I listen. I see various parts of my life swirling on the blackness around me. Some of the parts give me strength and others defeat me.

"Choose to follow only that which encourages you," his voice echoes through the cavern.

"As much as you want to give up and run away, remember one thing, your death will not make anything happen." His voice gets louder. "Hold on to every moment until you know. Make yourself know everything once again."

The voice stops and I feel the breath of my demons and I still can't move very well.

"It looks like you're done," it says coldly.

With all the strength I can muster, I move my left hand from under me. The pain in my chest rolls over my shoulders too. I manage to pull both arms to my sides and push up into a sitting position. My breath is short and panting, but I maintain its steadiness. It's one thing I can rely on in this moment. I slowly stand up with the most intense fire in every muscle.

I think of my father as I struggle to stay up. What a man, he had every reason to give up on life and refused. "Life is fragile, but you don't have to be timid," he would tell me.

Suddenly Illanamiqt stands in front of me. "Don't follow the past — learn from it. Take only the steps you know in your heart and connect them to your breathing. Your lungs are there to hug your heart, to reassure it with each breath . . . know that you know."

I begin screaming silently beyond my ear's capacity to hear and my mind's capacity to relate. "I — WILL — NOT — GIVE — UP . . . I KNOW I WILL PREVAIL . . . I WILL!

I walk and stumble painfully forward and the map appears from my heart. There is plenty of running water in Taquatsi and sometimes the sound is deafening. I'm weak from the lack of food, but drink the water. I feel a deep connection with Horse and Choti, with Illanamiqt, Ezkaya, Palqtlo and Xochina as I'm drawn through the darkness in pure steps of faith. This faith is imprinted with the love I've felt working with everyone in the Wirikuta. It's written on these walls of the Taquatsi and when I touch them I know exactly where to step and where to turn. I sense thousands of young teenagers that have gone through here before me. I feel Xochina. I experience every one of them as if they're me. The map unfolds in these senses more subtly than the five senses. I'm not counting and I'm not actually remembering . . . I know. It's the way and I'll walk until I emerge successfully. It is guaranteed.

All of a sudden Choti is rubbing against my leg as I walk. I grasp the now broken eagle feather in the sweat of my hands and walk alongside my good friend. Every step of my life and death exists in this moment. Every step is one of total faith and absolute certainty.

I emerge from the Taquatsi. It's evening but the light is too bright for my eyes. There's a combination of images before me as I slowly regain my senses. I see the outline of Illanamiqt standing in front of me and hear what sounds like the entire village greeting me.

I walk straight up to Illanamiqt and say to him, "That was you in there."

"No," he answers, "that was You in there."

Thirty Three

LEAVING HEAVEN

"You are not to stay here," Illanamiqt explains to me later in the evening. "You've completed your tasks and we must return you to the out-world."

This news sweeps in like abandonment, but the reality is that I'm listening to a great teacher who has guided me with precision. Therefore, I listen with the respect that is due and knowing this will be.

"All contact after you leave here will be through the spirit-body only," he continues. "To come back and forth would turn you into an oddity, not a teacher and we'd become the attraction. You are now to find the great one you've been destined to meet in this life. We will practice spirit-connection for the next few weeks while you are still here to make certain that it works accurately and you are comfortable in the discomfort."

In my guts this is the only place I can imagine living, but I don't have the time in this moment to process the sensations. All night we sing, drum and celebrate my graduation. I find out that I took longer than anyone they could remember, but then again, I'm the first 'outsider' to ever be here and the only outsider to ever navigate the Taquatsi.

They're telling me that by the end of the fourth day, the elders began spirit-connection in an attempt to track my location. When they saw that I was close to the exit point and going in the right direction they decided not to come in after me.

"Do you mean you could have found me in there?" I ask Ezkaya.

"Absolutely," she says, "Spirit leaves a trail. You can even track someone through multiple incarnations."

Everyone's at this celebration, even people I've barely seen in the time I've been here. I'm welcomed as never before. They've always been pleasant, respectful and loving toward me, but this evening they are engaging me like I am one of theirs and the language difference doesn't even show.

The words I know in their language are being used over and over and the larger conversations happen without words. I approach everyone, even the people I've never spoken to. They've all been through what I just completed.

I find Palqtlo's wife and share my gratitude. She was the angel who rescued me from my life. It was her wisdom that convinced me to come here. I find her among some elders and say to her, "I don't know exactly how long I've been here, but I want to thank you for causing all of this."

"It was your destiny," she says as she gives me the biggest hug. "You've been here for eleven months."

"I completely lost track," I respond. "All I can tell is that the seasons have changed a few times."

"Nice isn't it?"

"The Taquatsi was more than I ever expected," I tell her. "At one point I really thought I was not making it through."

"We all did that — mistakes are the most important part of success and progress," she explains gently. "In your culture mistakes are judged poorly, but in ours they're welcomed as a sign of progress."

"I lost sight of the map in my head." I tell her. "My focus fell apart and I was completely lost."

"You learned something very important from that experience," Xochina says joining our talk. "Your head is only there to support the heart by explaining the details. Your heart is the true seat of your power."

"Back where he comes from." Adltleena explains to Xochina. "Everyone uses their head for everything. The head makes all the rules."

Ezkaya joins us, "When a people are ruled by the head they live in a dangerous place."

Having heard our conversation from a little distance, Palqtlo puts his arm around my shoulders. "Until your heart took over, you were lost in the heavy judgment of your demons."

"I've dealt with that level of self-judgment," I explain.

"In the Taquatsi, that judgment turns to terror because of the amplification down there," he says. "That's the way the passages work, they amplify and magnify."

"That's why we all go through the Taquatsi," Adltleena says. "We're not really human until we open the heart."

"Did you go through what I did, all the demons and terror?" I ask them.

"Everyone does," Palqtlo answers. "We all reach the limit beyond our faith and meet our fear. You just had all that 'civilization' stuff to deal with." He starts to laugh.

"I got really angry at the end and it started to clear."

"You became determined," Adltleena adds. "That's the wise and focused use of anger."

"That determination supports the heart," Xochina says. "It heats the heart with passion and turns to compassion."

"Nice trick," I say.

I look at these siblings of mine and then around the rest of the evening's gathering. This is reality. This is the way God intended life to be lived. Living for the good in each other. Ignoring the worries that put us at odds and picking up the emotions that put us together. Living for each other. I feel from these people that I'm important here.

Illanamiqt joins us and looks at me with those gentle, piercing eyes and says, "Your only obstacle now is doubt. It will still come up from time to time. Some days this will all seem like a dream. When your life becomes complex this will seem far away." Looking very content he says. "Doubt is the curse of your modern world."

"At this moment I'm so grateful to be here and not in the outworld." I tell him. "I dread the idea of ever returning out there."

"Your brain has opened now," he says. "You can visit us whenever you want."

"I won't have to if I stay," I respond.

"This is not a choice," he calmly states. "You came here to learn, now you must go back to teach."

I acknowledge what he's saying with a nod as tears roll down my cheeks. I look around at everyone who's gathered around us now. I've become the center of attention at the celebration.

Illanamiqt continues addressing me for everyone to hear. "Hope is a ray that shines in the darkest hours. It's always there but it remains hidden until you connect with your heart. This connection is the commitment you've found in the Taquatsi. You discovered it in your darkest time. You discovered it when you committed to being You." He pauses and looks around at all of his friends and relatives. "Taquatsi gives you that gift in the pitch darkness where the solution's visible only in that tiny light of hope. This light is so small. We've all been to that altar and we forever remember its truth. You have been there to see that tiny light through the eyes of your heart. That light isn't visible to the head."

He gives me a huge hug and everyone applauds and walks around me with kisses and hugs. The tears running down my face are the sweetest ever. I keep looking at Palqtlo, Adltleena and Xochina.

"There it is," Xochina whispers. "The word is Maraakame — human consciousness that's connected to all things. This is who we are to each other."

Thank you, I think to myself, knowing she will hear this as I nod.

"You're welcome." She replies with her normal mammoth smile, revealing her beautiful white teeth in the darkness of her skin.

The celebration goes on for a few days with food and occasional rest. I see people taking naps all around the village, which has turned into a party town. There's drumming constantly as everyone has left what they might normally do and made this the event in their lives. I've been adopted.

After days, Illanamiqt comes to me and says, "You must fly in the world, so stay for one moon, and then you'll go back."

"I'll do this just like I did Taquatsi," I say. "But just like that it won't be easy."

"It'll be necessary for you to find the 'great man' when you reach the out-world," he tells me. "Without this you'll emerge from this dream and like a dream it will be forgotten over time."

"Who's this?" I ask.

"This great man will teach you to hold these treasures," he says without answering me.

"Who is this 'great man'?" I ask again.

"He'll appear," Illanamiqt replies.

"And how long till the world's ready to hear?" I ask.

"The world will be ready in the time of no time, but not until then," he says vaguely, "that's in about thirty years the way they measure it."

I'm shocked. I ask him what this means, but he goes off amongst his peers and makes it obvious to me that I'm not to ask any more.

Later that day, I come upon Ezkaya resting with Adltleena. "What's the time of no time?" I ask them. "Illanamiqt used these words today."

"What did he say this for?" Adltleena asks.

"He said that in the time of no time, the world will be ready to listen."

"He means when technology moves faster than the heart to control it," Adltleena answers.

"This is far away," I say.

"Not so long," Ezkaya gently tells me. "When you feel lost, you're believing the power of the illusion." She rests her kind hand on my knee, "Why believe that it's a long time . . . believe that it's a good time, my son."

When she says *my son* it soothes my concern about leaving. "Mother is saying, be a witness not a victim," Adltleena says and hugs me.

By now everyone's sweetly tired from the days of celebration and they're napping everywhere I look. Finding Choti hanging out by my side, I take her and look for Horse to take a ride up the mountain.

Over the remaining weeks I make this journey nearly every morning. I receive the company of nearly all the village dogs and Horse. Many days Palqtlo, Xochina and Adltleena accompany me. Riding along the river, I'm reminded of floating down into Taquatsi. Galloping up the mountain reminds me of the very first passage. My letters are fading into the desert, but are still readable. These rides refresh my consciousness with the inspiration of incredible people, all close to my own age. I guess I'm 22 now, not certain of what month it is. We sit around at the top of the mountain and chat about real life.

"What can I do now if I have to wait for so long before being heard?"

"Do whatever you do. That's not important. Hold your vision so that it's impossible to ignore, that's important," Palqtlo says. "People are going to get high just being around you if you can maintain this."

"What will I be able to do to maintain this?"

"You must become unshakable and unmovable," Adltleena answers. "I've lived with your societies and I know their widespread use of guilt. This guilt is sticky and it's easy to fall into its trap. Most of your old acquaintances will have trouble with your change."

We're an ancient culture with ways from eternal time," Palqtlo says. "Adltleena and I live our lives to unify ourselves. This is not about being a better person, this is about being a person period."

"You'll find that you must refresh yourself each day," Adltleena reminds me. "To tolerate the stress of your modern world, you'll have to create Taquatsi in your mind every day."

"For this reason you'll need to meet the 'great man' like Father says," Xochina explains. "He will teach you a discipline that will hold up in the pressure. I haven't been to the out-world, but I remember what you were like when you first arrived."

Everyone laughs at her point. Day after day we gather. We're beyond the feeling of love or bonded siblings; we're just many bodies with one mind, held in life by the same heart.

"The human opportunity," Adltleena reminds us, "is about reducing life to a simple process."

"In the 'out-world' you find the inhabitants unwilling to let go of their personal emotional chaos," Palqtlo adds. You must confront this unwillingness. It's a simple fear."

"Here we're blessed that Taquatsi teaches us to face this fear," I say. "What can we use in the out-world?"

"Consistency," he answers. "In your culture the processes become more complex and lack consistency."

"I've been there," I say. "This causes the purpose to be ruled by the process, your job, your possessions or your relations."

"That sounds really quite deadly," Xochina exclaims.

"And that's why people are into so much addiction."

"In a pure culture, we have kept the process of life simple," Xochina explains. "How could you have it any other way?"

And so we lie about and talk about how the out-world needs our help to change. We reduce it to its fundamentals and spend this time to develop our plan. I remember what they say as their lines of simple wisdom play over and over in my mind.

"The messenger of the soul is intuition."

"How completely you're able to trust the self is the measure of your connection."

"See beyond the illusions of this Great Reflection."

"You must take the step of risk with the strength of faith."

"When you see your reflection in everything, life begins."

On many of these days the little children chase us out into the wilderness. They run free in the countryside, afraid of nothing and extremely alert. On foot these children scale the mountain as if on an escalator.

"It's because they have no other thoughts in their heads," Palqtlo reminds me. "They're totally focused on the job at hand. Remember the elders on your first experience here telling you — when I walk up the mountain I'm only walking up the mountain."

"Well, you can take me out of Wirikuta," I tell them, "but you'll never take the Wirikuta out of me. The 'seed' Illanamiqt has spoken of is about to be planted."

Thirty Four

THE BEGINNING

On the morning we leave the Wirikuta, the entire village joins us for a grand sendoff, which becomes even more festive than when I arrived here eleven months ago. Not surprisingly, there is little sadness. Xochina even tells me, "I will not miss you — you are always here," as she holds her hands on her heart.

My experiences these months have taught me that we're always with each other, not just as an idea or a strong memory, but we are actually with each other. And when we aren't experiencing this, we are simply ignoring what is in fact very real. Of course, Choti and Horse are here and it's challenging not to miss them already but I make it through, hugging them one last time. Those two are so inside each moment. Having animals around us at all times is clearly vital to our health and happiness . . . they keep us present.

"Sadness is when we block our ability to experience our oneness . . . our union," Ezkaya says, with her hand on my shoulder. She can see my difficulty in parting from my four-legged friends who have been so loyal and probably saved my life on several occasions. When we have said everything there is to say, hugged everyone there is to hug several times over, we wave, turn around and walk into the total darkness of the cavern leading us from this paradise to the out-world. I chuckle remembering my attempted escape all those months ago when I tried to run from this heaven and back into the familiar hell of civilization. What an illusion our brain makes up of perception and perspective.

The trek out of the Wirikuta is now the four of us as a family; Palqtlo, Adltleena, Aramara, and I. We take a little more time walking through the dark — this extra time allows us to savor it and take the clarity back with us. At the opposite opening to the cavern we scale the wall using two ladders that have been stored inside. Palqtlo arranges them with one that stands upright from the floor of the ledge to halfway up the thirty-foot wall. The other ladder he hangs from a rope at the top. This is the same rope we used to lower ourselves down when we were coming in. He has set this whole thing up by climbing the rope hand over hand all the way to the top. When the three of us are done climbing the ladders, Palqtlo secures both ladders back inside the cavern and climbs the rope once again as if it's nothing.

When we arrive back at the adobe structure half submerged in the hillside, the one where we had cleansed ourselves on the trek in, I feel like we're meeting another one of my teachers from the past. It is here I experience my first obvious comparison between old and new patterns of thoughts and feelings. It's as if a young child walked through this building, on the way in to the Wirikuta, and now an adult is walking out eleven months later.

The same deep fragrance of sage and cedar greet us from the open walls and this time it's mixed with a little fuel oil smell. There sits the great friend 'truck' looking like a loyal dog on a master's front porch. Palqtlo is quite the mechanic I discover and even though the truck has been sitting all these months, we jump-start it by popping the clutch after he has primed the fuel lines and carburetor with sufficient gasoline.

Everything passes by like a life in reverse as we retrace our steps back through the Mexica backlands. It has been eleven months, but it might as well have been an entirely different universe. Even the swinging screen door on the little café that I fixed is a surreal reminder of who I was and who I have now become — same person – same places — vastly different perspectives. "Everything is a perspective," Adltleena reminds me as I stand there on the porch looking at the single screw that I put in last year. "We are just the observing," she adds. "We are not the observer and we are not the observed . . . we are just the observing."

During the drive, Aramara spends hours sleeping and sitting on my lap. This ignites a strong desire in me to be a father. "I'd love to have children," I tell them.

"You will," Adltleena says, as only a wise woman can. It's the kind of voice where there is no other reality or truth other than the statement she's speaking. "I can see it in your spirit."

The moment we cross the border into Texas, I call my parents from Customs and tell them a little about my adventure. "Sorry I was out of touch for so long," I explain with the love of hearing their voices again. "But once we got to where I told you I was going . . . well . . . it's really hard to express myself in this moment, but I will explain the entire adventure later on . . . I promise."

"We knew you were fine," my Mom tells me. "I could see this in my prayer every day." Having been raised by yogis, I have a distinct advantage over the generational gap that so often separates parents and children. We are simply one.

I have no idea what to say to my management team so I leave that phone call for later. The rest of my life will restart as it unfolds. In the first moments of actually meeting people in 'civilization' . . . "Oh God," I exclaim, ". . . what is this?"

We stop for gas in a tiny Texas town; this is the first time I've seen a mirror in over a year. I'm thin as a post, my hair curled and uncombed below my shoulders still with the colored ribbons tying it around and around. Speaking with people, even for brief moments is literally crazy-making. It will take a lot of practice, for with all the increased awareness comes a massive amount of information in every moment — not all of which is needed to be focused on a simple conversation. Just standing in someone's presence is like reading their entire book — their life history.

"You'll learn to deal," Palqtlo tells me as he sees me standing in my dilemma, "just like a newborn child does . . . what parts of the information are important and what parts can be ignored. The trouble with most people today is that they've determined that none of this information is important. They ignore it all and then walk through life in an unconscious state — unaware of the details that truly matter and even ignoring the information that could create true happiness, real health, and a connection to spirit. That is why we have the world as it is today, with all the wars and famines."

After a few days of driving we reach the ranch in Servilleta Plaza, New Mexico. The past eleven months are already becoming dreamlike, but being with Palqtlo and Adltleena reminds me that it's real. Palqtlo tells me one day, "In life, it's vital to prompt yourself from time to time, to remain aware of each moment — aware with each breath, otherwise true reality becomes a fantasy and the fantasy becomes real. The reality that is truth, the foundation of the Universe, quickly vanishes or fades into the background as the worldly experience takes over. There has to be a practice that you attach to each day to bring back that true perspective and perception of what is actually real in this world."

There's no way to know what's in store for me — what I'm heading back into, but Illanamiqt's words give me determination. *That which you can imagine — you can desire, and that which you can desire — you can manifest as your destiny. It's a cosmic law,"* he said. *"The universe always provides the exact time and exact space you need to pass your dreams into and this is even more absolute when your knowing is unwavering. We can carry our destiny through this keyhole of time /space except that which we doubt, fear, or refuse to forgive."*

Curious as to how I will hold this all together as I re-enter the places of civilization I ask Palqtlo, "Who do you think this great man is that your Father speaks of?"

"Ultimately, you will know that it's you," he says, "because your destiny is to become a world changer in this lifetime. In the time that comes in between now and then, the great man will come to you and teach you how to hold on to true reality in the face of all the illusion."

At the ranch, I immediately return to playing the guitar. Mine is in San Francisco with Dave, but there's a half-decent one here. The sounds that come out are totally different from anything I've played before. They aren't really songs — I have trouble playing songs right now, but I have a load of improvisational melodies with the pulsating rhythms from the Wirikuta.

Recuperating from the shock of returning to the world will never really happen and thank God. I spend time on the ranch milking the goats, taking long sweats and riding the horses. I walk the land to the top of the mountains and go on total silence for days at a time. But the genie is out of the bottle and there is no way and no need to put her back inside.

"Everything you wanted in life is with you right now," Palqtlo tells me. "Your eyes can see now. Remember in Seattle, how you saw into the future from the other side? Now you can go into each day with that same insight. That's why my Father told you to find the great teacher. This great teacher will show you how to preserve this power."

"It's going to be the new challenge," I respond, "but I'm definitely up for it."

"That's the nature of life," Adltleena says. "You have to be on top of it every moment, every breath. That's what we do here."

"Whenever you're overwhelmed," Palqtlo adds, "meditate on when you made your fires with the fire bow. It will slow you down so that life falls back into order. Go through each of the steps of how you would start with the dry grass, then the little twigs, the sticks and the logs. Remember, if you got this out of order, or tried to rush the process, you would put out the flame and have to start all over? This is a great meditation for getting things right again."

"After what I've experienced in the Wirikuta, it's hard to imagine how painful the illusion was for me before then," I admit.

"Yes, and that's why we must also practice the art of compassion and empathy," Adltleena reminds me. "From some perspectives, this world is a total mess and completely in slavery. People are afraid of what they truly feel and struggle with their lives without an ounce of guidance. You have to feel their pain and have compassion for them even when they offend you. Remember, they're lost and they spend their life worshipping money in order to buy their way out of this discomfort."

One day I climb the Sangre de Cristo Mountains in silence and imagine the more obvious things that the Wirikuta teachings can show this world. It's clear how people have lost the joy of community and now rely on their gadgets and their conveniences instead of each other. Every person needs the support of every other person around them or their dreams will seem impossible. Community is what we have in the Wirikuta and that's what we need to build here in the world. You can work all you want, but without a strong community supporting you, even the efforts with tremendous purpose will become exhausting. When this is missing it pulls people back into their fear and doubt and blocks the heart's connection — the connection that builds community.

I come off the mountain with a plan and within a few weeks I am determined to set my course toward this future. At this very moment I have no clue of where that future is, but I know that it is. The words to new songs are beginning to fill my head now and that is a sign of something.

Allow yourself to open the unknown doors
Don't ask how, determine when

Patience is not waiting — patience is knowing
Whatever you are to be, you already are
Time will sequence the events

I want to hitchhike back to the coast rather than fly. "I've got to become more grounded somehow," I explain to Palqtlo and Adltleena.

They tell me that they will go back into the Wirikuta to live and raise children . . . their work out here is done. We spend the next several days in deep connection and prayer in the 'aneepee' sweat lodge. We celebrate our collective journeys that they will fulfill our collective destiny. We celebrate the winds that brought our lives together and on the morning of the day I leave, they drop me on New Mexico State Highway #285, a road that has taken many turns for me ever since.

I pass through San Francisco just long enough to pick up my guitar from Dave and then surprise my parents in Seattle where we spend many loving days catching up. My mom tells me how she has been praying for me every day. *"The people my son is to meet he is meeting; the things my son is to do he is doing; the places my son is to be in he is in; and the joy my son is to experience he is experiencing."* My parents are the two people who have given me the life that is now unfolding as my dream.

Jimmy Greene doesn't quite understand why I'm not getting right back into my music. He asks me to sing at his club again and I explain, "The music is evolving and it will be back, but right now I have to allow it to evolve."

I still need to check in with San Francisco so after a couple of weeks I catch a S.F. bound Greyhound bus. It totally takes me back to my tour bus days. I arrive at the Haight Ashbury and Berkeley scenes that were once so fresh and innocent — they have now turned dark. Overrun with hard drugs — the streets are no longer the havens of the young dreamers. Now those lives and missions on the streets are fulfilling orders for heroin and cocaine. This has replaced the hopes and dreams and people's eyes look dead.

I hitch a ride across the Golden Gate Bridge remembering countless nights after concerts when Tex and I cast our wishes into the deep waters. I go to my management team's offices on the dock in Sausalito, but the sign is off the building and the windows are all papered up. I go to my old apartment in the city and a young lady living there says the owner has moved to Los Angeles.

I finally find where Tex lives. "Who is it?" she yells with that same powerful voice. "It's Frog," I call back.

"You got to be kidding," she says swinging open the door, "We thought you were gone forever." She's obviously high on something and just walks away from the open door. "Maybe you should've left it that way . . . gone forever," she says sitting back with her friends on the couch . . . all of them looking completely out of it.

I wanted a reunion, but I'm shocked into silence now . . . not quite sure if there is anything worth saying.

"You chickened out on me, Frog," she says.

I'm standing here gathering thoughts from the last eleven months of my life beyond my imagination and trying to weave a word or two into a room where no one gives a shit. "I just left a place where people actually fulfill their lives and reach enlightenment," I say, feeling awkward the moment it comes out of my mouth.

"That's such bullshit," she mumbles. "You haven't done anything, so stop fooling yourself."

I can't imagine playing music in a scene like this. I can hardly remember the times we spent together now. So I wish her my very best with a true prayer for her well-being and walk from the room and into the streets of a city gone terribly off course. *"Unlock the treasures of wisdom now,"* Illanamiqt whispers as I walk down the block, *"and do it while living in the center of the corruption."*

"Where?" I ask.

"Locate the great teacher in the space of your prayers," is his answer.

Around town I'm told that Julia and Bob have moved to Los Angeles. San Francisco doesn't feel like home anymore, so I pick up the rest of my belongings from Dave and head back out on the road.

It's January 1969 and I find Julia in Los Angeles — she's now a record company executive. "You look absolutely wild," she says. "It's so refreshing to see you again, we actually thought you'd disappeared into thin air. I called your Mom so many times and she just said that she was praying for you every day. We had no idea . . ."

We spend some time catching up on the things that have gone on in both of our lives over the past year. She lets me crash on her couch and it's a real trip after spending so much time sleeping on the ground. Even at my parent's home in Seattle I preferred to sleep on the floor of my old room. Bob hears that I'm in Los Angeles and asks me to come to his office the next day.

When I show up I bring my guitar but have no idea what's in store. We have the most heartfelt conversation I could have ever imagined. He has decided that the new musicians are a bit too "out there" for his world and has moved back to managing the big names that work in Las Vegas.

"That's right where you wanted me to end up," I laugh.

"You know I'm always here if you need anything," he assures me. "I can help your music even more than ever now."

"I didn't touch this guitar for nearly a year," I say pointing toward my case. "I'll have to find out what my music sounds like before I take you up on that."

"It'll be wild, knowing you," he laughs.

I leave his office near the corner of La Brea and Wilshire and walk down the boulevard . . . I really have no idea where I'm heading. A large and wildly painted school bus pulls over to the side of the road at a red light. We make eye contact and the driver calls out, "Hey man!"

"Hey," I answer back.

"Where're you going?" he asks.

"Same as you I guess," I say pointing straight ahead in the direction the bus is headed.

"We're going to a yoga class down on Melrose," he continues. "I don't know what this yogi has under his turban, but whatever it is — I can tell you, he's definitely the man . . . he's just arrived from India . . . name is Bhajan."

This description intrigues me and I'm up for just about anything. "Come on in," he says, swinging the bus door open. We drive to the corner of Melrose and Robertson in West Hollywood. 'Jules Buccieri Antiques' is the sign on the building. It's a small warehouse-type store, full of fancy old furniture and lines of young people carrying this stuff out of the store and into the parking lot. It looks like a bunch of ants at work making room for the class.

I brought my guitar, so I set up playing a bunch of chords and rhythms and the students make up words while we wait for the yogi to arrive. This is a real community feeling I think as I'm playing when the yogi walks into the room.

A tall man wearing a brightly colored turban above his piercing brown eyes and a long black beard stands as straight as a rod, just inside the doorway. He breaks into a pop song with the craziest sounding Indian accent trying to match my chords. *"What goes on cheek to cheek? What goes on, I really want to know?"* These are the words to Donovan's new hit song.

Immediately Illanamiqt's voice fills my ears, *"You have just met the man you've been looking for your whole life! If a master can act this humble and be this real . . . he is the great one."*

The Kundalini yoga he teaches this evening gets in me right away with deep breathing and postures that test my flexibility. I've done yoga all my life and this is a great addition to what I know. From the deep breathing and breath of fire I start having sensations in my body similar to times in the Wirikuta. It's the feeling of physical freedom that I always had around Illanamiqt and the other villagers . . . the complete sense that your body is really yours. A few moments into the class, Yogi Bhajan tosses a grapefruit that almost hits my head. I catch it and he's laughing. "That's the size of this Earth," he tells the class, his eyes looking intently into mine, "when it's seen from the eye of your soul. Don't ever forget this as long as you live and the problems of this world will never seem so large that you can't solve them."

The words of Illanamiqt echo in my brain. *"You'll know a great teacher by how small he says the Earth is."*

Yogi Bhajan — right on cue — says to the class as if he has heard Illanamiqt's words, *"It's not the life that matters, it's the courage you bring to it."*

And this is just the Beginning . . .

Epilogue

*M*y life has continued on to this present moment from the dirt trail visions and highways built of dreams that are depicted in this book. These paths have taken many turns, run into many roadblocks and had many breakthroughs that overcame the blocks in their ever-clarifying evolution. Goals and dreams have continued to sprout in my life like the seasons in nature and with every season there has been a brand new series of teachings, experiences and lessons.

Throughout this process one outstanding constant has been the realization that no matter who you are or where you live on this planet; life is an evolving sum total of the parts. It is an equation designed from the combination of our genealogical heritage (who brought our physical nature onto this Earth); our chronological time with all of its intentions, commitments, experiences and responses to these experiences; and our cosmological legacy (what we will be known for in posterity).

We are all like patchwork quilts, collages and calligrams; we continue to advance with our new and improved goals to the discovery of our vast deposits of buried treasures.

Our prayer is that your life is as healthy, happy and holy as you can possibly imagine. Bless your life with the courage to continue the journey from where you are to who you are. Bless your life to always pay as much attention to your heart-brain and its dreams, as you do to the brain in your head. And bless you to remember that "It's not the life that matters, it's the courage you bring to it."

With Blessings, Prayers, Love and Gratitude,

Guru Singh & Guruperkarma Kaur

Acknowledgments

*A*t our community of creativity — publishing and teaching what encourages and enables a healthy, happy and holy life — we set out to fulfill each goal with a committed, creative and highly qualified team. We love the experience of working as a team and every team has players at the center and players involved around this center. Just like parts of the body, every player is vital. Therefore, although I'm limited to the two dimensions of this paper to list and describe my gratitude for each of these persons, this order is by no means an order of importance. Each player is vital to the whole.

Every team requires players who keep the game rolling even when the nature of life takes on its jam-packed style. These are the team members who lead, codify and coordinate everything. These are the producer/directors who keep it all in alignment. Guruperkarma Kaur, my wife, is the vibrant center of this family. Her presence brings a personal style with her model of grace, inspiration and focus for the countless who participate in the global Kundalini yoga community.

The role of producers and creative directors belongs to Ram Prakash Kaur and Ram Prakash Singh (Nina and Mikhail) and for this we are deeply grateful. They have championed our website www.GuruSingh.com and now they've done the same with this book project — a project in the works for twenty years before they discovered it in my head and cracked the cosmic whip. This team is also a life-team as husband and wife. They raise their family in the same conscious way that they have raised this book and our website projects from their very infancy. Their never-ending enthusiasm, leadership and courage to respectfully get in my face also helps when needed and enables these multi-faceted projects to complete their journeys of destiny.

The editors on this project found my writing style — one that comes from all my songwriting — and brought it forward into the 21st century of literature. Now the reader can have the reading experience they deserve while leaving in just enough poetic license to keep up with the musical rhythms of the story. These angels are my wife Guruperkarma Kaur, project co-director Ram Prakash Kaur, Tamara Grace (Arjanpreet Kaur) and Jocelyne (Shant Joti). Tamara Grace is also the artist of the exquisite calligram in the epilogue of this book. We have not even come close to tapping into her full talents.

To the author Linda Sivertsen who encouraged this project when it was just the story of a memory in my brain some twenty plus years ago. She wrote about this in her first book and has been a dear friend ever since.

Then, there is the musical, artistic, digital and comical genius of Arvind Singh (Brian Kessler) — when you have a question he is never without an answer. Kevin Hutchings has been working with the idea of our projects of web and books with me through many incarnations for years. He is like glue in hanging diverse concepts together to make them work. Also, in this world of art, branding and graphics we are embraced by the best in this known universe. Lisa 'Gurudeep Kaur' Schiavello has been intuitively knowing our brand of graphic art for as long as we can remember. In addition to this she is a highly conscious hospice practitioner who accompanies people in their last days and moments in this physical body. What a blessing she is to so many. As is Sam Saddigh, of Knightsbridge Branding, who knows his way around the marketplace of consciousness so that the highest number of people who desire a conscious product have the opportunity to discover it while remaining in a state of grace rather than the hustle.

Once branded, even conscious events, products and brands are to be trademarked and again there is a need for someone who is highly purposeful and intuitive. Someone who is a student of infinity first and a trademark attorney somewhere down the list. Donna Rubelmann is just such an angel. She explains that you want to protect a Divine intellectual property so that it is never corrupted and able to spread the teachings of that highest purpose.

Mary and Ed Mohler have graciously housed my wife, our pups and I for years when we are on teaching tours and Mary is an editing talent that is only found in that writing and editing realm just adjacent to heaven.

Speaking of our teaching . . . teaching stimulates the juices to create projects such as this one. Many people coordinate the times and places where we all gather together as a class or seminar. We are grateful to Kewal Kaur and Adarsh Kaur at Yoga West in Los Angeles; Reinette Suraj Kaur Fournier and Thomas Paramatma Singh Speare of Tenth Gate Yoga in Newport, Rhode Island; Sada Simran Singh Khalsa of Gurugayatri Yoga in Seattle and Hari Singh Khalsa of Yoga West in Vancouver, Canada. Spreading the teachings of consciousness is a boon to the health and peace of this planet.

The front and back book cover and layout of our website is the guided vision of a man I have known since he was just about zero years old. I highly recommend Ditta Khalsa and his team at PranaProjects. The photographs that appear in all our projects are the genius talent of Marc Royce, photographer and dear friend.

Our work is all about enlightenment and family. We pride ourselves in living enlightened lifestyles in enlightened households. Archie, Vera, Dale and all the Bradleys — the birth family of Guruperkarma — encourage us in this pursuit by being exactly who they are. To Sada Anand Kaur (Dr. Melane' Sarkissian Ed.D.) a dear adopted daughter of ours who embodies the proof of respect, focus and will. She has worked with us to improve everything we do while pursuing her personal passion of true, effective childhood education. Guruperkarma Kaur and I have adopted many. They add nurture to the great nature of all family equations. The Garners: our son and daughter, Jason and Christy, with their children Nataly, Kevin and Jayden, along with Shaolin Master Wang Bo have joyously shared their enlightened household with elegance and grace. Along with the herbal genius of Jason and the medicinal foods and naturopathy of Christy, we have the young enthusiasm for growth of their three children proving that this lifestyle is not only just for the older adults.

To the memory of David Mimbu who is 'Dave' as I tell this story; he is and was a friend and part of my family since I was five years old. To his incredible wife Jocelyne (Shant Joti) who works with us on this and many projects and their magically talented daughter Jamie.

Louisa Wu, a Divine adoptee, met us eight years ago when we were teaching in Bora Bora, Polynesia and it was an instant kinship that has been a bidirectional support system ever since. Always in a state of quest for the best and the brightest in any field, she has guided us and many to connect with great kindred spirits and lasting relationships — so vital on this wisdom-path.

Family meals don't flourish as well without great baked goods and my wife and I believe that Azita Nahai, another Divine adoptee, is the best vegan gluten-free baker on planet Earth. She is also a long time practitioner/teacher of the Kundalini technology that moves people from 'Trauma to Dharma'. Her own story rivals that found in the pages of this book and she inspires us to keep up . . . often through our stomachs.

Judi Glova, Rudy Farmanara, Giancarlo & Jen Marcaccini bring spiritual nourishment into the business executive world and the world of professional sports and for this we are deeply grateful. This is a world that does not always find its way through the doors of conscious lifestyle centers, but many if not most of those involved in this world actually long for such a meal of consciousness.

Every family requires good and present medicine. Ours is no different, but our approach is. Paddy Canales is a Homeopathic practitioner who converted from designing the interiors of homes to designing the health that lives in the interior of our body homes when she began working with us. She keeps our team from falling down long before we are about to. Her daughter, Chaya Paloma Schapiro, is not only a college fencing star, but perhaps the best office help we have ever experienced in our careers.

Patrizia Paiar, Doctor of Traditional Chinese Medicine, keeps the needles flowing like super accurate darts that hit the spots that even we are unable to reach in our constant practice of Kundalini yoga and meditation. Alongside the Chinese needles is the masterful prayer work of Sandy Bertoli who holds projects like this one in the realms beyond time where they are already completed and thereby allows them to simply fit into what they already are. These two also take care of our home and two Chihuahuas (Miss Bean and Miss Belle) when we are on the road internationally and the pups can't fly along.

To all the musicians, comedians and artists of every kind who excel in their fields carving a destiny through the courage in their hearts and the creativity of their spirit. To Joseph Gannon, Bob Phillips and Julia who made many of these dreams, including my own, come true — even if in ways not known to any of us at the time. To Seal, Guru Ganesha Singh, and Thomas Barquee who teamed up with me many years ago to launch the newest version of my musical career. To those who teach the children how to develop their wonderfully creative talents — they are vital to the evolution of this planet and every creature that calls this planet their home. Yogi Bhajan always said that people live and prosper by the beauty of their music.

A film and web presence is vital to spreading wisdom and the real education required in today's world. We are deeply grateful for the unorthodox genius of Jimi Petulla and Brian Kraft in their work of generously helping our world in the realm of new technology and for truly educating people in what they love to do and doing it in such a way that they can then work in the field of their passion and pay their way through life. This is the magic creativity that is possible in education and has been lost today in the over-emphasis on educating only the logical side of the human brain.

To the indigenous people all over the world who are holding and preserving, for the benefit of humanity, all the wisdom traditions that work with the magical nature of nature. Like the Maraakame of the Wirikuta and the spiritual leaders from around the world, they work with Spirit in a way that can only be known to the wisdom that has developed over tens of thousands of years of practice through trial and error. If we were to lose this wisdom, the entire planet will suffer.

There are countless others who help so many aspects in so many ways — to you and for you we are truly grateful.

An Invitation

We invite you to sign up for our monthly newsletter and visit our website at www.GuruSingh.com to connect with Guru Singh and our global community. Here you will find inspiring blogs, podcasts, lectures, music, books and meditations. We also encourage submissions of community stories, inspirations and questions in our virtual Planet Ashram.

With love and blessings,

The GuruSingh.com Team

Made in the USA
Lexington, KY
22 August 2014